D1104515

THE COMMERCIAL RECIPROCITY
POLICY OF THE UNITED STATES
1774-1829

A Da Capo Press Reprint Series

THE AMERICAN SCENE
Comments and Commentators

GENERAL EDITOR: WALLACE D. FARNHAM
University of Illinois

THE COMMERCIAL RECIPROCITY
POLICY OF THE UNITED STATES
1774-1829

By

VERNON G. SETSER

DA CAPO PRESS • NEW YORK • 1969

A Da Capo Press Reprint Edition

This Da Capo Press edition of
*The Commercial Reciprocity Policy of the United States
1774-1829*, is an unabridged republication of the
first edition published in Philadelphia in 1937.
It is reprinted by special arrangement with the
University of Pennsylvania Press.

Library of Congress Catalog Number 76-90212

Copyright 1937 by the University of Pennsylvania Press

Published by Da Capo Press
A Division of Plenum Publishing Corporation
227 West 17th Street
New York, N. Y. 10011

Printed in the United States of America

THE COMMERCIAL RECIPROCITY POLICY
OF THE UNITED STATES
1774-1829

THE COMMERCIAL RECIPROCITY
POLICY OF THE UNITED STATES
1774-1829

By

VERNON G. SETSER

Philadelphia
UNIVERSITY OF PENNSYLVANIA PRESS
London: Humphrey Milford: Oxford University Press
1937

To
PAUL CHRISLER PHILLIPS
Professor of History
State University of Montana

PREFACE

THIS STUDY of the commercial foreign policy of the United States was begun in the Seminar of Professor St. George Leakin Sioussat at the University of Pennyslvania. The original plan was to treat the subject during the period from about 1840 to the Civil War. After extensive investigation, however, it became evident that many of the controlling laws and treaties had been adopted prior to that time, and that the early experience of the Government and the principles enunciated by the "Fathers" were extremely influential. Since no adequate study of early policies had ever been made, there seemed to be no alternative to my undertaking that task myself. I expect to continue my study of the subject until the record is complete to 1860 at least.

In addition to the debt owed to Professor Sioussat for encouragement and guidance, I am under great obligation to Professor Roy F. Nichols of the University of Pennsylvania and to Professor Samuel Flagg Bemis of Yale University. For essential financial assistance, I am indebted to the George Leib Harrison Foundation of the University of Pennsylvania, and to The George Washington University, whose grant of a Sanders Fellowship in History facilitated extensive research in Washington. Thanks are due also to the members of the staffs of the Library of the University of Pennsylvania, the Library of Congress, the Carnegie Foundation for World Peace, the New York Public Library, and the Archives Section of the Department of State. Miss Grace Gardner Griffin of the Manuscripts Division of the Library of Congress, and Dr. E. C. Burnett of the Carnegie Institution of Washington have been especially courteous and helpful, the former in advising on numerous bibliographical problems, the latter in granting the privilege of examining the material for the forthcoming volumes of *Letters of Mem-*

bers of the Continental Congress. My wife, Lucille Florence Setser, has assisted materially in checking references and preparing the manuscript for the printer.

V. G. S.

The National Archives,
Washington, D.C.

TABLE OF CONTENTS

ABBREVIATIONS

AAE—Archives des Affaires Etrangères, Paris

M et D, EU—Mémoires et Documents, Etats Unis

CP, EU—Correspondance Politique, Etats Unis

PRO, FO—Public Record Office, Foreign Office, London

AGI—Archivo General de Indias, Seville

AHN—Archivo Histórico Nacional, Madrid

AHR—American Historical Review

EHR—English Historical Review

HAHR—Hispanic American Historical Review

AHA, AR—American Historical Association, Annual Report

ASP, FR—American State Papers, Foreign Relations

ASP, C&N—American State Papers, Commerce and Navigation

Dip. Corresp.—Diplomatic Correspondence of the United
States, 1783-1789

I

INTRODUCTION

No LESS than twenty of the forty-five treaties[1] concluded
with foreign governments by the United States between 1778 and 1829 may be described as treaties of commerce, and articles in other treaties deal with commercial affairs. Dozens of separate acts of legislation by the national
Congress, in addition to tariff legislation, relate in some way
to the regulation of foreign trade—not to mention the ordinances of the Continental Congress and the acts of the state
legislatures in the period of the Confederation. Defenders of a
large and efficient diplomatic service have rested their arguments upon the aid rendered in the furtherance of trade.
Nearly every diplomat has felt the ambition to set his hand to
a commercial treaty. What have been the objectives pursued
by the United States in its commercial diplomacy and legislation? What principles were asserted, who formulated them,
and what were the circumstances of their origin? What success
has attended the efforts of government, and what has been the
effect of changing conditions from period to period?

The title "reciprocity policy" covers with reasonable ade-
quacy a fairly definite range of governmental activities in aid
of foreign trade. To trace the influence of commerce in general foreign policy has not been the purpose of this study.
Such an attempt would require consideration of the Mississippi and St. Lawrence navigation questions, the struggle for
neutral rights, the Monroe Doctrine—in fact almost every
subject arising in relations with foreign governments. The
writer has not attempted to relate the history of American
foreign trade, nor has he undertaken the futile task of estimat-

---

[1] The figures are approximate and would vary with the definition of the
terms "treaty" and "commercial."

ing the relative weight of governmental policy among those manifold factors influencing the increase or decrease of the volume of imports, exports, and registered tonnage. The investigation has been confined substantially to the formal diplomatic and legislative policy of the United States government—to the regulations directly applied to foreign commerce for commercial purposes, and to efforts to relieve trade from the adverse regulations of foreign governments. American trade with China has not been considered because there was never any question, during this period, of reciprocity in the commercial relations of the United States and the Celestial Empire. Because of the peculiar character of the various dealings with the states of North Africa and with the Ottoman Empire these matters have likewise been omitted.

In recent times the term "reciprocity," when applied to commerce, has come to mean mutual reduction of import duties by nations desiring to favor each other's trade. This interpretation was uncommon during the period from 1774 to 1829. In a broad sense, agreements resting upon reciprocity were agreements of mutual advantage and consent, and most governments recognized the principle in their commercial policies and treaties. American statesmen, in striving to solve peculiarly American problems, tended to give the word a more specific meaning. As officially interpreted after 1815, for example, reciprocity meant the abandonment, in compliance with the so-called reciprocity laws, of discriminating duties on shipping. As generally used, however, the term is as difficult to define as many of the political and diplomatic abstractions of the present day. The exact meaning depended upon the nature of the specific commercial grievances to which reference was intended.

On establishing independence, the United States assumed membership in a society of nations whose ideal was economic self-sufficiency. Each member attempted to monopolize all the world trade it could effectively control. The American colonies had developed a thriving commerce under the tutelage of one of these states, only to find their trade considerably restricted upon the severance of the colonial relationship. For a state in such circumstances, the obvious thing to do was to adopt the doctrine of freedom of trade to cloak its attacks upon the preserves of its selfish neighbors. Since the new nation had no colonial or other monopolies of its own to exploit, it was natural for its leaders to champion the principle that commerce, being a system of mutual exchanges, was also a system of mutual benefits and carried with it its own compensation. American commercial policy was, during the fifty-four years here discussed, a policy of attack, by force of argument, by example of "liberality" in commercial regulations, and by retaliation in kind, against the monopolistic and discriminatory commercial policies of European governments.

II

FIRST STAGES OF RECIPROCITY POLICY
1774-1783

COMMERCIAL ASPECTS OF THE REVOLUTION

THE EXIGENCIES of war, rather than the advantage of private business or the economic progress of the country, were the primary factors in commercial policy throughout the Revolution. The usual sources of supply were shut off at a time of crisis. New sources must be found, particularly new sources of munitions of war, if resistance were to continue to be offered to the British. This was the first and by far the most pressing commercial problem requiring solution by the new government. Secondly, it soon became apparent that the likelihood of America alone defeating the British was small. Commerce must serve as the medium of exchange for the purchase of such foreign assistance as might be needed. Political recognition by a European state was deemed a strong "support" of independence. Commerce must provide also the price to be paid for that.

In the system of resistance to Great Britain, commerce was thus made to occupy a highly important position. Its value was doubtless overestimated, but there was ample justification for holding it in high esteem. It was rather widely believed even in Great Britain that British power and wealth rested extensively upon the American trade, which constituted, after 1763, from about one-sixth to one-third the total for the whole empire, and reached the enormous value of four million five hundred and twenty thousand pounds in 1770.[1] When

---

[1] C. M. Andrews, *Colonial Background of the American Revolution*, p. 101. For statistical tables of the colonial trade, see Emory R. Johnson, *History of the Domestic and Foreign Commerce of the United States*, I, 121.

Lord Howe, seeking conciliation, proposed, in June 1776, a conference with American commissioners, he made it quite clear that England was fighting to prevent the American trade from passing into other hands.[2] Moreover, the French government in its program of weakening England assigned great weight to the consideration that the American trade was a "powerful vehicle for the growth of [English] industry and power."[3]

The commercial warfare passed through two phases. The first was simply the passive denial of the advantages of the trade to Great Britain, an effort to influence the British government through the "pocket nerves" of the merchants. This policy had proved highly successful in securing the repeal of the Stamp Act and the Townshend legislation. These easy victories doubtless served to increase the confidence of the Americans in their commerce as a weapon in foreign relations, and thus helped give it the prominence which it occupied in the diplomacy of the Revolution. Non-intercourse as a weapon broke against the obstinacy of the North ministry, and the next phase of the struggle was the turning of the advantages of commerce to foreign nations in exchange for assistance in the use of more deadly weapons. The decision

[2] Howe to Franklin, June 20, 1776, Francis Wharton, *The Revolutionary Diplomatic Correspondence of the United States*, II, 98. Franklin seized the opportunity to develop his opposing views upon commercial and political relations. "To me it seems that neither the obtaining or retaining of any trade, how valuable soever," he wrote, "is an object for which men may justly spill each other's blood; that the true and sure means of extending and securing commerce is the goodness and cheapness of commodities; and that the profit of no trade can ever be equal to the expense of compelling it and of holding it by fleets and armies." *Ibid.*, p. 104.

[3] Vergennes to Montmorin, June 20, 1778, in Henri Doniol, *Histoire de la participation de la France à l'établissement des Etats-Unis d'Amérique*, III, 140. Rayneval expressed the same idea more at length in his "Réflexions" in 1775: "England makes annually a profit of about two millions sterling on the trade which she does with her Colonies, and the King levies, besides that, a further sum of about two millions, by the different duties with which this trade is burdened; now this double profit would stop if the Colonies ceased to belong to Great Britain, because, free from all encumbrances, they would open a trade with the other nations of Europe, and would no longer frequent the ports of Great Britain, except so far as they would be attracted there by advantages equal to those they would experience elsewhere; from this would result an irreparable loss to English manufactures. . . ." AAE, M et D, EU, I, 59.

to make this last experiment was tantamount to a declaration of independence, and was made a considerable time prior to the official declaration.

THE CONTINENTAL ASSOCIATION AND THE NECESSITY FOR FOREIGN TRADE

The Continental Association of October 20, 1774, may be deemed the first complete piece of national commercial legislation.[4] In fact, in promulgating this series of regulations, the Congress assumed the position and imitated the forms of a sovereign legislative body, although loyalty to the English king was at the same time professed. The act forbade after December 1, 1774, the importation into the colonies of British and Irish goods and East India tea from any part of the world; molasses, syrups, paneles, coffee, and pimento from the British West Indies; wines from Madeira or the Western Islands; indigo, and slaves. Non-consumption of the prohibited goods was prescribed as an effectual security for the observation of non-importation. Ostensibly because of an earnest desire "not to injure our fellow subjects in Great Britain, Ireland, or the West Indies," though more probably in order that the current crops might be disposed of, non-exportation was "suspended" until September 10, 1775, but on that date was to be strictly enforced with regard to all articles except rice.[5]

The purpose of this rigorous enactment was clearly expressed as being to force Parliament to repeal all the objectionable legislation enacted since 1763, the various acts being specifically referred to.[6] The prohibitive measures were firmly enforced through local committees by means of the publication of the names of violators, by boycotts, and even

---

[4] A resolution had been adopted by Congress September 22 recommending non-importation, and a resolution of September 30 provided for prospective non-exportation. *Journals of the Continental Congress* (ed. W. C. Ford, G. Hunt, J. C. Fitzpatrick. Hereafter cited as *Journals*), I, 40-41, 51-52; A. M. Schlesinger, *The Colonial Merchants and the American Revolution*, pp. 427-428, 432-437.

[5] *Journals*, I, 75-81.

[6] *Ibid.*

by force.[7] The influence of the injured British merchants was not sufficient to induce the ministry to yield, however. Lord North attempted to make good his declaration that since the Americans refused to trade with England, they should trade with no one else, by passing through Parliament the restraining act of March 30, 1775.[8] This law prohibited the participation of the New England colonies in the Newfoundland fisheries, and all trade except directly with Great Britain, Ireland, and the British West Indies. The few "enumerated" articles produced in New England were even denied a market within the empire. These restrictions, excepting that regarding the fisheries, were·applied to New Jersey, Pennsylvania, Maryland, Virginia, and South Carolina by a similar act of April 13.[9] New York, Delaware, North Carolina, and Georgia were exempted from these laws, apparently because of a mistaken notion that they were loyal. The final arrow in the British quiver of commercial weapons was released December 22, 1775, when a law was enacted prohibiting completely all commercial intercourse with the thirteen colonies, and making colonial merchandise good prize when captured.[10]

By July 12, 1775, the majority of Congress was convinced, in view of the restraining acts, that non-intercourse was approaching the end of its usefulness. Military resistance had been begun in earnest, and foreign trade was necessary, if for nothing else, to provide the implements of war. The seriousness of this problem is unmistakable in the evidence that there were only about 80,000 pounds of gunpowder in the colonies in 1775.[11] British cruisers promised to become as effective instruments in enforcing the Continental Association as the patriot committees.

In the face of existing circumstances, it was a truly formidable task which Congress on July 12 gave to John Jay,

---

[7] Schlesinger, *Colonial Merchants*, pp. 535-536.
[8] 15 Geo. III, c. 10.
[9] 15 Geo. III, c. 18.
[10] 16 Geo. III, c. 5.
[11] O. W. Stephenson, "The Supply of Gunpowder in 1776," *AHR*, XXX (1925), 272-274, 277.

Franklin, Silas Deane, and Richard Henry Lee "to devise ways and means to protect the trade of these colonies."[12] Within three days Franklin brought in a motion, which was adopted, authorizing the breaking of the Association for the purpose of permitting the export of enough produce to pay for imports of arms and munitions.[13] The report of the committee, returned July 21, was such a recommendation as would satisfy those who had given up hope of a reconciliation, and were ready to recognize officially the state of war. It proposed two resolutions.[14] The first contemplated, on a day six months from the date set for putting the British restraining acts into force, the closing of the customhouses in the colonies, and throwing the colonial ports open "to the Ships of every State in Europe that will admit our commerce and protect it." The second offered "That we will to the utmost of our Power, maintain and support this Freedom of Commerce for two years certain after its Commencement, any Reconciliation between us and Britain notwithstanding. . . ." The Franklin plan had two objects in view. The first was political. Congress was divided between the "Hawk" and "Buzzard" policies of war and commercial boycott.[15] Opening the ports to foreigners would be an overt violation of law, and the radicals wished to commit Congress to a declaration of independence. The second was *bona fide* the protection of commerce. Briefly, it was proposed to invite foreign adventurers to run the blockade and supply America.

The Franklin plan was too advanced for the time, but the debates upon it show the current views upon the problem of trade. The weight of special interests and of the particularism of the several colonies and sections is evident. The conservatives had not abandoned hope of a reconciliation, although, as Samuel Chase admitted, the prospect was gloomy. Their solution of the problem of supply was to trade

[12] *Journals*, II, 177.
[13] *Ibid.*, II, 184-185.
[14] *Ibid.*, II, 200-201.
[15] John Adams to James Warren, July 23, 24, 1775, *Letters of Members of the Continental Congress* (ed. E. C. Burnett, hereafter cited as Burnett), I, 174-175, 176; John Adams, *Works* (ed. C. F. Adams), III, 29.

through the ports of the colonies exempted from the operation of the restraining acts. Continued non-intercourse, they feared, would ruin the credit of the country. On the other hand, the general opening of the ports would prematurely raise the question of independence. The decision to make an irreparable break should be delayed until a studied policy could be adopted.

The proposal to trade through the ports of the exempted colonies aroused strong opposition on the ground that it would cause jealousies and foment disunion among those not enjoying the privilege. Edward Rutledge favored keeping all the ports closed, believing that America could supply herself through the development of manufactures. Richard Henry Lee proposed complete non-intercourse in American ships, the country depending entirely upon foreigners to supply it. Representatives from the commercial colonies would hear nothing of this, asserting that native seamen and ships would seek service under foreign flags, and that the people would think Congress more oppressive than Parliament.[16] Among the radicals, few men had more influence in the attempted solution of the commercial problem at this stage than John Adams. He desired an immediate stroke for independence and was confident that America unaided possessed the means to achieve it. However desirable ideally, a continuance of non-intercourse was not, in his belief, at all practicable. There was not enough "Temperance, Fortitude, and Perseverance" among the people to enable them to endure such severe restrictions. He believed that if Congress would make the harbors safe from attack by the enemy, foreign merchants could be induced to send vessels to American ports. These, together with native blockade runners, would provide a suffcient marine to supply the country with necessaries.[17]

[16] For the debates on the question of opening the ports, see John Adams' notes in appendix of *Journals*, III, 476-481, 490-492. See also *ibid.*, II, 201, 202, 235, 253, 256; III, 258, 259, 268, 287, 291, 292, 301, 307, 308, 311, 312.

[17] John Adams to James Warren, Oct. 7, 1775, in Burnett, I, 218-220. See other Adams-Warren letters, *ibid.*, 236-237, 239-240, 243-244.

Rejecting the Franklin plan, Congress authorized a second committee "to take into consideration the state of the trade of America and report their opinion."[18] Enough conservatives were added to the old committee to give them control,[19] and the report presented September 30 expressed the views of the more cautious delegates.[20] It recommended that the non-intercourse resolutions be continued in force, although a few relaxations in certain cases might be permitted.[21] On November 1, it was resolved not to export any produce whatever before March 1, 1776, unless the permission of Congress should be obtained in particular cases, except for the purchase of military supplies.[22]

Time and events fought in the ranks of the radicals. The report of the second committee had little permanent influence. As mentioned above, the resolution to persevere in non-intercourse was amended so as to set a definite term to the Association. The date chosen, March 1, 1776, was only three months beyond that set by the Franklin report. In December, the King's speech and proclamation branded the Americans as rebels, and an act of Parliament outlawed all their commerce.[23] There was no longer any solution to the commercial problem but to open the ports to foreign nations, nullify the navigation laws, and institute a commercial system peculiarly American. On January 17, 1776, after having considered the problem anew in committee of the whole, Congress determined to take the step so long under consideration.[24] A committee was appointed to "consider under what regulations and restrictions the trade of these colonies ought to be carried

---

[18] *Journals*, III, 259.

[19] The new members were John Rutledge, Peyton Randolph, Thomas F. Johnson, and Thomas Willing. *Ibid.*

[20] *Journals*, III, 268-269.

[21] These would allow the export of flaxseed to Ireland and provisions to Bermuda, the exports to be exchanged in each case for military stores or other specified articles in great demand.

[22] *Journals*, III, 314.

[23] In December also, the threat of a salt famine in the South made it necessary to authorize exportation for a supply of that necessity. *Journals*, III, 464-465.

[24] Richard Smith's Diary in Burnett, I, 316-317.

on after the 1st of March next."[25] Debate on the subject began on February 14.[26] If Adams' notes give an adequate report of the discussion, there was no longer any serious opposition from conciliationists. Attention was directed almost entirely to the subject of the expediency of the measure and to perfecting its details. Some of the delegates feared that the enemy army would be supported by their warships preying upon defenseless American merchant vessels. Others, as for example, George Wythe of Virginia, thought that the declaration of independence ought to precede the bid for trade with foreign countries, since foreign courts would hardly fall in with a plan to encourage trade with people still professing to be British subjects. Adams himself believed that the added expense of the enemy navy would amount to more than double the value of the goods which might be seized, and he had great faith in the power of trade as an inducement for the friendship of foreign nations.[27]

Although the Association was to terminate, according to the November resolutions, on March 1, 1776, it was not until April 6 that Congress adopted the series of resolutions which established on the domestic side the commercial system of the war period. These resolutions may be fitly called the declaration of the commercial independence of the United States. They authorized the export of all goods, except staves and empty casks, from the colonies "by the inhabitants thereof, and by the people of all such countries as are not subject to the King of Great Britain, to any parts of the world which are not under the dominion of the said King . . . ," and the importation of all merchandise except East India tea, slaves, and all goods from the British Empire, "from any other parts of the world to the colonies, by the inhabitants thereof, and by the people of all such countries as are not subject to the said King." A clause was inserted reserving the right for Congress and the states to adopt such commercial regulations

---

[25] *Journals,* IV, 62.
[26] *Journals,* IV, 113, 148, 153, 154, 159.
[27] Adams' notes in *Journals,* VI, 1071-1074.

as should in the future be thought just and necessary. It was recommended to the various colonies to establish port offices and appoint officials to enforce the regulations adopted and perform other duties usually falling within the province of the customs service. Goods imported from Great Britain, except prize goods, were made subject to confiscation.[28]

THE BID FOR FRENCH AID

There lay in the background of all this discussion and legislation the conviction that the coöperation of foreign merchants, and perhaps of foreign navies, was essential to success. As early as Bonvouloir's mission[29] to Philadelphia in December 1775, if not earlier, the American leaders had understood that France might be disposed to aid them. The probable need of it had, of course, been noted before.[30] Until late in the year 1776, when the disheartening military situation damped the enthusiasm of the patriots, the trend of opinion was opposed to any sort of foreign political connection. In June 1776, John Adams asserted that he wished "for nothing but commerce, a mere marine treaty" with France.[31] Silas Deane expressed the same opinion.[32] This was the policy which controlled in the appointment of Franklin, Deane, and Arthur Lee as Commissioners at Versailles, and in the formation of the first treaty plan, and the first instructions to the plenipotentiaries. Not until late in 1776 did a political and

---

[28] *Journals*, IV, 257-259.

[29] Achard Bonvouloir, confidential agent of the French foreign ministry, arrived at Philadelphia in December 1775, and held secret conferences with a committee of Congress. Although careful not to commit himself or his Government, his visit justified the inference that France was ready to give aid as opportunity offered. Wharton, I, 333-335; Doniol, I, 153-159, 287-292.

[30] For example, in the debates in the summer of 1775, Samuel Chase declared that "we must treat with foreign nations upon trade. They must protect and support us with their fleets." *Journals*, III, 478-479. Another delegate, Carter Braxton, held back from approving a declaration of independence, because he thought an alliance with a naval power essential for the protection of the trade necessary in carrying on the war. Burnett, I, 420-421. See also C. H. Van Tyne, "French Aid Before the Alliance of 1778," *AHR*, XXI (1925), 20-40.

[31] Adams to John Winthrop, June 23, 1776, in Burnett, I, 502.

[32] Wharton, II, 128, 138.

military alliance begin to be strongly advocated, although Deane had been instructed to sound Vergennes on the subject of such an alliance in the first interview.[33]

Congress entered into relations with France, then, with the expectation of buying the support of Louis XVI, offering as compensation the opportunity of gaining the larger fraction of the trade of the thirteen colonies. That, in attempting to collect, France might be forced into a war with Great Britain was of course considered probable, though not inevitable; but Congress wished to assume no additional obligations on that account. The Committee of Secret Correspondence[34] instructed Deane, March 3, 1776, "that it is likely a great part of our commerce, will naturally fall to the share of France, especially if she favor us in this application, as that will be a means of gaining and securing the friendship of the colonies; and that our trade was rapidly increasing with our increase of people, and, in a greater proportion, her part of it will be extremely valuable."[35]

The policy of appealing to Europe to supply America soon began to produce results. In January 1776, prior to the formal opening of the ports, two French merchants, Pliarne and Penet, appeared before Congress and gave assurances that trade could be carried on with France. Frequent references are made in the correspondence of the members of Congress to the arrival of French ships during January, February, and March.[36] On January 10, Richard Smith recorded in his diary that foreign goods were beginning to come in, and that he had bought some linen from St. Eustatius.[37] In August, the Comte de Vergennes officially assured Deane

[33] Wharton, II, 79.

[34] The Committee of Secret Correspondence, established by Congress, November 29, 1775, to carry on the diplomatic correspondence, was transformed into the Committee of Foreign Affairs, April 17, 1777. In 1781, the committee was replaced by a Department of Foreign Affairs, with Robert R. Livingston as Secretary. See Gaillard Hunt, *The Department of State*, chs. I-III.

[35] Committee of Secret Correspondence to Deane, March 3, 1776, Wharton, II, 79-81.

[36] Burnett, I, 299, 304, 313-314, 327, 341, 407.

[37] *Ibid.*, p. 307.

that he might consider himself "perfectly free to carry on any kind of commerce in the kingdom which any subject of any other state in the world might, as the court had resolved their ports should be equally free to both parties."[38]

Since the French government was in a position to exact commercial concessions from the United States, the fact that it demanded none is not easy to comprehend. On the whole, its policy was to fall in as far as conditions warranted with the plans of the Americans. Certain broad reasons for general abstention from demanding concessions appear. The nature of French relations with the rest of Europe made a strong self-seeking policy inadvisable. Spain could not be expected to support France in a war of aggrandizement, nor would the rest of Europe be certain to remain quiet in such a war. Important also is the fact that France was bidding against Great Britain for the American alliance. Fear and jealousy of France as the traditional enemy had to be overcome in America.[39] The ease with which the American peace commissioners were brought to distrust the French government during the peace negotiations of 1782 shows that Vergennes was wise in not asking favors for France. There is still another explanation, however. Throughout the war, the government displayed no great enthusiasm over the possibilities of commercial advantages. The hopes of many Frenchmen were aroused at the prospect, it is true, and Rayneval[40] gave commercial gain sec-

[38] Deane to the Committee of Secret Correspondence, Aug. 18, 1776, Wharton, II, 114.

[39] For the European situation see S. F. Bemis, *Diplomacy of the American Revolution*, chs. II, VI; E. S. Corwin, *French Policy in the American Alliance*, chs. II, III. American distrust of France as the traditional enemy had an influence of considerable importance in Revolutionary diplomacy. See De Kalb's report (1768), in Yela Utrilla, *España ante la independencia de los Estados Unidos*, II, 3; and Vergennes' instructions to Guines in Wharton, I, 333-334. Vergennes scrupulously adhered to his resolution of self denial. Cf. his statement in his "Considerations" of March 12, 1776: "That if France and Spain give help, they must only seek the value of it in the momentary political end at which they aim, reserving to themselves to decide in the sequel according to events and conjunctures." *AAE, M et D, EU*, I.

[40] Joseph Mathias Gérard de Rayneval, Vergennes' private secretary, who prepared a memoir late in 1775, justifying French aid for the Americans. *AAE, M et D, EU*, I, 59.

ond place in his list of advantages which would result from assisting the rebels. Spanish statesmen believed that French policy in the American alliance was largely influenced by the desire to secure control of the trade. Vergennes denied this, and declared that, with American commerce open to the competition of the entire world, it could be for France only *un objet minime*.[41] In so far as trade was a motive, the government seemed to emphasize taking it away from Great Britain rather than gaining it for France. Mercantilists, who exercised the paramount influence upon French commercial policy, could not see the value of uncontrolled trade, and, of course, France could never possess the American trade in the mercantilistic sense.[42] Franklin found the commercial argument very distasteful to the French court, and considered it necessary to caution Secretary Livingston in 1782, with regard to this principal point of American diplomacy. "Trade," he wrote, "is not the admiration of their noblesse, who always govern here."[43]

The extravagance of the idea of Americans of the value of their trade in foreign relations is abundantly shown in the treaty plan of 1776. The committee for drafting it was chosen on June 12, and was composed of John Adams, John Dickinson, Benjamin Harrison, Robert Morris, and Franklin. According to Adams' recollection there was no great difference of opinion among the members as to what the plan ought to contain. Franklin marked some clauses in a collection of treaties and Adams embodied them with some others in the final draft, which was adopted with only stylistic changes by Congress on September 7, 1776.[44] Adams' statement of the policy which he wrote into the draft is interesting. "I contended for the same principles which I had before avowed and defended in Congress, namely, that we should avoid all alliances which might embarrass us in after times, and involve us in future European wars; that a treaty of commerce which would operate as a repeal of the British Acts of Navigation

[41] Doniol, III, 140.
[42] Corwin, *op. cit.*, pp. 12-18.
[43] Wharton, V, 215.
[44] *Journals*, V, 768-779.

so far as respected us, and admit France into an equal participation of the benefits of our commerce, would encourage her
manufactures, increase her exports of the produce of her soil
and agriculture, extend her navigation and trade, augment
her resources of naval power, raise her from her present deep
humiliation, distress and decay, and place her on a more equal
footing with England, for the protection of her foreign possessions, and maintaining her independence at sea, would be
ample compensation to France for acknowledging our independence, and for furnishing us, for our money, or upon
credit for a time, with such supplies of necessaries as we
should want, even if this conduct should involve her in
war."[45]

The plan was never accepted by any foreign state, although
it provided the outline for the French treaty, which superseded it as a model. But it is significant as indicating what
Congress believed the United States ought to offer, or rather
receive, in a commercial way.[46] First and most important, it
proposed that each party should give the subjects of the
other all the "privileges, immunities, and exemptions" in
trade which it allowed to its own nationals, the clause being
worded so as to give Americans the same privileges as the
French monopolistic companies. Thus was laid down at
the beginning the basis, not of free trade, but of complete
equality of treatment, no distinction being made between
foreigner and native.

The French Caribbean islands received special attention.
Although the subject was covered in the clause proposing
general national treatment, another article suggested a special
guarantee that higher duties would not be charged upon
West Indian goods when exported to the United States than
when exported to France. Further, the French government
was to be asked to bind itself never to impose an export duty
on molasses when exported from the French islands to the
United States. No equivalent was offered by the latter. Two

[45] John Adams, *Works*, II, 516-517.
[46] The treaty plan is in *Journals*, V, 768-779.

other interesting propositions were included. Each party, it was proposed, should obligate itself to admit the merchant ships of the other to its armed convoys, and to guarantee to them the same protection that it offered those of its own subjects. France was to be asked to afford, without equivalent, the same protection to American vessels against the Barbary pirates, which Great Britain had furnished before the war began.

The instructions which were to accompany the treaty plan were approved September 24.[47] These indicate with emphasis that the articles of the plan contained the maximum demands of Congress. That the primary object was to meet the immediate military requirements appears in the authorization to drop everything, if need be, except the clause providing that France protect American ships in French seas and admit them to French convoys. The instructions did not authorize the envoy to specify any very costly concessions on the part of the United States. Most-favored-nation treatment might be substituted for national treatment, but no other solution of the problem of commercial regulations was authorized. It might be stipulated that the United States would never acknowledge allegiance to Great Britain nor "grant to that nation any exclusive trade; or any advantages, or privileges more than to his most christian majesty." Even in case the Most Christian King should be drawn into the war in consequence of his agreeing to the treaty, Congress would bind itself to nothing except to refrain from assisting Great Britain "in such War, with Men, Money, Ships, or any of the Articles in this treaty denominated Contraband Goods."[48] There was no suggestion of political or military alliance. The plan was, on the face of it, a simple commercial treaty.

John Adams' conception of the purchasing power of the American trade, as he remembered it in later years, was not identical with that of certain members of Congress, however. He himself reported, in his account of the treaty plan, that

[47] *Journals*, V, 813-817.
[48] See Article VIII of the treaty plan, *Journals*, V, 770.

"many motions were made to insert in it articles of entangling alliance, of exclusive privileges, and of warranties of possessions, and it was argued that the present plan reported by the Committee held out no sufficient temptation to France, who would despise it and refuse to receive our ambassador."[49] But the majority was and remained with Adams. Even in December, when the disastrous defeat at New York and its sequel seemed to be bringing the laboriously raised structure of independence tumbling about their ears, Congress continued to hold out for freedom from commercial bondage.[50] However, one small concession in trade was offered in the additional instructions of December 30, 1776. In return for military assistance, the carrying trade between the United States and the West Indies would be shared an equal terms with France, to the exclusion of all other nations.[51]

The French government was quite willing to extend to the Americans all the tangible things demanded in the draft treaty as far as the immediate requirements of the war were concerned, except the recognition of independence which the signature of the treaty would announce. Franklin and Deane described the attitude of the court in May 1777 as follows: "Our treaty of commerce is not yet proceeded on, the plan of this court appearing to be not to have any transaction with us that implies an acknowledgment of American independency while their peace continues with England. To make

---

[49] John Adams, *Works*, II, 516-517.

[50] A memorandum by John Witherspoon, written apparently in 1783, throws some light on the instructions of December 1776. According to this statement, several members of Congress, feeling that the bid for an alliance was not high enough, were in favor of offering France an exclusive trade with the United States for a term of years, and of granting special tariff treatment to imports from France. However, "it was the opinion of a very considerable Majority of Congress to make no such Proposals; that they were contrary to the very spirit of our undertaking; that if we were to be independent we would be independent of the whole world. . . ." Burnett, *Letters of Members of the Continental Congress*, unpublished material.

[51] This was the only commercial concession. There were others concerning the fisheries and the conquest of the West Indies. *Journals*, VI, 1055. For a statement indicating that great exclusive privileges had been offered, see Vergennes to Montmorin, March 17, 1778, in Doniol, II, 837. Vergennes boasted that his government had refused to take any notice of them.

us more easy with this, they tell us we enjoy all the advantages already which we propose to obtain by such a treaty, and that we may depend on continuing to receive every indulgence in our trade that is allowed the most favored nations. Feeling ourselves assisted in other respects, cordially and essentially, we are the more readily induced to let them take their own time, and to avoid making ourselves troublesome by an unreasonable importunity."[52]

Less than a year later the French government, in consequence of the American victory at Saratoga and renewed steps toward conciliation on the part of Great Britain, decided to throw in its lot with the colonists. A treaty of alliance and a commercial treaty were signed at Paris, February 6, 1778.[53] The declared purpose of the former was "to maintain effectually the liberty, sovereignty, and independence absolute and unlimited, of the said United States, as well in matters of government as in commerce." The American negotiators were unable to obtain in the treaty of commerce the grant of national treatment for their fellow citizens which the draft treaty proposed. Most-favored-nation treatment in the King's European dominions and admission to the established free ports in the colonies was all that Vergennes would concede. A significant qualification of the usual most-favored-nation clause was introduced in the second article. As commonly expressed in eighteenth-century treaties, this clause provided that if one of the contracting parties should grant a special commercial favor to a third nation, the second party should immediately obtain it without granting an equivalent. By a special proviso, however, the Franco-American treaty stipulated that the second party should enjoy the favor only on allowing equivalent compensation if the third nation had paid a price for it. This proviso became thenceforward an important, though troublesome principle of American reciprocity policy.

It has been assumed by most writers on commercial policy

[52] Franklin and Deane to the Committee of Secret Correspondence, May 25, 1777, Wharton, II, 324.
[53] *Treaties and Other International Acts of the United States* (ed. Hunter Miller), II, 3, 47.

that the new principle was included in the treaty at the instance of the American government or its plenipotentiaries. There is, however, no mention of it in American documents. The evidence points to French authorship. It was apparently inserted for the purpose of demonstrating to the world that, as far as the French government was concerned, the United States remained perfectly free to make commercial arrangements with any country whatever without France benefiting therefrom because of her prior treaty.[54] The demand of the United States for equality of treatment as the only principle compatible with independence was readily acquiesced in by the French government, and Vergennes took pride in the fact that he had demanded no special privileges.[55]

Although the preamble of the treaty declared it to be the purpose of the two nations to avoid all special preferences and to leave each country complete control over its internal regulations, one special arrangement modifying the declaration of principle was included in the original treaty.[56] The prohibition of export duties on molasses from the West Indies to the United States proposed in the American treaty plan, although in keeping with French fiscal policy, was unacceptable to the government as a treaty provision without an equivalent concession by the United States. Gérard, French plenipotentiary, suggested that a similar exemption on tobacco exported to any of the French dominions would be a satisfactory equivalent. The commissioners objected to this because any partiality as to articles would arouse sectional ill feeling at home, and offered to exempt from export duty every production of the United States when shipped to the French Islands. This was quite acceptable to the French agent.[57]

These provisions occasioned a disagreeable quarrel among

[54] V. G. Setser, "Did Americans Originate the Conditional Most-Favored-Nation Clause?" *Jour. Mod. Hist.*, V (1933), 319-323.

[55] Vergennes to Gérard, March 29, 1778, Wharton, II, 523-526.

[56] Miller, *Treaties*, II, 10-11.

[57] Ralph Izard to Henry Laurens, Feb. 16, 1778, Wharton, II, 497-498. Deane to the President of Congress, Oct. 12, 1778, *ibid.*, pp. 764-765.

the commissioners, which places in exaggerated relief some of the forces active in the formation of commercial policy. Arthur Lee objected at first that the American equivalent was too large for the concession purchased. Franklin and Deane, demonstrating the bad policy of export duties, which could be used by America only to her own prejudice, prevailed upon him to consent, and the treaty was agreed to, though not signed. Lee, perhaps moved to some extent by jealousy of his colleagues, soon thought of another serious objection. Ralph Izard, awaiting in Paris an intimation that he would be *persona grata* as minister to the Grand Duke of Tuscany, supported him. "Should the article in question be agreed to," he argued, "the French might lay what duty they pleased upon their European exports, and even upon their sugar, coffee, and other productions of their islands, without our having any check upon them whatever. For if, in consequence of any such duty imposed by them, a duty were to be laid by America on any of her exports to France, the French vessels would have nothing to do but clear out for the West Indies and sail directly for Europe, or touch first at one of their islands."[58]

Lee asserted that he did not believe molasses to be of sufficient importance to justify "tying both our hands with the expectation of binding one of their fingers," nor did he wish to sacrifice agriculture for the benefit of commerce, which "whatever temporary advantages it may give, will be permanently pernicious to the peace and welfare of our country."[59] Later he and Izard affected to believe that Deane and Franklin were merely striving to advance the interests of the rum distillers, and classed them both as New Englanders.[60] In short, Lee would not sign the treaty with the objectionable articles included. Gérard refused to drop the articles, since they had already received the royal assent, but a verbal promise to void them in case Congress desired it

[58] Wharton, II, 477-479.
[59] Wharton, II, 481.
[60] Izard to Laurens, Wharton, II, 497-501, 710-714.

was given. The majority of Congress agreed with Izard and Lee, and demanded the suppression of the articles.[61] The episode is not to be attributed solely to the quarrels of jealous agents. It shows how deep was the influence of local interests in the actions of all except the greatest of the public men of the time, how serious was the fear of the toils of wicked Old World diplomacy, and how strong the desire to preserve as complete isolation as possible.

THE EXTENSION OF COMMERCIAL
PROPAGANDA AND DIPLOMACY

France was not the only country whose friendship Congress attempted to purchase through extending the opportunity of competing for a share of America's liberated trade. The question as to whether other countries than France ought to be appealed to had been raised early in the consideration of foreign policy. Franklin's influence had been exerted in opposition. In 1777 he wrote: "But I have never yet changed the opinion I gave in Congress, that a virgin state should preserve the virgin character, and not go about suitoring for alliances, but wait with decent dignity for the application of others."[62] He was overruled, apparently at the urging of Silas Deane. The attentions of certain foreign agents at the French court aroused the enthusiasm of the latter and led him to believe that more could be accomplished through the commercial argument than was actually the case.

"Would you have universal commerce," he wrote to the Committee of Secret Correspondence, October 1, 1776,[63] "commission some person to visit every kingdom on the continent that can hold any commerce with America. . . . It is of importance, as I have mentioned in my former letters to have someone deputed and empowered to treat with the King of Prussia. I am acquainted with his agent here, and have already received some queries and proposals respecting Ameri-

[61] *Journals*, IX, 459-460; Wharton, II, 482-483, 485, 498, 574-575, 582-583; Miller, *Treaties*, II, 32-34.
[62] Franklin to Arthur Lee, March 21, 1777, Wharton, II, 296.
[63] Wharton, II, 154-157.

can commerce, to which I am preparing a reply. I have also an acquaintance with the agent of the Grand Duke of Tuscany, who proposes fixing a commerce between the United States and Leghorn, but has not as yet given his particular thoughts. France and Spain are naturally our allies; the Italian states want our flour and some other articles; Prussia, ever pursuing her own interests, needs but be informed of some facts relative to America's increasing commerce to favor us: Holland will pursue its system, now fixed of never quarrelling with anyone on any occasion whatever. In this view is seen at once the power we ought to apply to and gain a good acquaintance with."

An earlier dispatch from Deane had already brought Congress to the decision to follow his recommendations. On October 16, 1776, additional instructions were prepared, authorizing the commissioners in France to negotiate with other powers with a view to inducing them to recognize American independence, and to conclude treaties of peace, amity, and commerce.[64] These instructions did not necessarily imply that the United States had decided to go about "suitoring" for alliances, but that the agents were authorized to receive proposals when made. But on December 30, 1776, it was "Resolved, That Commissioners be forthwith sent to the Courts of Vienna, Spain, Prussia and the Grand Duke of Tuscany."[65] The terseness of the resolution seems to speak eloquently of the recent military reverses about New York. The commercial policy expressed in these missions differs in no important respect from that of the French mission. The commissioners were to conclude no treaty which would be inconsistent with any treaty previously made with France, nor which was not based upon equality and reciprocity.[66] In no case was the extension of American commerce the primary purpose in sending the envoys.

[64] *Journals*, VI, 884.
[65] *Ibid.*, 1054.
[66] For the instructions for these envoys, see *Journals*, VI, 884. Wharton, II, 359-361; III, 352-353; IV, 201-203, 224.

In the history of commercial policy, the principal importance of these missions is that the envoys became agents for the spread of commercial propaganda. Numerous memorials were written and circulated where it was thought they would do most good, and the amount of oral propagandizing at conferences, dinners, and private conversations cannot be estimated. For example, William Carmichael went, at the request of the Prussian commercial agent at Paris, to Berlin to discuss trade with the ministers of Frederick the Great. On the way, he stopped at Amsterdam to try to interest Dutch merchants in a direct trade between the Netherlands and the United States, and to prepare a memoir on commerce for the benefit of the Russian minister to the Netherlands.[67] Deane sent home a memoir on the commerce of Tuscany, which the Grand Duke's envoy had given him in exchange for one on American trade. He learned that the Tuscan government had taken off "somewhat secretly" the duties on American produce as an encouragement to trade.[68] Early in 1777, Arthur Lee was inquiring into the difficulties under which American commerce was struggling at Bordeaux, and the means of removing them. A little later, he circulated a memorial in the Netherlands, demonstrating how that country could profit from the American trade.[69] Copies of a commercial memorial dated in January 1777 found their way into both the French and the Spanish archives.[70] Perhaps the most important service performed by Francis Dana at St. Petersburg was the preparation of a discourse on the advantages to Russia of the development of channels of commercial intercourse with the United States.[71] These are only a few

[67] Wharton, II, 166-167, 184, 187, 194; Samuel Gwyn Coe, *The Mission of William Carmichael to Spain*, pp. 3-4. Carmichael was at this time a volunteer aide to the American commissioners in France.

[68] Deane to Committee of Secret Correspondence, Nov. 26, 1776, Wharton, II, 194.

[69] Arthur Lee to the Committee of Secret Correspondence, Feb. 18, 1777, Wharton, II, 288, 543.

[70] *Stevens Facsimiles*, No. 614; Yela Utrilla, *op. cit.*, II, 28-30.

[71] Wharton, V, 529-531. Dana's purpose was to refute British propaganda which asserted that the free commerce of an independent America would be in-

illustrative cases of the activities by which the official agents and their helpers kept before the eyes of European public men and others the American view of the advantages which would accrue to Europe from the liberation of American commerce. Similar, though less extensive work of this character, was doubtless performed by the various commercial agents, many of whom were or had been merchants, designated by the Secret Committee,[72] by its successor, the Commercial Committee, by Congress itself, by the Commissioners in Europe, or by the individual states. It is not surprising that Franklin found the argument wearisome to the courtiers of Louis XVI.[73]

---

jurious to Russia because American products, especially naval stores, would come into competition with those of Russia. The American agent contended, on the other hand, that friendly commercial relations would discourage the production in America of competing articles, which had been stimulated in the past by British bounties; and that Russia would profit through obtaining American goods directly from the producer rather than from the British middleman.

[72] The function of the Secret Committee, appointed Sept. 18, 1775, which is not to be confused with the Committee of Secret Correspondence, was to arrange for the purchase of supplies for the Continental service and for the exportation of produce to pay for them. In July 1777, it was reconstituted and its name changed to Commercial Committee. *Journals*, II, 253-254; IV, 40, 53, 97, 169; VIII, 533-534; Burnett, II, xi, 474-475; IV, 177, 254; V, 50.

[73] Perhaps the best known of these agents in foreign ports were Oliver Pollock, who served at New Orleans from 1777 to 1782, and William Bingham, resident at St. Pierre, Martinique, from 1777 to 1780. Stephen Ceronio occupied for a time a similar position at Cape François, Haiti. Robert Smith was appointed agent at Havana in 1781. The Commissioners in France were empowered to appoint agents at the French seaports. Jonathan Williams served under them, as did William Hodge, Jr. Of commercial agents designated by individual states, Abraham Van Bibber at St. Eustatius is an example. Another is Philip Mazzei, whom Virginia sent to Tuscany to seek a loan. Thomas Barclay took up the duties of consul general in France in 1782. The principal duties of these agents were to purchase and supervise the shipment of supplies for the Continental service. However, through the connections they made and other means they undoubtedly advertised American commerce abroad. A large part of Pollock's correspondence is in Papers of the Continental Congress, 50, I and II; Bingham's, *ibid.*, 90, I; Barclay's in 91, I-II; Williams', *ibid.*, 90, II. See also Wharton, II, 162-163, 173, 181, 283, 287, 405-406, 561, 587-590; III, 35, 191, 823; V, 796; *Journals*, X, 139; J. F. Jameson, "St. Eustatius in the American Revolution," *AHR*, VIII, 685 (1903); R. F. Nichols, "Trade Relations and the Establishment of the United States Consulates in Spanish America, 1779-1809," *HAHR*, XIII (1933), 290; Howard R. Marraro, "Philip Mazzei, Virginia's Agent in Europe," *Bulletin of N. Y. Pub. Lib.*, XXXVIII (1934), 155-175, 247-274, 447-474, 541-562; R. C. Garlick, *Philip Mazzei*, 59-96.

Next to France, Spain appeared to Americans to be the most eligible candidate for abettor in the attempt to throw off the British yoke. This view was undoubtedly derived from the consideration that Spain was a close ally of France by virtue of the Bourbon Family Compact, that she was the third naval power of the world, and that the nearness of the Spanish colonies marked them out as convenient sources of supplies. In 1777, Arthur Lee visited Spain in the hope of inducing the government to commit itself to energetic assistance. He stressed the advantage to Spain of depriving Great Britain of the American trade.[74] About the same time, Congress designated Franklin envoy to Spain. He was well aware of the fruitlessness of further efforts to influence the Spanish government and remained in Paris.[75]

The government of Charles III was distinctly opposed throughout the Revolution to a formal connection with the American rebels. The advantage to Spain of the disruption of the British Empire was obvious. To assist in bringing it about, the government was quite willing to join with France in granting secret aid, and to allow Americans in Spanish ports the same commercial privileges enjoyed by subjects of other nations.[76] However, the encouragement of colonies to rebel against the authority of their mother country was a dangerous policy for the greatest of colonial powers. When Spain finally entered the war in 1779, it was for distinctly Spanish objectives: the recovery of Gibraltar, Minorca, and Florida, and the destruction of British contraband trade in the Gulf of Mexico. Spanish statesmen realized that the United States was potentially a serious threat to Spain's American provinces. They were determined to take every precaution possible to avoid removing the British danger only to set up

[74] Valentín Urtasún, *Historia diplomatica de América*, I, 248; Yela Utrilla, *op. cit.*, I, 161-180; Lee's Memorial to the Court of Spain, Wharton, II, 281-282; Grimaldi to Florida Blanca, March 5, 1777, Yela Utrilla, II, 76-79.

[75] Committee of Secret Correspondence to Franklin, Jan. 1, 1777; Franklin to Arthur Lee, March 21, 1777, Wharton, II, 242, 296-297; Urtasún, *op. cit.*, I, 249-250.

[76] Arthur Lee to Grimaldi, March 17, 1777, Wharton, II, 290; Urtasún, I, 248.

another in a free United States.[77] The events transpiring in
America were carefully watched by the agents of Charles
III. Early in 1778, Juan de Miralles, a Havana merchant,
was sent to Philadelphia as "unofficial observer." He was especially active in keeping his government informed of events
in the United States, especially those occurrences which might
affect Spanish interests in Florida and the Mississippi valley.
Gérard reported to Vergennes that Miralles was convinced
that the United States was bound to become a future enemy
of Spain. He died in 1780 while on a visit to Washington's
winter quarters at Morristown, N. J., one purpose of the
visit being to induce the American commander to send sufficient reinforcements to South Carolina to prevent the
British from detaching troops to check the Spanish reconquest
of Florida. He was succeeded by his secretary, Francisco
Rendón.[78]

In 1779, Congress appointed John Jay as envoy to Spain.
He was never formally received at court. His instructions required him to propose that Spain agree to a treaty similar to
that concluded between the United States and France, and
to ask, in addition, the free navigation of the Mississippi below the southern boundary of the United States.[79] A little
later, Congress adopted an additional instruction that Jay
should use his "utmost endeavors" to obtain for Americans
the privilege of taking salt from the island of Sal Tortugas
and of cutting logwood and mahogany along the Gulf of
Honduras.[80] Inasmuch as one of Spain's objectives was to

[77] Grimaldi to Aranda, Feb. 4, 1777, Yela Utrilla, II, 62; A. P. Whitaker,
The Spanish American Frontier, 7; S. F. Bemis, *Pinckney's Treaty*, 16; Yela
Utrilla, I, 143-157; Urtasún, I, 248, 404-405.
[78] A ministerial note, without date, suggesting the appointment of an American agent and outlining his duties is in Manuel Conrotte, *La intervención de
España en la independencia de los Estados Unidos de la América del Norte*,
254-255. The correspondence of Miralles and Rendón with the Captain General
of Cuba and other officers is in AGI, Papeles Procedentes de Cuba, legajos 1281-
1283, 1291, 1301, 1319, and 1354; Gérard to Vergennes, July 25, 1778,
Doniol, III, 293-294; Yela Utrilla, I, 384-399; Urtasún, II, 95-99; Miralles
to Diego Josef Navarro, April 15, 1780, AGI, Papeles de Cuba, legajo 1281.
[79] *Journals*, XV, 1118; Wharton, III, 352-354.
[80] *Journals*, XV, 1140-1141; John Jay, *Correspondence* (ed. H. P. Johnston),
I, 248-250.

abolish British privileges in the Gulf of Honduras, it can be imagined that Jay's proposals were received with little favor. Florida Blanca, the Spanish foreign minister, heard the envoy, however, and showed considerable interest in the possibility that the United States, in return for money and military supplies, might furnish ships and naval stores for the Spanish fleet.[81]

Discouragement due to the existing military and financial situation of the United States induced Congress early in 1781 to make a more serious attempt to purchase the assistance of Spain. Jay was authorized to yield the claim to the navigation of the Mississippi south of the American boundary.[82] In September 1781, he obtained a conference with Florida Blanca, at which the latter discussed the subjects at issue in the relations of the two countries, apparently with a view to a formal negotiation. He said that Spain could, without difficulty, grant American commerce most-favored-nation treatment in Spain by treaty, but that trade to her American dominions could not be similarly legalized. The minister again inquired about the ability of the United States to supply Spain with ship timber and naval stores in exchange for pecuniary aid.[83]

After the conference, Jay submitted a rough summary of propositions to serve as the basis for a treaty. His commercial articles proposed mutual most-favored-nation treatment, with the proviso that the United States would declare contraband any branch of trade desired by the Spanish government. This

[81] Florida Blanca to Jay, March 9, 1780; Jay to Florida Blanca, April 25, 1780, Yela Utrilla, II, 278-280, 294-296.

[82] *Journals*, XIX, 152-153.

[83] Jay's notes of a conference with Florida Blanca, Sept. 19, 1781, John Jay, *Correspondence*, II, 118. Cuban ports were thrown open in 1779, because of the interference of the British navy with the usual supply trade from Spain. At the instance of Robert Morris, the principal American merchant interested, Congress sent two commercial agents to Havana, first Robert Smith, then Oliver Pollock. The ports were closed after the conclusion of peace in 1783. The subject of the Cuban trade is treated by R. F. Nichols, *op. cit.*, pp. 289-313. The right to obtain military supplies at New Orleans was granted in 1777. Certain trade rights at Havana were promised at the same time. Lee to Grimaldi, March 17, 1777, Wharton, II, 290-291; and Lee to Gardoqui, Dec. 4, 1778, *ibid.*, 848. See also J. A. James, "Oliver Pollock, 'Financier of the Revolution in the West,'" *Miss. Valley Hist. Rev.*, XVI (1929), 67-80.

clause, though no details were specified, seems to point to the readiness of Jay to bind his government to aid in enforcing Spanish regulations to prevent contraband trade to the American colonies. If this is true, the offer is one of the most important commercial concessions ever proposed to a foreign nation by the United States.[84] Florida Blanca seemed prepared at this time to enter a negotiation, at least to the extent of finding out the ultimate terms which Congress would offer. He informed Jay that the King was disposed to appoint a person to confer with him on the treaty.[85] However, the Spanish commissioner designated was not empowered to negotiate. A pretense of awaiting a proper occasion for entering on a negotiation was continued up until the conclusion of the treaty of peace with Great Britain.[86]

Deane's plan of turning the interest of the Prussian government to America's advantage seemed for a time very promising. The matter which first brought the American agents and Prussian officials together was the problem of the supply of tobacco for the royal monopoly. Prices were high, and toward the end of 1776, the article was almost unobtainable in the usual markets. The government wished to learn of the possibilities of a supply direct from Virginia. In addition, Frederick had long been interested in building up the trade of Emden and a market for Silesian linens. However, the impossibility of obtaining insurance on shipping, the lack

---

[84] Jay's propositions are in Wharton, IV, 760-761. In March 1782, Rendón, the unofficial representative of Spain in Philadelphia, apparently on his own initiative, addressed inquiries to Livingston regarding the military, financial, and commercial resources of the United States. He asked a statement of the commercial advantages of the proposed treaty with Spain, and to what extent the United States would coöperate to check illicit trade to the Spanish colonies. In his reply, Livingston intimated that, in the event of a general treaty, his government might be willing to assume some unspecified active responsibility for the prevention of smuggling. Rendón to Josef de Galvez, April 20, 1782, AGI, Papeles de Cuba, legajo 1319; Livingston to Rendón, March 6, 1782, Wharton, V, 226-227.

[85] Autograph note of Florida Blanca, Sept. 22, 1781, Yela Utrilla, II, 350-351; Jay to the President of Congress, Oct. 3, 1781, Wharton, IV, 763.

[86] Jay to the President of Congress, Feb. 6, Oct. 13, 1782, Wharton, V, 150, 809; Carmichael to the Committee of Foreign Affairs, Oct. 5, Nov. 17, 1781, Wharton, IV, 769, 842.

of a Prussian merchant marine and navy, and the danger from offending England were obstacles which American diplomacy could not overcome. The chief American objective in the Prussian adventure was the acquisition of a Baltic port wherein privateers could seek refuge, refit, and sell their prizes. In 1777, Arthur Lee tried to interest the King on that basis, pointing out that American produce could be brought by American ships, which could then go on privateering voyages, return and load for America with Prussian produce. This plan was very shortly dismissed by the King. In February 1779, Schulenburg, Frederick's minister of state, gave William Lee formal assurance that American ships would receive most-favored-nation treatment in Prussian ports. Lee thought this indicated a strong desire for trade, and advised the Committee for Foreign Affairs to encourage American merchants to send their ships to Prussia.[87]

Francis Dana spent a great deal of his time at St. Petersburg in devising a scheme for extending American commerce to Russia. In the spring of 1782 he transmitted to Secretary Livingston an account of Russian commerce, with a statement of the share of each foreign nation in it. There was a great demand in America for Russian hemp, cordage, sail cloth, and linens, which had been furnished previously through England. However, Russia bought few American articles, except some rice and indigo. Because of this, according to Dana, a

[87] The Prussian documents dealing with this negotiation are in General Controlle, Königl. Geheimes Ministerial Archiv, Tit. LVIII, No. 7, vols. I and II. The following documents in Vol. I are significant: Schulenburg to Montessuy, Sept. 12, 1776; Schulenburg's report of a conversation with Carmichael, Nov. 30, 1776; the King to Schulenburg, Dec. 2, 1776; Schulenburg to the King, June 21, 1777; the King to Schulenburg, June 23, 1777; Schulenburg to the King, July 3, 1777; Carmichael to Schulenburg, Nov. 2, 1777. And in Vol. II, the following: Schulenburg to A. Lee, Jan. 16, 1778; the King to Schulenburg, Feb. 1, 1778; Schulenburg to the King, March 30, 1778; Schulenburg to the King, July 25, 1778; William Lee to Schulenburg, Dec. 1, 1778; the King to Schulenburg, Dec. 19, 1778. See also F. Kapp, *Friederich der Grosse und die Vereinigten Staaten*, 16-20; Franklin and Deane to the Comm. of For. Aff., March 12, May 25, 1777, Wharton, II, 288, 322; A. Lee to Schulenburg, June 20, 1777, *ibid.*, II, 346; Schulenburg to A. Lee, June 26, and Oct. 8, 1777, Wharton, II, 350, 407; William Lee to Comm. of For. Aff., Feb. 25, 1779, Wharton, III, 65-67.

direct trade between Russia and the United States would not be likely to flourish; but he thought it would be possible to develop a prosperous circuitous trade by exchanging American produce for West Indian and French goods and carrying them to Russia.[88] He became so enthusiastic about the possibilities of his scheme that he believed it justifiable to pay the Russian ministers heavy bribes in order to secure a commercial treaty.[89] However, before the envoy seemed to have any prospects of being received by the Empress, peace had been made with England, and the main reason for a treaty with Russia, the securing of "support" for independence, had passed away. He was grudgingly given authority to make the treaty, but not to pay the necessary bribes, and he gave up the attempt.[90]

The well-known propensity of the Dutch for trade marked them out as ideal subjects for American propaganda, and a great deal of missionary work was done among them. Although the Dutch public was apathetic with regard to the American cause, the merchants, pursuing opportunities for gain, did all that could have been expected of them in supplying America. Dutch powder filled a large proportion of patriot powder horns and cartridge boxes during the early years of the war, and French supplies frequently came by way of Holland and in Dutch bottoms. The Dutch West India colony of St. Eustatius became the principal supply depot of the Revolution, until it was captured and sacked by Admiral Rod-

[88] Dana to Livingston, March 30, 1782, Wharton, V, 281-283. He recurred to the subject in a dispatch of Nov. 1, 1782, *ibid.*, V, 840-842. See also p. 24 above.

[89] Dana's dispatches to Livingston, Feb. 10, March 21, June 24, Aug. 17, 1783, Wharton, VI, 249-250, 327-328, 503, 655. He reported June 24, 1783, that the first ship flying the American flag in Russian waters had lately arrived at Riga, seeking a cargo of hemp.

[90] *Journals*, XXIV, 348-357. Madison's comment in his notes on the discussion of this matter in Congress is enlightening: "The disagreements on the questions relating to a Treaty of Commerce with Russia were occasioned chiefly by sympathies, particularly in the Massachusetts Delegation with Mr. Dana; and by an eye in the navigating & ship building states to the Russian articles of Iron and Hemp. They were supported by S. Carolina, who calculated on a Russian market for her rice." Madison's notes, *Journals*, XXV, 966. See also *ibid.*, 958, for explanation of Madison's opposition.

ney.[91] The prominent part played by the Netherlands as a neutral in supplying America and her allies caused Great Britain to force that country into the war in 1780. The draft of a commercial treaty, drawn up in 1778, in an unauthorized negotiation between William Lee, an American diplomatic agent, and Jean de Neufville, representative of the magistrates of Amsterdam, became the instrument which precipitated hostilities. The document was found among the papers of Henry Laurens, who was captured at sea while on his way to his post as United States minister to the Netherlands. Although the paper was unimportant from every point of view, the British government magnified its preparation into an un-neutral act.[92]

In sending Henry Laurens and then John Adams as envoys to the Netherlands, Congress was not concerned primarily about commercial regulations, but was anxious to obtain a loan. In fact, by the time Adams' importunity had induced the Dutch government to recognize him in his official capacity and show some interest in a commercial treaty, Congress had lost interest, partly because its members were disgusted at the procrastination of the States General, and partly because Yorktown had somewhat reduced the urgency of a Dutch connection.[93] The treaty which Adams finally concluded on October 8, 1782, contained no important new departure in commercial policy. Since the conclusion of the treaty with France, that instrument superseded the original model treaty, and placed a limitation upon the introduction of new proposals. Adams was obliged to drop the demand for the privileges of Dutch nationals in the Netherlands, and agreed to

[91] J. F. Jameson, "St. Eustatius in the American Revolution," *AHR*, VIII, 683-708; Bemis, *Diplomacy of the American Revolution*, pp. 116-117.

[92] William Lee to the Committee of Foreign Affairs, Sept. 12, Oct. 15, 1778, Wharton, II, 715, 787-788; Adams to the President of Congress, Nov. 16, 1780, *ibid.*, IV, 153-154; Bemis, *Diplomacy of the Revolution*, pp. 157-161. The treaty is in Wharton, II, 789-798. It is interesting to note that this draft contained a stipulation for mutual national treatment, a provision which was not admitted into the French treaty of 1778 nor into the treaty with the Netherlands of 1782.

[93] Livingston to Adams, Nov. 20, 1781, Wharton, IV, 850-851.

most-favored-nation treatment. The conditional clause was omitted. One interesting stipulation which held promise of possible great future advantage to the United States was included—a clause providing that the United States should enjoy the privileges of the most-favored-nation in the Dutch colonies. This concession, which was somewhat more liberal on paper than the clause regarding the colonial trade in the French treaty, was obtained by Adams with some difficulty.[94]

WAR-TIME ATTITUDES TOWARD TRADE WITH GREAT BRITAIN

Although some thought was given during the course of the war to the future commercial relations of the United States and Great Britain, the problem did not impress itself strongly upon the minds of the American leaders until the terms of peace came to be discussed. War-time bitterness gave rise in certain quarters to a feeling that hostility ought to be perpetual, and that the British should never be permitted to participate again in the trade. In 1776, Deane drew up articles for a proposed alliance between the United States, France, and Spain, one of which provided for the permanent exclusion of British ships from the United States and the French and Spanish colonies. He communicated this document to French government officials and to the Spanish minister to France. Carmichael reported in 1782 that the foreign diplomatic corps in Spain expected the French government to use its influence with Congress to secure the outlawry of British trade.[95] The various propositions for giving special privileges to France, of course, connoted the exclusion of her chief rival, but, as has been seen, none of these met with much favor. In fact, no plan received earnest support which could be construed as interfering with the right of American citizens to trade to the best markets.

Many Americans failed to support the outlawry of Brit-

[94] Livingston to Adams, July 4, 1782, Adams to Livingston, Oct. 8, 1782, Wharton, V, 592-593, 803-805; Miller, *Treaties*, II, 59-90.
[95] Wharton, II, 215-216, and footnote; V, 64. See also James Lovell to Franklin, Sept. 6, 1779, Burnett, IV, 421-422.

ish trade even during the war. In 1781, General Sullivan, then serving in Congress, wrote Washington that "the traffic carried on with the enemy is alarming, as it not only serves to furnish them with necessaries, but tends to reconcile our citizens to the idea of renewing their connection with Great Britain, and of course disaffects them to our Government."[96] Several channels were used to introduce British goods in exchange for American produce. In addition to the overland trade between the towns occupied by British troops and the adjacent country, collusive captures were concerted between British and American captains. Partly in order to supply the United States, particularly the southern states, with salt, and partly as a friendly gesture toward a neighbor, Congress permitted trade with Bermuda. This offered an excellent opportunity for introducing British goods. The ordinary neutral trade brought in articles indirectly from the British Isles. Also the permission sometimes given to individuals to bring in personal effects was taken advantage of for importing British manufactures.[97]

With the object of putting an end to this injurious and disgraceful traffic, Congress, with the approval and probably at the urging of the French minister, included in an ordinance regulating captures at sea, passed in December 1781, a clause providing for the seizure and condemnation of all produce of Great Britain and its dependencies, even in neutral bottoms, when taken within three miles of the American coast. A little later, it was recommended to the states to enact laws providing for the seizure of such merchandise when found on land.[98]

[96] Sullivan to Washington, March 6, 1781, *Correspondence of the American Revolution* (ed. Jared Sparks. 4 vols. Boston, 1853), III, 253.

[97] Samuel Adams to Caleb Davis, April 3, 1781, Burnett, VI, 43-44; The Virginia Delegates to the Governor of Virginia, Aug. 7, 1781, *ibid.*, VI, 170; President of Congress to the Governor of Maryland, Aug. 15, 1781, *ibid.*, VI, 185-186; Virginia Delegates to Governor of Virginia, June 25, 1782, *ibid.*, VI, 375; Madison to Edmund Randolph, July 9, 1782, James Madison, *Writings* (ed. G. Hunt), I, 215-216.

[98] Va. Delegates to Governor of Va., Jan. 8, 1782, Burnett, VI, 288-289; Pres. of Cong. to the Governors of the States, Jan. 6, 1782, *Pa. Archives, 1st series*, IX, 475; Madison to Edmund Pendleton, Jan. 8, 1782, Madison, *Writings*, I, 169; *Journals*, XXI, 1152-1158.

In an instruction to Adams, Livingston represented this legislation as adding attractiveness to the opportunity for foreigners to capture American trade. "You will also observe," he wrote, "that it uses means to put an entire stop to all kinds of commerce with Britain or in British manufactures. In consequence of this, new habits and new fashions must be introduced. Wise nations will not neglect this favorable moment to render them subservient to the interests of their own commerce and manufactures."[99]

In preparing their peace terms, Congress gave little attention to commercial arrangements. Two conclusions may be drawn from the nature of the few efforts which were made to deal with the subject. In the first place, the delegates expected that the British, while yielding political sovereignty, would endeavor in the peace negotiations to retain control of American commerce. Secondly, it was felt that, once independence was recognized, the United States would be courted with regard to trade. In the first committee report on proposals of peace to be offered the enemy, the following was included: "It may be stipulated that the subjects of the United States shall not trade to the East Indies, or engage in the slave trade, if adequate compensation can be obtained." The report also recommended that no exclusive privilege of commerce be allowed to Great Britain.[100] That part of the report regarding the East Indies and the slave trade was not adopted, and the only stipulation regarding commerce which remained constantly in the peace proposals was that forbidding the granting of exclusive privileges to Great Britain.

New England was much more concerned about the Newfoundland fisheries than the West India trade. In the instructions to the peace commissioner, which were adopted August 13 and 14, 1779, was a clause pledging the government neither to agree to a treaty of commerce nor to carry on any commerce with Great Britain except with the unanimous consent of the states until the rights of the Americans to the

[99] Wharton, V, 73-74.
[100] *Journals*, Feb. 23, 1779, XIII, 242-243.

fisheries should be guaranteed.[101] The commissioner was expected to govern himself by the treaty with France, to grant no privilege to Great Britain which had not been given to France, and to admit no "peculiar restrictions or limitations whatever in favor of Great Britain." "In all other matters," stated the instructions, "you are to govern yourself by your own discretion, as shall be most for the Interest of these States, taking care that the said Treaty be founded on principles of equality and reciprocity, so as to conduce to the mutual advantage of both nations, but not to the exclusion of others."[102]

John Adams was elected September 27, 1779, minister plenipotentiary for negotiating a treaty of peace and a treaty of commerce with Great Britain. The determination of Congress to secure complete independence in commercial matters is again fully shown in an additional instruction to Adams, dated October 18, 1780. It stated

. . . that in a treaty of peace it is the wish of Congress not to be bound by any public engagements to admit British subjects to any of the rights or privileges of the United States, but at all times to be at liberty to grant or refuse such favors according as the public interest and honor may dictate, and that it is their determination not to admit them to a full equality in this respect with the subjects of his most Christian Majesty unless such concession should be deemed by the said ministry preferable to a continuance of the war on that account.[103]

Adams, a few months after arriving in France, proposed to communicate his power for a commercial treaty to the British government, arguing that knowledge of the willingness of the United States to carry on commerce on the basis of reciprocity would encourage sentiment for peace among the people of Great Britain. A serious disagreement with Vergennes resulted, the French minister insisting that Adams keep his commission secret until Great Britain had shown a willingness to recognize American independence. Vergennes' influ-

[101] Wharton, III, 296-297. Jay to Franklin, Aug. 14, 1779, *ibid.*, 303-304.
[102] *Journals*, XIV, 955-967.
[103] Wharton, IV, 100-101.

ence caused Congress to revoke the commission for a commercial treaty, July 12, 1781.[104] From that time onward, there was no specific power held by any American agent for a commercial treaty with Great Britain, although the general authority of the peace commission which replaced Adams probably covered the conclusion of a commercial arrangement within the peace treaty. On October 27, 1781, a committee composed of James Lovell, Madison, and Daniel Carroll presented a report of instructions to the peace commissioners as to the best means to secure in a treaty of peace the demands which Congress did not desire to make *ultimata*. It was deemed the best plan to secure the intervention of the French government. In dealing with commerce, the committee declared that

... it is the wish and policy of the United States to preserve their commerce as unfettered as possible with stipulations in favor of nations with which they are now unconnected, and particularly of that with which they are now at War; that this policy cannot but coincide with the sentiments of his Majesty, since it alone will leave to his allies the future opportunity of manifesting their preference of his interests to those of his enemies and rivals; that Congress do for these reasons most earnestly desire, expect and entreat that his Majesty will spare no efforts that may be necessary to exclude from a treaty every article which would restrain the United States from imposing on the trade of Great Britain any duties, restrictions or prohibitions which may hereafter be judged expedient. ...

On January 22, the report was sent to another committee, and, when again presented, the paragraphs relating to commerce had been stricken out. The whole report was ordered recommitted, and seems never to have been brought up again.[105]

It was not until 1782 that American leaders began to consider seriously the commercial problems with which they would be obliged to deal in a settlement with Great Britain. Perhaps the more serious application to the subject at this

[104] Adams to Vergennes, July 17, July 26, 1780, Wharton, III, 861-863, IV, 7-11; Vergennes' observations on Adams' letter of July 17, *ibid.*, 3-6; Vergennes to Franklin, July 31, 1780, *ibid.*, 18-19; *Journals*, XX, 746.
[105] *Journals*, XXIII, 480-481, 524.

time was influenced by the fact that during the last years of the war it was difficult to carry on any trade at all, so closely were the ports guarded by the British cruisers.[106] Secretary Livingston was the first high official to place emphasis upon the importance of securing the West India trade in the treaty of peace and its importance in the general commercial system of the country. In a letter to Adams July 4, 1782, he called attention to the value of the sugar island trade in the intercourse of the United States with the Dutch.[107] On August 29, he reverted to the subject, with more particular reference to the importance of the market for lumber and provisions in the British islands.[108]

In letters to Franklin and Jay, he continued urging care for commerce, and particularly the West India trade. Franklin was instructed to "press earnestly" the latter subject in the negotiation with the British. The French West Indies were also included in his discussion. If provisions were excluded from the islands, he argued, American agriculture would suffer. In the readjustment which would inevitably follow, the colonial powers would have to pay. Consumption of their sugar would decline, and Americans would turn more and more to manufacturing. It would be to the advantage of England and France for the United States to remain agricultural, and thus furnish a growing market for their manufactures. If any depression in the agriculture of the metropolis resulted from throwing open the colonial trade, it would be compensated for by the cheapening of the costs of manufacturing through reducing the outlay necessary for provisions and for ocean transportation.[109] Livingston also favored an attempt to secure a share in the logwood and mahogany trade, if the British were able to retain their old privileges in the Bay of

[106] Livingston to Franklin, May 22, 1782, Wharton, V, 434-435. See Robert Morris' "state" of the American trade and plan for its protection, *Journals*, XXII, 264-274; Wharton, V, 395-396.

[107] Wharton, V, 592. Francis Dana had touched upon the subject in his despatch on Russian trade March 30, but this did not reach Livingston until September 1782. Wharton, V, 741.

[108] Livingston to Adams, August 29, 1782, Wharton, V, 677-679.

[109] Livingston to Franklin, Sept. 5, 1782, Wharton, V, 697-698; Livingston to Jay, Sept. 12, 1782, *ibid.*, 720-724.

Campeche and the Gulf of Honduras. The English, he thought, could not oppose the granting of the privilege to the United States without weakening their own title, which rested upon the same ground of long usage. On the other hand, Spain would gain nothing by excluding Americans because such action could have no other effect than to give a monoply to her rival.[110]

Also of interest in this period is a paper entitled "Thoughts on the West India Trade," which was presented as a memorial to Congress by an unnamed petitioner. This memorial became the basis of a report which was read November 21, and referred to the Secretary for Foreign Affairs and by him sent to the representatives abroad "as a useful material of information."[111] This treatise introduces its subject by stating that the American people were beginning to turn their attention to the situation of their trade, and that,

. . . eased of the oppressive monopoly with which they were kept down by England, they look forward to an extension of their European commerce, and readily discern the vast advantage which will accrue to them by the liberty of carrying their produce to the markets where it is likely to sell to most advantage, and of purchasing the goods necessary for their own consumption, wherever they can be got cheapest and best.

Since the English policy had always been to confine the colony trade to themselves, no indulgence could be expected from that quarter. The plan proposed was one of joining with France to develop her sugar islands, the United States contributing supplies of cheap provisions. The opening of this market to the United States would also increase their capacity to consume French sugar and manufactures.[112] The French government was not inclined, however, to unreservedly throw open the ports of the French West Indies to the United States. In a letter to Luzerne, dated October 14, Vergennes had noted the growing American interest in the matter, and had declared that French maritime industries, which were largely dependent

---

[110] *Ibid.*, 697-698.
[111] *Journals*, XXIII, 747; Livingston to Franklin, Jan. 6, 1783, Wharton, VI, 198.
[112] Papers of the Continental Congress, No. 25, II, 153.

upon the colonial monopoly, could not be sacrificed for the benefit of the United States.[113]

COMMERCE IN THE PRELIMINARY PEACE DISCUSSIONS

When the British and American agents met to begin the negotiations for a treaty of peace, neither party was at all certain what the attitude of the other would be with regard to commerce. Furthermore, the British Government was in doubt as to what sort of arrangement would be best for British interests. Strange to say, each party was prepared to demand liberal concessions on the part of the other. In his conversation with Oswald, July 9, 1782, Franklin reverted to the original "Plan of Treaties," and proposed reciprocal national treatment in matters of commerce. This appeared in his list of "advisable" articles, which he offered as preparing the ground for a return of friendship between America and England.[114] The Earl of Shelburne feared some sort of secret arrangement between France and the United States, and he also feared that the latter was determined to restrict trade with England. On a draft of instructions to Oswald, he wrote,

Insist in the strongest manner that if America is Independent, she must be so of the whole world. No secret, tacit, or ostensible connection with France. . . . It is reasonable to expect a Free Trade, unincumbered with duties to every part of America.[115]

Instructions of July 31 proposed "that in future an unreserved system of naturalization should be agreed upon between Our Kingdoms and the American Colonies."[116] Weeks of quibbling about the powers of the British plenipotentiary and the method by which the independence of the United States should be recognized intervened before the negotiation really got under way. In the meantime, close contact between the allies had been interrupted because of the belief of Adams and Jay that the "perfidious" Frenchmen

[113] AAE, CP, EU, XXII.
[114] Oswald to the Earl of Shelburne, July 10, 1782, Shelburne Papers, LXX.
[115] Shelburne Papers, LXXI.
[116] Shelburne Papers, LXX.

had sold their brothers into Egypt in order to advance purely Franco-Spanish interests; and the British had won two victories at Gibraltar. In this series of events, in all probability, the Americans lost their first good opportunity for a satisfactory regulation of Anglo-American trade by treaty.

In the first draft of articles, which was made October 5, and which Oswald agreed to send home for the opinion of his principals, was inserted a commercial article, which stipulated "that the navigation of the river Mississippi, from its source to the Ocean, shall forever remain free and open, and that both there and in all rivers, harbors, lakes, ports, and places belonging to his Britannic Majesty or to the United States in any part of the world, the merchants and merchant ships of the one and the other shall be received, treated and protected like the merchants and merchant ships of the sovereign of the country," except that the monopolies of the British chartered companies were to remain intact.[117] In reporting to Livingston, Franklin did not enclose a copy of the articles as agreed upon, but merely summarized them. This summary did not indicate that in the draft, national treatment of British subjects by the American government was set off against a stipulation of reciprocal national treatment of Americans by the British government. This resulted in a misunderstanding which elicited the first official declaration by the United States government that it intended to adopt the "reciprocity" article (Article II) of the French treaty as its permanent policy, and demand compensation of a specific nature when admitting another power to most-favored-nation privileges. Congress instructed the commissioners to word the commercial articles so as to make it perfectly clear that the United States granted the favor in question in return for a similar concession on the part of Great Britain. Livingston wrote:

You will see that without this precaution every ally that we have that is to be treated as the most favored nation, may be entitled to the same

[117] Wharton, V, 807.

privileges, even though they do not purchase them by a reciprocal grant.[118]

It was just before the preparation of these articles that Jay made the suggestion that the British try to reconquer Florida with the troops from the garrison at New York. One of his strongest arguments in the effort to induce Oswald to recommend the plan to the ministry was that Florida, along with Canada, would afford an excellent depot for supplying the United States with manufactures. "By which means," wrote Oswald, paraphrasing Jay, "upon the whole, England, having those two keys in its hand, may still enjoy an exclusive monopoly of a large share of North American commerce; and consequently may not happen to be in point of Trade, so great a loser by the change, as is generally imagined."[119] At another time he wrote: "One of the commissioners tells me that we shall lose nothing (in the way of trade), and should be saved the expense and trouble of governing them." This last, which was one of the chief arguments used the following year by Lord Sheffield in the famous pamphlet demanding the application of the Navigation Acts to the trade between the United States and the British colonies, sounds strange in the mouth of an American official. At this time also, Oswald proposed that the United States and Great Britain agree to refrain from hostile acts at sea against each other's merchant ships during the course of the negotiations. He said that Jay was willing to consent that the British issue their proclamation, believing that American ship captains would voluntarily refrain, but that engagements with France would prevent a public act by Congress. Franklin at first seemed favorable, but, after conferring with Jay, decided that it would not be loyal to France to take such action.[120]

Several considerations doubtless contributed to Shelburne's

---

[118] Franklin to Livingston, Oct. 14, 1782, Wharton, V, 811; Livingston to Franklin, Jan. 6, 1783, *ibid.*, VI, 198; *Journals*, Dec. 31, 1782, XXIII, 838.

[119] Oswald to Shelburne, Shelburne Papers, LXX, 405-406. For a discussion of the British plan to use Canada as a base for supplying manufactures to the American back country, see G. S. Graham, *British Policy and Canada, 1774-1791*, 43-45.

[120] Oswald to Townshend, Oct. 5, 1782, Shelburne Papers, LXX.

decision to reject the commercial article of October 5. He probably had, personally, no objection to it, for he several times expressed his opposition to commercial monopoly.[121] However, his entire conduct in the negotiation seems to indicate that he was determined to grant at the dictation of a victorious enemy no more than was absolutely necessary to secure peace. His loudly trumpeted plan of reconciliation had one immediate object, and that was to induce the Americans to loosen themselves from French guidance. It is worthy of note that none of Franklin's "advisable" articles received much consideration, and they constituted the real reconciliation program. The commercial article was submitted for expert criticism to Francis Baring, perhaps the outstanding English merchant of his day. He was convinced of the necessity of maintaining substantially intact the monopoly of the colonial trade. "The West India Merchts.," he wrote, "are large owners of shipping & will probably make the greatest clamor if a measure is adopted so directly opposite to our act of Parliament."[122] In an instruction dated October 20, Shelburne informed Oswald that the Administration had no power to alter the Act of Navigation.[123]

The Shelburne government, however, proceeded to prepare the way for a renewal of commerce between Great Britain and the United States. The prime minister called upon John Pownall, former secretary of the Board of Trade and consulting expert on American affairs, to report as to what legal barriers stood in the way.[124] In February, the same agent submitted the draft of a bill authorizing the King to enter upon a negotiation with the Americans for a treaty of commerce, and to arrange temporary commercial regulations.[125] When the treaties were laid before Parliament, Shelburne defended them on the ground that it was best to strike with

---

[121] Fitzmaurice, *Life of William, Earl of Shelburne* (2nd ed.), pp. 11, 14, 181, 236-241.
[122] Baring to Shelburne, Oct., 1782, Shelburne Papers, LXX.
[123] Instructions to Oswald, Oct. 20, 1782, Shelburne Papers, LXXXVII. Franklin to Livingston, Dec. 5, 1782, Wharton, VI, 113.
[124] John Pownall to Shelburne, Jan. 30, 1783, Shelburne Papers, LXXII.
[125] Pownall to Shelburne, Feb. 7, 1783, *ibid.*

America before French habits became so common as to interfere with the marketing of British manufactures.[126] On February 22, however, the ministry was defeated in the House
of Commons on the question of the treaty, and the task of
providing a substitute for the colonial relationship devolved
upon the Fox-North coalition. Before the coalition had assumed full control, William Pitt introduced a bill for re-
establishing commercial relations on a most liberal basis, but
it made little progress in Parliament.

THE HARTLEY NEGOTIATION AND THE RESUMPTION OF TRADE

When negotiations were resumed in April 1783, David
Hartley, an earnest, professorial *philosophe*, succeeded Oswald at Paris. He was an old friend of Franklin, and had
long been a staunch defender of American rights in Parliament. He was much given to verbose discussion and the writing of long memorials. It cannot be said that his government
sent him for the mere purpose of amusing the American envoys until an American policy could be determined upon, but
that was the most important function which he actually performed. However liberal individual opinion may have been,
there was no one in England with the power to make a really
generous gesture toward America. Parliament was leaderless,
and broken into jealous factions. But there did exist in certain
quarters a fear of an American navigation act and restrictions
upon the introduction of English manufactures. The coalition
had no policy, except the excellent one of waiting for time and
events to point the way. While waiting, it was desirable to
keep the road open for a conciliatory policy if events should
make that desirable, and to lull the American plenipotentiaries into a sense of security.

The American diplomats, in spite of the fact that the
French alliance could no longer be relied upon to support the
negotiation, believed that they still had one excellent trump
card. This was the power to refuse the reopening of American
ports to British goods and British shipping. Franklin called

---

[126] William Cobbett, *Parliamentary History*, XXIII, 373-435, and notes for
this speech in Shelburne Papers, LXXXVII, 209 ff.

the attention of Congress to the point shortly after the conclusion of the preliminary treaty. "As the British ministry excluded our proposition relating to commerce," he wrote Livingston, "and the American prohibition of that with England may not be understood to cease merely by our concluding a treaty of peace, perhaps we may then, if the Congress shall think fit to direct it, obtain some compensation for the injuries done us as a condition of our opening again the trade."[127] It is to be noticed that it did not seem to occur to him that it would be necessary to use it as a means to prepare the British Government for "opening again the trade." Jay thought that "they mean to court us, and in my opinion we should avoid being either too forward or too coy."[128] Adams felt that he was perhaps in a more favorable position than he had ever been before as diplomat.

I said to my brothers, [he wrote] I shall be very ductile about commerce. I would agree at once to a mutual naturalization, or to the article as first agreed on by Dr. Franklin and Mr. Jay, with Mr. Oswald; or, I would agree to Mr. Hartley's propositions, to let the trade go on as before the war, or as with Nova Scotia; I could agree to any of these things, because that time and the natural course of things will produce a good treaty of commerce. Great Britain will soon see and feel the necessity of alluring American commerce to her ports by facilities and encouragements of every kind.[129]

Hartley arrived in Paris April 24, armed with two papers, one a "Proposal for a supplemental treaty," and the other entitled "General memorandums upon the proposed supplemental treaty." He believed the views which he had embodied in these papers expressed the policy of his principals, and he had left copies of them with Fox.[130] In his instructions, the opening of the British and American ports was given first place in the list of the objects of the negotiation. Secondly, he was to treat with the American plenipotentiaries "upon any Arrangements of Trade, on the Footing of Reciprocity and mutual convenience." Finally, he was to treat for the purpose

[127] Franklin to Livingston, Dec. 5, 1782, Wharton, VI, 113.
[128] Jay to Livingston, April 22, 1783, Wharton, VI, 388.
[129] John Adams, *Works*, III, 363.
[130] Hartley to Fox, April 27, 1783, PRO, FO, Series 4, II.

of concluding the definitive treaty of peace. He was limited strictly to "treating," and must send to London any articles which might be agreed upon.[131] It was not until the American envoys objected to negotiation with him on that account that his government sent him a full power—along with instructions to make no use of it except to pacify the American commissioners.[132] A private instruction from Fox, dated April 10, outlined what the Secretary for Foreign Affairs considered a fair commercial arrangement. Obviously, the most important concern was for the abolition of the war-time legislation closing the ports. Further than that, it would be desirable to secure the admission of British manufactures into America, and American raw materials into Great Britain without any other duties than those payable before the war. "With respect to the West Indies," he wrote, "there is no objection to the most free intercourse between them and the United States, and the only restriction intended to be laid upon that intercourse is forbidding American ships carrying to those Colonies any other merchandise than the produce of their own country." Also, it would be necessary to forbid American vessels carrying other than their own produce to Great Britain.[133]

The American commissioners submitted their first proposition April 29. It was substantially the same article as that included in the draft treaty of October 5, 1782. The opening of trade on the basis of exchange of the privileges of nationals was made contingent upon the prior evacuation of all posts within the boundaries of the United States.[134] The ground taken was assumed with skill, and if the commissioners could have depended upon their power to open the ports or to keep them closed, their position would undoubtedly have been a strong one. Hartley, preferring the American proposal to that outlined by his government, sent the articles to London. In return, he was severely disciplined by Fox, and the infinitesimal degree of liberty in negotiating which he possessed was further restricted. He was instructed to consult the Duke of

---

[131] Instructions to Hartley, April 18, 1783, *ibid.*
[132] Fox to Hartley, May 15, 1783, *ibid.*
[133] Fox to Hartley, April 10, 1783, *ibid.*
[134] Wharton, VI, 396-397.

Manchester, British ambassador to France, on the problems which arose in his conversations with the Americans. "I will freely own to you," wrote the Secretary, "that it appears to me by the First Article which you have sent over, that you have either not attended to or misunderstood my Instructions; in which it is particularly expressed that the Admission of American ships as British should be confined to such ships only as are laden with American Produce, where as it appears by your Article that it will be competent to the ships of the United States to bring into our Ports any commodities which it is lawful for a British ship to bring. I hope that notwithstanding this seeming sense of the words, no such idea is entertained by the American ministers, because if it be, it will be an insuperable Obstacle to any Agreement upon the subject; but words must be used in the Article to put this Question out of Doubt."[135]

American policy in the Hartley negotiation was partly directed toward bringing pressure to bear upon France, with the object of inducing that nation to grant a freer commerce with the United States. The suggestion came from Livingston, who had expressed to Franklin his regrets over the exclusion of the commercial article from the preliminary treaty. "It would have been very important to us," he declared, "to have got a footing at least in the British West Indies, as a means of compelling France to pursue her true interests and ours by opening her ports also to us."[136] After the first proposal, which stipulated mutual national treatment, had been made to Hartley, Franklin ostentatiously forwarded a copy to Vergennes. That veteran statesman, however, disdained to bargain with his late protégés. On May 20 he submitted to Franklin two explanatory articles which he proposed to add to the treaty of 1778, which would explain away the "conditional" principle in Article II, and oblige the United States, if the British should accept the article proposed, to give Frenchmen the privileges of American citizens, but without the right to require compensation from France. Franklin neg-

---

[135] Fox to Hartley, May 15, 1783, PRO, FO, Series 4, II.
[136] Livingston to Franklin, March 26, 1783, Wharton, VI, 344.

lected to send the Vergennes articles to Congress until after the signature of the definitive treaty. But when revising its commercial policy in 1784, Congress agreed to a declaration that it did not intend to admit any nation to greater commercial privileges than France.[137]

Upon the rejection of the American proposal, the plenipotentiaries proceeded to the consideration of a temporary convention which would serve the purpose of opening the ports, leaving time for the development of a permanent convention. Upon what principle should it be drawn? The American principle was that of "literal" reciprocity, which the commissioners were ready to accept to any degree which the British might choose, from the slightest of mutual concessions to the most complete naturalization. The British could not accept this principle at the moment, but were willing to compromise on an arrangement which would afford "virtual" reciprocity. Restoration of trade as before the war would be such an arrangement, and Hartley formally proposed it May 21. The American commissioners demanded whether or not he had authority to sign such an article. It appeared that he had not, whereupon they refused to consider it. Hartley had gathered from their conversation that they were willing to accept the *ante bellum* status temporarily if offered *in toto;* i.e., if the privilege of American ships to carry directly from the West Indies to Great Britain were included. Without that concession they would not accept the principle. He believed that he could have concluded an article immediately if he had been able to concede the point.[138]

[137] The documents in regard to this affair are printed in *Treaties and Other International Acts of the United States* (ed. Hunter Miller), II, 158-161. See also Commissioners to the President of Congress, September 10, 1783, Wharton, VI, 691. An interesting comment by Hartley on American relations with France at this time is in Hartley to Fox, April 30, 1783, and June 2, 1783, PRO, FO, Series 4, II.

[138] The several projects and counter-projects exchanged are in Wharton, VI, 396-397, 442-444, 460-462, 465-469. The more important correspondence dealing with the negotiations is as follows: Henry Laurens to Livingston, June 17, 1783, Wharton, VI, 491-493; Adams, Franklin, and Jay to the President of Congress, Sept. 10, 1783, *ibid.*, 687; Fox to Hartley, May 15, June 10, 1783; Hartley to Fox, April 30, May 3, May 20, June 2, June 20/22, 1783, PRO, FO, Series 4, II.

In a letter dated June 10, Fox declared that if the Americans would accept the principle with the restriction, "no time need be lost in finishing this business," even though the United States should in return prohibit non-British produce in British vessels.[139] But he sent no instructions to sign. In his next dispatch, Hartley demanded frantically, "Give me leave upon this occasion to beg of you, that you will send me specifically an article that I may sign." At this point, a report from private sources arrived that the American ports had been opened by an order of Congress of April 24. Both sides agreed that this development affected the negotiation fundamentally, and discussions were suspended until official information arrived, and Hartley could consult his court. In the course of the delay, the commissioners saw in the pamphlet recently published by Lord Sheffield the crystallization of a policy contrary to that formerly professed.[140] This view was borne out by the issue of an order in council on July 2, which restricted American imports into the British West Indies and confined them to British vessels. The negotiation for a commercial treaty was dropped, in spite of Fox's protestation that his government had not changed its views and was willing to agree to a liberal arrangement.[141]

The report which occasioned the suspension of the negotiation was erroneous, although in fact the ports were shortly opened to British vessels and goods; and the British government was doubtless informed of the great eagerness on the part of the American merchants to resume trade. But Congress resisted the pressure of the merchants, those of Philadelphia being particularly importunate, and refused to declare that the cessation of hostilities repealed the restrictive laws enacted for the duration of the war.[142] The French minister, Luzerne, was consulted and advised against it,

---

[139] Fox to Hartley, June 10, 1783, *ibid.*

[140] John Baker Holroyd, Lord Sheffield, *Observations on the Commerce of the American States with Europe and the West Indies* (London, 1783).

[141] Hartley to Fox, June 20/22, 1783; Fox to Hartley, July 29, 1783, PRO, FO, Series 4, II.

[142] The North Carolina Delegates to Governor Martin, Sept. 26, 1783, *N. C. State Records*, XVI, 885; Burnett, VII, 309-310.

showing that the restrictions would give the British a motive to hasten the evacuation of the posts still held in America. He added in a dispatch to Vergennes that delay would also prolong the exclusive market at the time enjoyed by French merchants in the United States.[143] Avarice found a way, however. Philadelphia judges held that the proclamation of cessation of hostilities terminated the state legislation against British goods, and the Philadelphia papers of April 29 and 30 carried notices that the port was open to the vessels of all foreign countries.[144] The other states followed suit.[145]

In other ways great eagerness was shown to renew commercial relations with Great Britain. Luzerne wrote that the arrival of news of the signature of the preliminary treaty of peace caused a considerable drop in the price of exchange on France, while the few bills on London negotiated for the subsistence of the British prisoners of war were in great demand, and merchants were preparing expeditions to British ports. In July, he reported that all the shipyards were busy constructing vessels for the West India trade. In the meantime, American vessels were rushing to British markets. As early as February 5, a ship flying the American flag was reported in the Thames. It had gone there from a French port with a cargo of oil, upon hearing the news of the armistice. On April 15, the two leading vessels of a fleet carrying wheat and flour from New England arrived at London.[146]

Although the negotiation for a commercial treaty was suspended, one commercial article remained under discussion at Paris. The British government was very desirous of doing something to protect the interests of the fur traders in the

---

[143] Luzerne to Vergennes, April 15, 1783, AAE, CP, EU, XXIV; Minutes of a verbal communication from Luzerne to Livingston, March 22, 1783, Wharton, VI, 330-332; *Journals*, XXV, 588-589. The *Pennsylvania Packet*, April 17, 1783, contains a forceful editorial advocating keeping the ports closed as a means of inducing the British to evacuate New York.

[144] *Pennsylvania Packet*, April 29, *Pennsylvania Gazette*, and *Pennsylvania Journal*, April 30, 1783; the North Carolina Delegates to the Governor of North Carolina, Sept. 26, 1783, Burnett, VII, 309-310.

[145] For example, the Virginia laws were repealed by act of the legislature May 17, and those of Massachusetts in the same way June 4. *Pennsylvania Journal*, May 28, and *Boston Independent Chronicle*, June 5, 1783.

[146] *Pennsylvania Packet*, June 7, 1783.

northwestern territory of the United States. The Quebec merchants had shown alarm as soon as the boundary settlement had become known, and Fox had given Hartley special instructions on the matter.[147] In his propositions for a definitive treaty, the latter proposed "equal and free participation of the different carrying places and the navigation of all the lakes and rivers of that country, through which the water line of division passes between Canada and the United States," together with complete free trade across the boundary. The American commissioners preferred to postpone this whole matter, except freedom of navigation in the waters crossed by the frontier line, for a treaty of commerce.[148] In later proposals, the Americans seem to have considered favorably making a special grant of national treatment for the trade between the British North American Colonies and the United States, but included a demand for the free navigation of the St. Lawrence.[149] However, the respective viewpoints were by this time too far apart to admit of reconciliation, and the articles of the preliminary treaty were signed as a definitive treaty without alteration.

[147] Memorial of the Quebec Merchants, Feb. 6, 1783, Shelburne Papers, LXXXVII, 463; Hartley to Fox, April 10, 1783, No. 1, PRO, FO, Series 4, II.

[148] Wharton, VI, 469-472.

[149] "Project for a definitive treaty of peace," July 27, 1783, Wharton, VI, 601-606. Americans in the Lake Champlain area were also interested in the regulation of trade across the northern frontier. Simon Metcalfe of Prattsburgh Township presented a memorial to Congress on behalf of those living on the tributaries of the St. Lawrence, praying that their interests be looked after in the treaty of peace. The memorial was dated October 7, 1782. In addition to the free navigation of the St. Lawrence, Metcalfe desired the privileges of building ships and boats on the river, of discharging and reshipping cargoes along its banks, of using the roads along the river, free "egress and regress" for persons and servants, and free access to the Indian country of the Northwest, with the privilege of wintering in the country and carrying on trade with the Indians without license from British officials, and also the liberty of fishing in the Gulf of St. Lawrence and of cutting wood and drying fish on the shores and islands of the Gulf and the coasts of Labrador. The memorial was referred to the Secretary for Foreign Affairs. In another memorial of March 1783, Metcalfe angrily complained that nothing had been done in the preliminary treaty with regard to his demands. Papers of the Continental Congress, No. 41, VI, folio 299; No. 42, V, folio 277; Journals, XXIII, 640-641; XXIV, 194, 212-213.

III

DISILLUSIONMENT AND CONFUSION
1783-1789

THE EVENTS following the peace soon demonstrated that the United States, in spite of the recognition of independence, remained an English colony in economic status. The acts of trade and navigation appeared to have been little more than paper regulations. The real restraining bond was an organization which had grown up to meet the needs of the American settlements. The establishment of permanent commercial connections with Continental Europe required more than the conclusion of liberal treaties. The Continental merchant must barter his manufactures for native American produce. He must study the peculiar needs of the Americans, and adapt his products and methods to American tastes and customs. The meeting of these conditions required an elaborate credit and marketing structure. The British had the advantage because they already possessed an efficient organization, and knew the requirements of the American market.

The desire of the Americans for European goods was insatiable. The only apparent limit was the capacity to pay. Payment with specie was out of the question. Within a short time after the peace, all the specie accumulated during the war through the expenditures of the French and British armies had been returned to Europe to balance the unfavorable exchange. The southern states suffered less than the others. Tobacco, indigo, and naval stores were in demand abroad. The northern and middle states, particularly New England, found themselves in a very difficult situation. The European market for wheat, flour, lumber, ships, fish, and whale oil was small. In the disposal of these articles it was necessary to compete with well-established European industries, usually enjoying governmental protection.

Prior to the war, the trade between the continental and West India colonies had been fundamental in the economic structure of the British empire. Without the livestock, provisions, and lumber, together with the ships to carry them, from the North, and the northern market for rum and molasses, the profits of the sugar planters and the productiveness of their estates must of necessity have declined. No other adequate market existed for those articles which the mainland colonists must sell in order to settle their debts for manufactures purchased in England. The New England shipping industry was especially dependent upon this commerce, which fed the coasting trade, the African slave trade, and a large part of the direct trade with Europe. Close economic relations fostered similar political doctrines, and it is possible that only a conviction of the futility of island communities struggling against a great naval power prevented the sugar colonies from joining in the war for independence.[1] It was assumed in America that the former mutually profitable connection would be restored with the establishment of peace.

The almost simultaneous application of restrictive regulations in the West Indies by Great Britain, France, and Spain took the country by surprise.[2] Both French and English mer-

---

[1] H. C. Bell, "The West India Trade before the American Revolution," *AHR*, XXII (1917), 272-274, 276-278, 286-287; Ragatz, *Fall of the Planter Class*, ch. v.

[2] The British Order in Council of July 2, 1783, excluded the very important articles of meat and fish, the produce of the United States, and limited all intercourse to British vessels. About the same time, the French ordinance of 1778, which authorized relatively free trade to the French West Indies, was withdrawn, and the decree of 1767 was again enforced. This excluded flour and other foodstuffs, the produce of the United States, permitted the export from the islands of rum and molasses only, and limited entry to two ports. American shipping was, however, admitted freely to the trade. Spain promptly restored the old colonial monopoly, and reinforced it by expelling, in February 1784, all foreigners from Cuba. H. C. Bell, "British Commercial Policy in the West Indies," *EHR*, XXXI, 429-441; F. L. Nussbaum, "The French Colonial Arrêt of 1784," *South Atlantic Quarterly*, XXVII, 63-64; Nichols, "Trade Relations," *HAHR*, XIII, 289-291.

chants, after the cessation of hostilities, flooded the ports with manufactures. To Americans, it seemed that this was all done in a hostile spirit by nations jealous of the potential power and prosperity of the country. It was widely held that England and France had entered upon a secret convention to throttle American trade.[3] In anticipation of a great expansion of trade after the war, the shipyards were filled with vessels under construction. The enforcement of the restrictions made the vessels useless, and some were allowed to rot on the stocks. The ports rapidly filled with English shipping.

Once the actual situation became clear, the American leaders turned their attention to the means of adjustment. The merchants themselves undertook one means, that of finding a new commerce to replace that lost to them, and began to send their ships to the Far East; but the China trade was for some time in the experimental stage and could not serve as substitute for the short, peddling voyages between continental ports and the Caribbean islands. A gesture was made toward reviving the voluntary boycott of British goods. The Chamber of Commerce of Philadelphia named a committee of correspondence to keep in touch with similar bodies in other ports with the purpose of concerting measures of resistance. An assembly of merchants at New Haven bound themselves not to accept commissions from merchants in ports closed to American shipping, and appointed a committee to make every effort to prevent the disembarkation of cargoes from such ports brought in foreign ships. Boston merchants took similar action.[4]

[3] The charge that a combination existed among the colonial powers, the purpose of which was to exclude the United States from the West Indies, was given currency in the dispatches of John Adams. Adams, *Works*, VIII, 74, 85, 90, 98; Wharton, II, 533-34. Jay informed Otto that it was generally believed and that he himself could not help believing that there was a secret convention on the matter between England and France. Otto to Vergennes, Aug. 13, 1786, AAE, CP, EU, XXXII. See also Luzerne to Vergennes, Dec. 1, 1783, *op. cit.*, XXVI. Vergennes denied the existence of any international understanding hostile to American commerce but was delighted at American resentment caused by British restrictions, believing it would benefit French trade. Vergennes to Luzerne, Dec. 24, 1783, Feb. 15, 1784, *ibid.*, XXVI, XXVII.

[4] Luzerne to Vergennes, Dec. 8, 1783, AAE, CP, EU, XXVI; George Bancroft, *History of the United States* (New York, 1888), VI, 139.

However, general reliance was placed in governmental regulation of a retaliatory nature. John Adams recommended an American navigation act in no uncertain terms as soon as he learned of the British Order in Council of July 2,[5] and continued regularly to urge that policy. Jay and Laurens, though not so outspoken, were doubtless of the same opinion.[6] Franklin was very cautious. It would be for Congress to decide

... whether it will be most prudent to retort with a similar regulation in order to force its repeal, which may possibly tend to bring on another quarrel, or to let it pass without notice, and leave it to its own inconvenience, or rather impracticability, in the execution, and to the complaints of the West India planters, who must all pay much dearer for our produce under those restrictions.[7]

There was not a great deal of opposition to the principle of retaliation, although there was some criticism by southern statesmen who feared a northern monopoly of shipping. As the plan for defense developed, it displayed two main features. In the first place, unfavorable foreign regulations were to be countervailed by similar regulations in this country. To make this plan effective, Congress would need to be invested with authority for the control of foreign trade. Secondly, a new policy for commercial treaties was to be formulated and a new commission sent abroad to negotiate with the European states. It was believed that Europeans were so much interested in gaining a share of American commerce that they would be inclined to bid against each other in granting favors to the United States, and that if one colonial power would relax the restrictions in its islands, the others would be obliged to do likewise.[8]

The possibilities of negotiation were not unpromising in the year 1783. The American commercial propaganda aroused

---

[5] Adams to Livingston, July 14, 1783, Wharton, VI, 541-542.

[6] Laurens to Livingston, Sept. 16, 1783, Wharton, VI, 700; Laurens to Thompson, March 28, 1784, *ibid.*, 790-91; Jay to Morris, July 20, 1783, *ibid.*, 577-578.

[7] Franklin to Livingston, July 22, 1783, Wharton, VI, 581.

[8] Jefferson to Jay, March 12, 1786, Jefferson, *Writings* (ed. P. L. Ford), IV, 199.

wide interest in Europe, both among governments and private individuals, although it had failed to induce cautious rulers to brave Britain's rage to aid in winning independence. No sooner had the recognition of independence by Great Britain become known than government agents and commercial people began to approach the American plenipotentiaries with regard to the means of extending commercial interests in the new nation. Franklin was the recipient of most of these inquiries and proposals.

One of the first overtures was made by the government of Sweden, and the result was the third commercial treaty concluded by the United States—the first unsolicited recognition. From the American point of view, there was nothing new in the Swedish treaty. The policy was that of the treaty of 1778, the only effect of which would be to prevent discrimination against the United States as compared with other foreign nations. Franklin reverted to the principle of the French treaty, and stipulated that a privilege acquired by one nation by a reciprocal concession could be secured by another only on granting an equivalent.[9] In its instruction to Franklin, Congress declared that "the direct and essential object of the treaty is to obtain the recognition of our Independency by another European power."[10] The Swedes were interested in finding a market for iron. Even before the conclusion of the treaty, the Baron de Hermelin was dispatched to the United States to examine political and economic conditions.[11] Swedish consuls were commissioned to reside at Philadelphia and Boston.[12]

[9] Adams was very critical of the treaty with Sweden, both from jealousy of Franklin, and because he did not think the treaty was in the interest of American navigation. Prior to agreeing to the treaty, the Swedish government had reduced the duties on American produce when imported in Swedish vessels. Adams believed that the commercial treaties ought to prevent discrimination in favor of the subjects of the contracting parties. Adams to Livingston, Aug. 3, 1783, Wharton, VI, 631-632; Adams to James Warren, Sept. 10, 1783, *Adams-Warren Letters*, II, 222. The treaty is in Miller, *Treaties*, II, 123-150.

[10] *Journals*, Sept. 28, 1782, XXIII, 623-624.

[11] A. B. Benson, *Sweden and the American Revolution*, 47-48 and note.

[12] *Journals*, XXVII, 659; *Secret Journals of the Acts and Proceedings of Congress*, III, 555.

Among the other governments which made inquiries of the American envoys in France were those of Denmark, Saxony, Portugal, Tuscany, Ragusa, Prussia, and the Empire.[13] Franklin began the negotiation of treaties with Portugal and Denmark.[14] The city of Hamburg applied directly to Congress, and sent John Abraham de Boor to bear the letter and receive a reply.[15] Prince Kaunitz, the Austrian Chancellor, and the "elder brother of the King of Bavaria" applied to Franklin for the "names and solidity" of American merchants. He declined to give the desired information as being improper coming from him, but recommended that investigators be sent to the United States.[16] The need of personal investigation was much stressed by Franklin. When the Neapolitan publicist, Gaetano Filangieri, inquired about the advisability of removing to America, Franklin refused to advise it without his first examining the possibilities on the spot. He suggested that Filangieri apply to the Neapolitan government for an appointment as commercial investigator.[17] The Republic of Genoa proposed to send a consul in 1784, but Franklin discouraged this until a commercial treaty should have been agreed upon.[18] Saxony sent Philip Therriot across the Atlantic in 1783 to exercise the function of special commercial commissioner.[19] The Austrian government sent Baron de Beelen-Bertholff in 1784 to represent the interests of the Austrian Netherlands.[20]

---

[13] Wharton, VI, 539-540, 580-588, 609-610.

[14] Franklin to Livingston, June 12, 1783, Wharton, VI, 480.

[15] Senate of Hamburg to Congress, March 29, 1783, Wharton, VI, 351-352; Journals, Oct. 29, 1783, XXV, 758.

[16] Franklin to Ingenhousz and Deux Ponts, May 16 and June 14, 1783, Franklin, Writings (ed. Smyth), IX, 43-44, 50-51. He overstepped the self-imposed line of scrupulousness, however, in recommending Mr. Richard Bache of Philadelphia and Mr. Williams of Boston to the Saxon Minister. W. E. Lingelbach, "Saxon-American Relations," AHR, XVII, 521 and note.

[17] Franklin, Writings (ed. Smyth), IX, 1-3.

[18] Franklin to Spinola, Sept. 13, 1784. Dip. Corresp., I, 506-507.

[19] Lingelbach, op. cit. 524-525.

[20] Hans Schlitter, Die Berichte Baron de Beelen-Bertholffs, 235-238.

THE MOVEMENT FOR CONGRESSIONAL CONTROL
OF COMMERCE

The movement in Congress for a centralized commercial system as the essential preliminary in any war upon injurious foreign systems began with a report by a committee composed of James Duane, John Rutledge, Thomas Fitzsimons, Elbridge Gerry, and Stephen Higginson, which was adopted September 29, 1783.[21] The assigned task had been merely to report upon the correspondence of the ministers abroad, but the committee went beyond the usual summary and suggestions. The hints of retaliation, negotiation, and greater energy in government which had been thrown out in the dispatches of the commissioners were seized upon and transformed into a thoroughgoing program for the aid of commerce, which became the foundation of the commercial policy of the Confederation period. The injurious nature of the British regulations, and of those expected soon to be promulgated by France was briefly described, and the remedy declared to be retaliation. This could be successfully carried out "only by delegating a general power" for regulating commerce. A special committee was proposed to prepare an address to the states, reporting the facts and pointing out the measures which the situation required. Further, if the United States were to "become respectable" in the eyes of Europe, it must be by means of more energy in government. European jealousy of American prosperity required that new political and commercial arrangements be instituted. A committee was recommended to consider this subject—a committee to devise means to strengthen the union. A third committee was proposed to study and report plans for the negotiation of commercial treaties with foreign powers.

[21] *Journals*, XXV, 628-630. While the Articles of Confederation were under consideration in 1778, the legislature of New Jersey declared in favor of conferring complete authority over foreign trade upon the central government. The prevention of unfair taxation by New York and Pennsylvania of imports into New Jersey was the object, rather than the retaliation of foreign regulations, however. *Journals*, June 25, 1778, XI, 648; W. C. Hunter, *The Commercial Policy of New Jersey*, 26-27.

Compared to this original report the product of the special committee[22] on the address to the states was a tame affair. The facts were set forth in general terms lacking in vigor, the only forcefulness being in the annexed abstracts of the Adams and Franklin letters. The most noteworthy statements were to the effect that it might be expected that all Europe would follow the example of Great Britain, and that, while all the states would not suffer alike, if the least important should suffer, it would behoove all the others to aid in obtaining relief. The recommendation was without strength. "The several states being sovereign and independent possess the power of acting as may to them seem best. Congress will not attempt to point out the path which should be pursued."[23] Congress recognized the inadequacy of the address, recommitted the report, and reconstituted the committee, adding members until it contained three of the ablest men in Congress: Gerry, Hugh Williamson, a strong nationalist from North Carolina, and Thomas Jefferson.[24]

A revised address was reported April 22, 1784. Its recommendations were made to rest upon broad considerations of national policy. It was the duty of Congress to be attentive to the conduct of foreign nations and to take measures to prevent proceedings that might prove injurious to the interests of the United States. Injury to trade was not looked upon as harming a part of the Union only; but

. . . the fortune of every citizen is interested in the fate of commerce, for it is the constant source of industry and wealth; and the value of our produce and our land must ever rise or fall in proportion to the prosperous or adverse state of trade. . . . It will certainly be admitted that unless the United States can act as a nation and be regarded as such by foreign powers, and unless Congress for this purpose shall be vested with powers competent to the protection of commerce, they can never command reciprocal advantages in trade; and without such reciprocity, our foreign commerce must decline and eventually be annihilated.

[22] The members were Fitzsimons, Duane, and Arthur Lee.
[23] *Journals*, Oct. 9, 1783, XXV, 661-664.
[24] *Ibid.*, 664 and note.

For the purpose of securing such reciprocity two clear-cut recommendations were made. The states were advised to vest Congress for the term of fifteen years with full authority, first, to prohibit the import or export of goods in vessels belonging to the subjects of any state with which a treaty of commerce had not been concluded; and, secondly, to prohibit the import in the vessels of any state having a treaty, of goods not the produce of that state.[25]

The energetic enforcement of laws based on these proposals would have gone a long way toward replacing the United States in the position occupied before the premature opening of the ports in 1783. The first proposition would have enabled the diplomatic agents to say to foreign governments: "Sign treaties satisfactory to us or we will close our ports to your flag." The second proposition contemplated a system whereby the trade of the United States would be limited to American ships and those of the country producing the goods given in exchange for American produce. Such a plan, carried into execution, would not only have proved a strong stimulus to American shipping, but would have struck a heavy blow at Great Britain's position as middleman between the United States and the rest of the world. It is to be noted that the address envisaged nothing further than a navigation act, and did not propose any means of direct retaliation against tariff discriminations or prohibitions of American produce. Presumably, it was believed that pressure upon the shipping of states having an important merchant marine would be effective in forcing an arrangement of these matters also.

The address was adopted April 30 with surprisingly little opposition, although an amendment was added requiring the consent of nine states to any legislation under the powers sought.[26] There was little opposition among the states to the content of the recommendations. The reason for the failure of the plan lies in inertia and the inefficiency of the political

[25] *Journals*, April 22, 1784, XXVI, 269-271.

[26] *Journals*, April 30, 1784, XXVI, 317-322. The Rhode Island delegation and one member from Connecticut favored an amendment simply requesting the states to take the action desired. *Ibid.*, 321-322.

machinery, which prevented the people from carrying their intentions into effect. Three states—Virginia, Maryland, and Pennsylvania—had voted to confer the necessary authority even before Congress requested it.[27] But the states were slow to pass the desired acts, and when passed, they differed from each other so much that Congress could not be said to have a uniform authority in all the states. A committee reported March 3, 1786,

. . . that four states have complied, three others have also complied, but have determined the time of commencement so that there will be a dissimilarity in the duration of the power granted; that three other states have passed laws in pursuance of the recommendations, but so inconsonant to them, both in letter and spirit, that they cannot be deemed compliances; and that three other states have passed no acts whatever.[28]

The attention of the states was again called to the problem,[29] and after another delay, some progress was made. When the status of the measure was again examined in October 1786, it was found that all the states had passed acts in compliance with the recommendation, and it only remained for New Hampshire and North Carolina to revise their acts in some degree, before Congress began to exercise its authority.[30] But the movement for a complete revision of the Articles of Confederation was soon in full swing, and interest in the recommendations of 1784 disappeared. It had been demonstrated that something was wrong with the governmental system when it was necessary to allow three years to elapse after an injury had been inflicted before the country could be placed in a position to resist it.

Certain members of Congress anticipated the probable difficulties involved in the procedure adopted, and foresaw serious defects which would not be remedied even if the address of April 1784 should be complied with completely. A committee of which Monroe was chairman recommended

[27] Jefferson to B. Harrison, April 30, 1784, Burnett, *Letters*, VII, 508.
[28] *Journals of the American Congress from 1774 to 1788*, IV, 621-622.
[29] *Ibid.*
[30] *Ibid.*, 715-716.

March 28, 1785, that the ninth article of the Articles of Confederation be amended to vest in Congress a blanket power to regulate trade between the states as well as with foreign nations. It was proposed to send an address to the states, which would demonstrate that such authority would be necessary to enable the United States to execute treaties in good faith, and to insure success to further negotiations. It would be very difficult for thirteen states acting separately to agree upon the interpretation of a treaty, or concur in measures to counteract foreign discriminations. A temporary power, such as that proposed in the address of April 30, 1784, would be insufficient, since the same problems would always require the same remedies.[31] The report, which was considered during the summer of 1785, encountered, said Monroe, a "respectable" opposition. Southern leaders, while willing to permit a navigation act for fifteen years, provided nine states desired it, balked at a larger authority which would exist perpetually. A monopoly of shipping by New England must be avoided. In debate on the proposed amendment, opponents pointed out the danger in concentrated power. The eight northern states had a common commercial interest, and it would be to their advantage to combine and shackle the other states. The proposal to amend was in reality an attack upon the Confederation, and its effect would be to weaken the union by arousing discontent.[32] No action was taken upon the Monroe report.

The failure of the plan for a national commercial system did not, however, mean that no retaliatory action was to be taken against the adverse policies of foreign states. State governments displayed more vigor in passing direct legislation than in conferring powers upon the central government; and not long after the imposition of the restrictions upon the Brit-

[31] *Journals*, XXVIII, 201-205.

[32] Monroe to Jefferson, July 15, 1785, Monroe, *Writings* (ed. S. M. Hamilton), I, 95; Monroe to Madison, July 26, 1785, *ibid.*, I, 97-99; J. McHenry to Washington, Aug. 1, 1785; David Howell to William Greene, Aug. 23, 1785; also a letter of Nathan Dane to an unnamed correspondent, Jan. 20, 1786, Burnett, *Letters*, unpublished material.

ish West India trade all the states except Connecticut had
some sort of discriminatory legislation upon their statute
books.[33] The legislation differed much from state to state, but
in the main, the objects and the principles were the same.
Heavier tonnage duties were levied upon foreign ships than
upon those of the United States, and higher duties were
charged upon goods when imported in foreign ships. In a
few cases, efforts were made to exclude British ships entirely;
in some cases, only those coming from West India ports were
to be refused admittance. In an effort to prevent foreign
shipping from monopolizing the coasting trade, several states
limited the entry of foreign vessels to a few specified ports,
and at least one refused to admit any foreign vessel coming
from a port in another state. Great Britain was not the only
country discriminated against. The exclusion by the Portuguese government of foreign flour, rice, and indigo drew re-
torts from the American states in the form of discrimination
against Portuguese wines and fruits.[34] In a few cases, retaliation was expressed in the form of exemptions in favor of powers having treaties of commerce, and Virginia laws of 1786
provided for the admission of French wines and brandies free
of duty, while levying two pence per gallon on all other
liquors.[35]

State regulations of this nature, however well conceived
and effectively enforced, contained certain inherent weak-
nesses, which were thoroughly understood by contemporaries.
Lack of uniformity was responsible for two grave dangers.
For example, one state could, as Connecticut did, adopt a
policy of free trade with Great Britain, and so by becoming
a sort of entrepôt, completely nullify the navigation acts of
the neighboring states. Secondly, the existence of thirteen
distinct systems would give to Great Britain an excuse for
the enforcement of that part of the navigation act limiting

[33] A. A. Giesecke, *American Commercial Legislation before 1789*, 128-130,
137-140.
[34] De Melho e Castro to Chevalier del Pinto, Jan. 4, 1786, *Dip. Corresp.*,
II, 575-578.
[35] *Statutes at Large of Virginia* (ed. W. W. Hening), XII, 289.

the vessels of any foreign state to the carriage of the produce of that state. By treating each of the American states as a separate sovereign, Great Britain could destroy what remained of New England shipping, for that shipping depended largely on the carriage of the produce of the Southern and Middle States. Americans really expected this misfortune to happen, as is shown in the report of September 29, 1783, previously referred to.[36] Further, embarrassing disputes with foreign nations were bound to result, and it was a foregone conclusion that their governments would begin to deal in the end with the powers whose legislation was actually affecting their interests—not with Congress but the individual states. An example of the danger appeared in the complaint of the minister from the Netherlands in February 1787, with regard to the Virginia law exempting from duties French brandies when imported in French and American ships. Since the Netherlands had concluded a most-favored-nation treaty with the United States, the vessels of that country were obviously entitled to the same concession.[37] The French government complained and even began to consider retaliation against particularly drastic navigation laws proposed by Massachusetts and New Hampshire in 1785.[38]

Whether the state legislation was of any great value to commerce is, in the absence of statistics and of information as to the effectiveness of enforcement, very difficult to determine. Channing found that the commerce of New England

[36] *Journals*, XXV, 628-630.

[37] Van Berckel to Jay, Feb. 20, 1787, *Dip. Corresp.*, III, 437-439; for Jay's report to Congress on the matter, see *ibid.*, 439-442. In analyzing for Congress the complaint of the Netherlands, Jay contended that although the treaty with the Netherlands contained the most-favored-nation clause in the general form, the conditional principle was implied. Therefore, if France had purchased the favor for her shipping, the Netherlands could obtain it only by granting an equivalent favor to the United States. Jay concluded, however, that the concession to France had been freely given and therefore should be extended to the Netherlands without the requirement of an equivalent. This was the first expression of the American interpretation that the conditional principle was implied even in the unqualified statement of the most-favored-nation clause.

[38] Marbois to Vergennes, Aug. 14, 1785, AAE, CP, EU, XXX, 211-212; Castries to Vergennes, Sept. 25, 1785, *ibid.*, XXX, 314.

had by the end of 1786 entered upon a period of fair prosperity.[39] It seems very probable that the state protective legislation may have had some effect in enabling American vessels to compete more favorably in the direct trade between the United States and Europe. British merchants engaged in the American trade complained to the Committee of the Privy Council for Trade in 1787 that the tonnage duties and additional duties on goods in foreign ships was resulting in preference for American shipping. In 1791, they were of the opinion that the state regulations had been more injurious to British interests than the new discriminative measures of the federal government.[40] These efforts were not successful in securing the repeal of adverse regulations, however.

THE NEW COMMERCIAL FOREIGN POLICY

It is evident that one purpose of Congress in seeking authority for a navigation act was to provide something with which to bargain in negotiating. A plan for negotiation advanced *pari passu* with that for domestic regulation. Franklin's Swedish treaty, ratified July 29, 1783, was the final step in the war-time policy of making commercial treaties to secure political recognition. The commercial policy from 1783 onward was primarily for commercial ends. It was not promulgated suddenly and in complete form, but was the product of a long period of discussion, hampered by the slackness of delegates in attending and by pressing domestic business.

Incomplete steps toward a reorganization of policy were made in the summer of 1783 while the commercial treaty with Great Britain was still in expectation. A committee reported May 1, 1783, that such a treaty should be made as soon as possible, not only because of its value to commerce, but because of the effect it would have in inducing other nations to

[39] Edward Channing, *History of the U. S.*, III, 412-413.
[40] "Memorial of the Committee of Merchants trading to North America, March 30, 1787," PRO, FO, Series 4, V; *A Report of the Lords of the Committee of the Privy Council appointed for all matters relating to Trade and Foreign Plantations, on the Commerce and Navigation between His Majesty's Dominions, and the Territories belonging to the United States of America. 28th January, 1791.*

make concessions, and because "the present conjuncture may be more favorable to the views of these states than a future period." This committee believed that Congress should require all treaties to be submitted to it for study and revision before conclusion.[41] On May 6, Secretary Livingston submitted to Congress the project of a treaty with Great Britain which was referred to a committee of which Madison was a member.[42]

Madison began at this time to use his influence to develop a commercial policy which would suit the interests of his state and the rest of the South. Writing to Jefferson, he pointed out that the aim of the Livingston plan was to secure not only a direct trade between the United States and the West Indies, but also the privilege of carrying from the islands to other ports in the British Empire, and to Continental Europe. The South, he declared, was little interested in any but the direct trade between the United States and the islands; the rest would benefit only the North. Livingston proposed, moreover, in return for these concessions, to admit British subjects to the privileges of American citizens. Madison thought that would be disadvantageous to the South and that the direct trade could be obtained more cheaply. "The interest of these [the southern states] seems to require," he wrote, "that they should retain at least the faculty of giving any encouragement to their own merchant ships or mariners, which may be necessary to prevent a relapse under Scotch monopoly, or to acquire a maritime importance. The Eastern states need no such precaution." The Virginia legislature approved Madison's views and instructed its delegates in Congress to insist that treaties be referred to Congress for revision before conclusion.[43]

The influence of the South, then, and of Virginia in par-

----

[41] *Journals*, May 1, 1783, XXIV, 320-321.

[42] "Notes of Debates in the Continental Congress, by James Madison," *ibid.*, XXV, 164.

[43] Madison to Jefferson, May 1783, Madison, *Writings* (ed. G. Hunt), I, 463-464; Madison to Edmund Randolph, May 1783, *ibid.*, 464-468; Madison to Jefferson, June 10, 1783, Wharton, VI, 478-479.

ticular was thus exerted to delay or prevent further commercial treaties, and was successful in preventing them until the following year. The full powers for the treaty with Great Britain, authorized by resolution of May 1,[44] were never issued, and the commissioners had no authority for negotiating with that government after the conclusion of the definitive treaty of peace. The committee on the Livingston plan reported instructions June 19, 1783, authorizing a treaty with Great Britain, making the direct trade between the United States and the islands a *sine qua non,* and reserving to Congress the right to revision. Treaties with Portugal, Naples, and Tuscany were also recommended. However, no action was had upon this report,[45] nor on a similar report of another committee presented September 1.[46]

The news of the July order in council and the failure of the Hartley negotiation, together with decisions by France and Spain affecting adversely American trade, stimulated Congress to give the subject more careful consideration, and initiated the movement for the twofold scheme of defense already referred to. The Duane committee in September, in the same report which recommended centralized control of commerce, proposed a committee to prepare instructions for treaties, and the proposal was adopted.[47] This committee, of which Duane, Samuel Huntingdon, and Arthur Lee were members, reported a set of instructions October 29, which were agreed to, although no commissions were ever issued under them. The commissioners were to encourage the advances of the European commercial powers.

In negotiations on this subject, you will lay it down as a principle in no case to be deviated from, that they shall respectively have for their bases the mutual advantage of the contracting parties, on terms of the most perfect equality and reciprocity. . . .

Treaties so negotiated

[44] *Journals,* XXIV, 321.
[45] *Journals,* XXIV, 404-405.
[46] *Ibid.,* XXV, 531-532.
[47] *Ibid.,* 621-622.

. . . shall not be finally conclusive until they shall respectively have been transmitted to the United States in Congress assembled, for their examination and final direction, and that with the drafts or propositions for such treaties, shall be transmitted all the information which shall come within the knowledge of the said ministers respecting the same; and their observations, after the most mature inquiry, on the probable advantages or disadvantages and effects of such treaties respectively.[48]

Perhaps the most difficult task in the formation of commercial policy was that of deciding upon the formulae regarding the regulation of commerce, which should be included in the treaties.[49] European statesmen had, in the course of long experience, developed two such formulae. The most-favored-nation clause was the most common. Under the circumstances existing at the end of the eighteenth century, the most-favored-nation clause conferred no privileges of any great importance, for the general rule was to treat all foreign nations as equals. Most-favored-nation treatment then, meant not favored treatment, but merely a guarantee against being less favorably treated than other foreign nations. It placed no

[48] *Journals*, Oct. 29, 1783, XXV, 754-755. A group of New Englanders in Congress looked upon the policy of the October instructions as being pro-French and perhaps engineered by the French minister. With regard to them, Gerry wrote Adams January 14, 1784: "Those proceedings appeared to me calculated to defeat every treaty and confine our commerce to France and Holland; for after you had formed the projects, as they are called, and sent them to America, projects of another nature would have been contrived here to have made alterations, which would have in effect rendered null your proceedings." John Adams, *Works* (ed. C. F. Adams), IX, 521. See also Samuel Osgood to John Adams, Dec. 7, 1783, Burnett, VII, 378-388; Stephen Higginson to Sam Adams, May 20, 1783, *ibid.*, 166-169; Gerry to Stephen Higginson, May 13, 1784, *ibid.*, 522-524. Osgood attributed the change in policy in 1784, with regard to referring the treaties, to the change in the membership in Congress. Samuel Osgood to John Adams, January 14, 1784, *ibid.*, 414-416.

[49] The problem of treaty formulae is discussed or touched upon in the following documents: *Journals*, May 7, 1784, 357-362; April 1, 1784, XXVI, 176-177; Monroe to Jefferson, April 12, 1785, Burnett, *Letters*, unpublished material; E. Gerry to Jefferson, Feb. 1785, Burnett, *Letters*, unpublished material; Jefferson to Monroe, Dec. 10, 1784, Jefferson, *Writings* (ed. Ford), IV, 19-20; Jefferson to Monroe, June 17, 1785, *ibid.*, IV, 54-59; Jefferson to John Adams, July 31, 1785, *ibid.*, IV, 79-81; Report of John Jay on a Plan of a Treaty of Amity and Commerce, May 17, 1785, *Dip. Corresp.*, I, 529-531.

obstacle in the way of a nation which desired to adopt a highly protective policy in favor of its own industry.[50] By another formula, each signatory agreed to make no distinction in commercial regulations between its own subjects and those of the other party to the treaty. Liberality of this sort was usually reserved for very close allies.[51]

Neither of these formulae conformed to American ideas of "strict reciprocity." Although all the commercial treaties which the United States had concluded declared in the preamble that they took complete reciprocity for their basis, every American knew that it was not so—American trade was relatively free, European generally restricted. Several attempts were made to get rid of the most-favored-nation clause, and develop a method to guarantee complete reciprocity by treaty. Gerry described the most-favored-nation formula as a system of cobwebs to catch flies. "Attend to it," he wrote, "as it respects restrictions, prohibitions, and the carrying trade, and it is equally distant from a rule of reciprocity, which is the only equitable and beneficial rule for forming commercial treaties."[52]

The stipulation of reciprocal national treatment would, of course, have admitted Americans to the trade with European colonies, and relieved them of alien duties wherever such were chargeable against their ships and goods. This formula had been included in the original plan of treaties of 1776, but had been refused by the French. The restoration of the principle in the new policy was advocated in Congress, but weighty reasons against it were now discovered. Madison's advice that Virginia retain the power to protect her own commercial in-

[50] For the early history of this clause, *vide* Stanley K. Hornbeck, *The Most-Favored-Nation Clause in Commercial Treaties*, pp. 8-16, and Joseph Koulischer, "Les traités de commerce et la clause de la nation la plus favorisée du XVI au XVIII siècle," *Rev. d'histoire moderne*, VI (1931), 3-29.

[51] The Bourbon Family Compact between France and Spain, dated Aug. 15, 1761, is an example of a treaty conferring national treatment. *Recueil des traités de commerce et de navigation de la France* (ed. D'Hauterive and De Cussy), I, 382-385.

[52] Gerry to Jefferson, Feb. 1785, Burnett, *Letters*, unpublished material.

terest has already been referred to, and the same argument was used by other members. Further than that, national treatment by treaty could not guarantee that American produce would not be in effect discriminated against by loading it with heavy duties, since the United States provided Europe's supply of certain articles without a great amount of competition.

Another plan strongly advocated was one for establishing a separate conventional arrangement with each country, including a conventional tariff, and thus avoiding any relationship between American regulations and those of third powers. Gerry proposed this at the time of the adoption of the new instructions in May 1784, and moved that the commissioners be instructed to stipulate in the treaties that each state should levy on the imports from the other, the average of the duties collected by it. The proposal was rejected because of the practical impossibility of executing it,[53] but the idea of separate conventional arrangements persisted. Secretary Jay was much opposed to most-favored-nation treaties. With his usual extreme *penchant* for orderliness, he desired a complete and logical commercial policy to be adopted before any more treaties were concluded. The settlement of domestic questions of a commercial nature would be impeded, if treaties should be concluded first, and that would be particularly true of most-favored-nation treaties.[54] Even after the new instructions were adopted, the question continued to be considered. Early in 1785, a committee was appointed to consider revision of the instructions. It recommended that the United States

Connect with each power independently of other powers, and (to) extricate us from the complicated system with which their connections with each other is involved, a system which they will understand, have been long accustomed to the exercise of and to turn to their particular advantages by every possible means of fraud and chicane.[55]

[53] Jefferson demonstrated the absurdity of the idea of equal imposts in a letter to Monroe, June 17, 1785, *Writings* (ed. Ford), IV, 79-81.

[54] Report of John Jay on a Plan of a Treaty of Amity and Commerce, May 17, 1785, *Dip. Corresp.*, I, 529-531.

[55] Monroe to Jefferson, April 12, 1785, Burnett, *Letters*, unpublished material.

The report was, however, not adopted, but all these considerations had an effect upon the negotiations in Europe.

The new attitude upon this matter was shown in the report, made October 22, of the committee on the treaty with Denmark, the same committee which prepared the instructions of October 29. This treaty had been drawn up on the basis of that with Sweden, and was consequently a most-favored-nation treaty. The committee found that the proposed treaty provided equality and reciprocity only in appearance. A clause which proposed to admit trade to all places where it was not prohibited was not equal, because there were no places where trade was prohibited in the United States, while Denmark possessed several, some of them being the ports to which it would be most convenient for the United States to trade. The Danish government had complained of the most-favored-nation clause, because there was no favored nation in commercial relations with the United States, while there were such in Danish trade. The committee proposed to obviate both objections by amending to provide for national treatment in admission to ports, and most-favored-nation treatment only as far as duties were concerned. Although this amendment was not adopted by Congress, the effect of the whole proceeding was to postpone the Danish treaty.[56]

Because of pressing domestic problems, Congress was unable to devote the requisite attention to foreign policy until March 1784. At that time a committee of which Jefferson was a member presented a report of instructions, which was eventually adopted without essential alteration. The urgent need of the northern states for some sort of relief for their commerce induced the delegates from the South to give up their contention for the reservation of a right of revision by Congress. A commission of plenipotentiaries all of northern antecedents was still suspect,[57] but it was decided that a south-

---

[56] *Journals*, XXV, 720-721. For the views of the Danish government on a proper treaty with the United States see "Explanation of the counter project of a treaty of Amity and Commerce received from Denmark," Wharton, VI, 525-527.

[57] *Vide* Monroe to Benjamin Harrison, March 26, 1784; Burnett, *Letters*, VII, 477-479.

ern member on the commission would provide a sufficient safeguard. Jay's request to be relieved, and his election to the Secretaryship of Foreign Affairs provided the opportunity, and Jefferson was elected to the vacancy on the commission.[58]

The instructions which were to guide the commissioners were adopted May 7. The most significant departure from previous instructions was contained in the section regarding trade to the colonies of European powers. It was desired that the new treaties should admit Americans to trade with the colonies under the same regulations as with the mother countries, or to an unrestricted trade with specified free ports. The minimum which might be accepted was the free admission of American vessels to a direct intercourse between the colonies and the United States. Every treaty should guarantee that neither party would charge, on the ships or goods of the other, higher duties than those paid by the most favored nation. The most-favored-nation clause should contain the conditional principle. The danger of separate arrangements with individual members of the American union was noted in the provision that the United States should be recognized in all treaties as one nation. It was proposed to negotiate with all the European commercial powers, including France, Sweden, and the Netherlands. Supplemental treaties with the latter countries were desired in order to bring the existing treaties within the bounds of the new American policy.[59]

These instructions were not entirely satisfactory to all the delegates in Congress, and the ill success of the commissioners gave rise to renewed discussion. In the spring of 1785, a committee, of which Monroe was a prominent member, was appointed to recommend any needed alterations. The report contains some very careful reasoning on the subject of American commercial relations. It pointed out that the first problem to be solved was that of the commercial power of Congress, for without authority to impose restraints "reciprocity means nothing and foreign powers may follow what policy they

[58] *Journals*, May 7, 1784, XXVI, 355-356.
[59] *Journals*, May 7, 1784, XXVI, 357-362; June 3, 1784, XXVII, 529-530.

please." It advocated the careful consideration of the interest of each individual nation in American commerce, when treaty provisions were being prepared. Treaties with nations without colonies were unnecessary and should be avoided. Such nations had as much to gain as the United States in mutual intercourse, and engagements with them might interfere with more advantageous treaties with colonial powers. France and Great Britain, on the other hand, could more properly demand perfect reciprocity, since most of America's trade was with them. Those nations might insist, in return for opening their colonies, on special advantages, from the enjoyment of which other countries should be excluded. Before granting such exclusive privileges, the United States should first try the power of retaliation. It was recommended that no engagement be entered into with any state having possessions in the West Indies which did not open those colonies in some degree. The report was not adopted, but a part of the policy recommended was actually carried out by the commissioners, as will be seen.[60]

Congress took one further step in the spring of 1784, of importance in the commercial policy of the period. On May 11 it adopted a resolution declaring that "it will be our constant care to place no people on more advantageous ground than the subjects of his [Most Christian] majesty." This was the American response to Vergennes' proposal of the preceding year for a convention nullifying the "conditional" qualification in the most-favored-nation clause in the treaty of 1778. The resolution explained the inability of Congress to agree to the convention because "these states are about to form a general system of commerce by treaties with other nations" and "at this time we cannot foresee what claims might be given to those nations by the explanatory propositions from the Count de Vergennes." But the effect of the resolution was to accede to the demand of the French minister, and bind the United States to give freely to France any commercial concession which might be purchased by another nation.[61] This

[60] Monroe, *Writings*, I, xlii-xlvi.
[61] *Journals*, May 11, 1784, XXVII, 368-369.

stipulation, which Vergennes required Franklin to present as a formal declaration, was a further limitation upon the power of Congress in establishing a commercial system.[62]

THE NEGOTIATIONS OF 1784-1786

It is customary for historians to fit the account of the American commercial negotiations of 1784-1786 into the introduction to the movement for the Constitution, and to attribute the failure of diplomacy to Europe's lack of respect for an ineffective government. Such a presentation gives a very imperfect image of the real situation. That diplomacy failed is a fact, but it is also a fact that it never succeeded in an equally ambitious program even when backed by a more perfect union. It is true that Great Britain was hostile. It can hardly be said that the rest of Europe held aloof when Frederick the Great, the Emperor, the Kings of Spain, Portugal, and Denmark,—all the important commercial states, except Great Britain, with whom the United States did not already have treaties—sought treaty connections. The really important fact is that the United States was demanding special consideration, privileges such as no European country had ever granted to another. Governments refused to alter their established policies at the demand of a new nation which had little to offer in return.

The Danish government made overtures early in 1783 to Franklin and to Carmichael at Madrid. The negotiation, begun at Paris, was delayed by the American claim for indemnification for certain prizes which John Paul Jones had sent into Danish ports and which the Danes had turned over to the British. Franklin proposed a treaty based upon that between the United States and the Netherlands. The Danish government insisted on maintaining a monopoly of the colonial

---

[62] In his conversation with Pitt, August 24, 1785, Adams claimed the United States could still require compensation from France, but the resolution will not bear that interpretation. Adams to Jay, August 25, 1785, John Adams, *Works*, VIII, 307-308. For Jefferson's comment on the difficulties caused by the connection with France, see his letter to Monroe, June 17, 1785, Jefferson, *Writings* (ed. Ford), IV, 58-59.

trade, particularly the trade between the Danish West Indies and Europe. The Danish counter-project became the subject of an adverse report by the committee to which it was referred in Congress.[63] Little progress was made under the new American commission. Jefferson gave Walterstorff, the Danish minister at Paris, a copy of the draft treaty, which he and the other commissioners had prepared to conform with the new instructions, and the Danish minister took it home to discuss with his principals. It was not acceptable.[64] In 1788 the Danish foreign minister suggested a renewal of the negotiation, but the commission of the American envoys had long since expired.[65]

The Prussian government approached Adams through Baron von Thulemeier, the ambassador at The Hague, and it was there that the treaty of 1785 was concluded. Since there were no conflicting commercial interests in the relations of the United States and Prussia, no questions of importance were raised. The Prussians had the same objects in view that moved them in the discussions during the war; namely, a supply of tobacco, and a market for Silesian linens.[66]

This treaty, as far as trade was concerned, was simply a repetition of that of 1778—a most-favored-nation treaty, although the preamble describes it as being based upon the

[63] Rosencrone to Walterstorff, Feb. 22, 1783, Wharton, VI, 261; Carmichael to Livingston, March 3, 1783, *ibid.*, 295-296; Franklin to Rosencrone, April 15, 1783, Franklin, *Writings* (ed. A. H. Smyth), IV, 29-30; Franklin to Livingston, April 15, 1783, *ibid.*, 30-31; Rosencrone to Franklin, July 8, 1783, Wharton, VI, 519-527; *Journals*, XXV, 720-722, 754-755.

[64] Jefferson to Walterstorff, Feb. 3, 1785, *Dip. Corresp.*, I, 548-549; Jefferson to Jay, May 12, 1786, *ibid.*, 731-733.

[65] J. P. Jones to Bernstorff, April 5, 1788; Bernstorff to Jones, April 5, 1788; Jefferson to Bernstorff, June 19, 1788, *Dip. Corresp.*, II, 153-155, 167-168.

[66] Adams to the President of Congress, March 9, 1784, Wharton, VI, 784-785. The counter-project of this treaty is in *Dip. Corresp.*, I, 520-529, and also the answer of the commissioners, I, 554. See also letter of Von Thulemeier, *ibid.*, I, 579. The Prussian papers dealing with this negotiation and treaty are in *Preussischer Geheimes Staatsarchiv, Berlin-Dahlem, General Controlle, Rep. XI, 21a, Conv. I, Amerika, Verein. Staaten*, No. 5. Of particular value are Thulemeier's dispatches dated Feb. 20, March 12, May 18, Dec. 10, 1784; Schulenberg to the King, Dec. 24, 1784, and Schulenberg to Thulemeier, April 21, 1785.

principles of equality and reciprocity.[67] One clause expressed
an aspect of the new American policy. By the provisions of
Article IV, each party might import into the ports of the other
its own produce not only in its own vessels but also in those
of any other country. However, if the United States should
decide, for example, to retaliate against that part of the British
Navigation Act which prohibited American vessels from carrying to Great Britain other than American produce, they
might then prohibit the importation of Prussian produce in
British vessels. Secretary Jay, although he recommended ratification, was opposed to the principles of this treaty, chiefly
on the ground that they would interfere with the establishment of a complete system of commercial regulations by the
United States.[68]

Franklin had also begun a treaty with Portugal at about
the same time as that with Denmark. He favored the policy
of continuing to offer the French treaty to all the European
states. Adams thought him careless in looking out for American commercial interests, and expressed the hope that either
the Portuguese would send an envoy to Congress or Congress
a representative to Lisbon to complete the treaty. Although
the opening of the Portuguese colonies could not be expected,
Portugal and its nearby islands offered great potential markets for the United States. Adams thought it would be advantageous to establish in the Azores a depot for sugar, coffee,
and cocoa from Brazil. The Portuguese ambassador in London
had told him that those articles could be purchased there
fifteen per cent cheaper than similar produce from the British
West Indies. Portugal could also use American grain and
flour, fish, rice, and indigo. Obviously a treaty with Portugal
which would secure these advantages would be a great success
for American diplomacy.[69]

The Portuguese government also saw the possibility of

[67] Miller, *Treaties*, II, 162-184.
[68] Report of Secretary Jay on the Prussian Treaty, *Dip. Corresp.*, I, 598-599.
[69] Adams to Livingston, July 12, 1783, Wharton, VI, 538; Franklin to
Livingston, July 22, 1783, *ibid.*, 583. For the treaty project, see *ibid.*, 588-
591. Adams to Livingston, Aug. 1, 1783, Wharton, VI, 626-628.

advantage in an American treaty. The peace treaty of 1783 between France and Great Britain contained a provision that a commercial treaty between the two countries should be concluded by 1786.[70] It was expected that the proposed treaty would admit French wines into Great Britain at the same rate as Portuguese, which had in the past practically monopolized the British market. If the treaty were concluded, a direct trade with the United States would perhaps preserve a part of the market. Lisbon officials were averse to treating in Paris, however. An exchange of ministers was proposed, but for the United States that would have been a needless expense. The negotiation was transferred to London, where the Chevalier del Pinto, the Portuguese representative in Great Britain, carried it on with Adams. A treaty was signed toward the end of April 1786, after Jefferson had made a special trip to London for the purpose. But Portugal's ruler refused to ratify it. The commissioners had insisted on the removal of a prohibition on the importation of flour, and this was resisted by Portuguese milling interests. Jefferson believed that the treaty might have been agreed to except for the fact that the Anglo-French negotiation was at the time encountering difficulties. The Portuguese government remained cordial, and ordered its cruisers to protect American ships from the Barbary pirates. It was quite willing to renew the negotiation at Lisbon. Jay favored sending an envoy, but Congress failed to take action.[71]

[70] Vergennes, who advocated economic liberalism and who hoped to put an end, by means of close commercial relations, to the continued enmity between Great Britain and France, was responsible for the article. He expected his country to profit greatly from the enlarged market for wines. The British government delayed entering the promised negotiation for several years. In retaliation, France excluded a number of important British manufactures. In March, 1786, Pitt sent William Eden to Paris to begin the negotiation, and a treaty was concluded September 26, 1786. It reduced the British duties on French wines to the level of those on the wines of Portugal, and widened considerably the market in France for British manufactures. J. H. Clapham, "Pitt's First Decade," *Cambridge History of British Foreign Policy*, I, 164-170; Levasseur, *Histoire du commerce de la France*, I, 534-546.

[71] Jefferson to Jay, Oct. 11, 1785, *Dip. Corresp.*, I, 653-654; Adams to Jay, Nov. 5, 1785, *ibid.*, II, 527-533; Jay's report to Congress, May 11, 1785, *ibid.*, I, 674-675; Adams to Jay, Jan. 21, 1786, *ibid.*, II, 560; Melho e Castro

The negotiation with Austria was first delayed by the slowness of the United States in adopting a commercial policy, and then by that of the Austrian government in obtaining the views of the various local governments and in settling a quarrel with the Netherlands.[72] That there was an interest in commerce is shown by the formation in Trieste of a company to trade with America. Beelen-Bertholff, the Austrian agent in the United States, pointed out to his government the value of a treaty as protection against the discriminatory legislation of the American states.[73] It was early in 1786, before the Imperial government was ready to undertake the negotiations, and by that time the powers of the American commissioners had only a short time to run, and American policy had undergone a readjustment.

The Italian states were of importance to the United States because of their ability to consume fish, rice, and other American products. Two of these states, Sardinia and the States of the Church were not disposed to regulate commerce by treaty, although quite ready to receive American ships and seamen in their ports.[74] The King of Naples was prepared to consider the negotiation of a treaty, but consumed so much time in deliberation that the commissioners lost interest.[75] Tuscany,

---

to Pinto, Jan. 4, 1786, *Dip. Corresp.*, II, 575-578; Jefferson to Jay, April 23, 1786, *ibid.*, I, 725; Jefferson to Jay, March 12, 1786, *ibid.*, I, 720-721; W. S. Smith to Jay, April 11, 1786, *ibid.*, III, 22; the Commissioners to Jay, April 25, 1786, *ibid.*, I, 602; Adams to Jay, June 27, 1786, *ibid.*, II, 578; Jefferson to Jay, August 13, 1786, *ibid.*, I, 804-805; Pinto to Adams, Sept. 7, 1787, *ibid.*, II, 803; W. S. Smith to Jay, Sept. 12, 1787, *ibid.*, III, 72-74; Jay's report to Congress, March 12, 1788, *ibid.*, III, 83-84; Jefferson to Jay, March 12, 1789, *ibid.*, II, 277-278.

[72] Franklin to Argenteau, July 30, 1784, Wharton, VI, 817; Argenteau to Franklin, *ibid.*, VI, 820-821; Franklin to Thomas Mifflin, Dec. 25, 1783, Franklin, *Writings* (ed. Smyth), 132-133; Hans Schlitter, *Die Beziehungen Österreichs zu den Vereinigten Staaten von Amerika*, 91-94; 108-118; Jefferson to Jay, Jan. 27, 1786, *Dip. Corresp.*, I, 714-715.

[73] Schlitter, *Die Beziehungen Österreichs*, 94-109; *Berichte Beelen-Bertholffs*, 588-594; Beelen-Bertholff to Prince Kaunitz, Oct. 18, 1785, *ibid.*, 535-538; Beelen-Bertholff to Count Mercy-Argenteau, Feb. 25, 1786, *ibid.*, 596-600.

[74] Scarnafis to the Commissioners, Feb. 2, 1785, *Dip. Corresp.*, I, 551; Archbishop of Selucie to the Commissioners, Dec. 15, 1785, *ibid.*, I, 561-562.

[75] Pio to the Commissioners, Jan. 22, 1785, *Dip. Corresp.*, I, 549-550; Jefferson to Jay, Oct. 11, 1785, *Dip. Corresp.*, I, 654.

under the enlightened rule of its Hapsburg Grand Duke, Leopold I, who was making great efforts to increase the economic well-being of his people, had shown interest in American trade from the beginning of the Revolution.[76] No great difficulty was encountered in agreeing upon a project, but the exchanges of counter drafts took time, and the Americans were not sorry to see their commissions expire before the treaty was concluded.[77]

The commissioners were also authorized to negotiate supplementary treaties with France, Sweden, and the Netherlands.[78] In each case, the object to be obtained was the opening of the colonial trade, and removal of discriminations in favor of nationals.[79] Jefferson reported that the French were not averse to favorable arrangements, but that the government did not desire to write them into a treaty. Holland was "so immovable in her system of colonial administration, that as propositions to her on that subject would be desperate, they had better not be made." Sweden would probably convert St. Bartholomew into a free port, which would render a conventional arrangement unnecessary.[80]

Of the various governments to which proposals of negotiation were made, the Russian was the only one which made no response. The commissioners judged a negotiation with the Ottoman Empire to be too expensive.[81] Saxony made enthusiastic overtures for a commercial connection with the United States, but was treated with uniform coolness by the representatives of the American government, perhaps because Saxony was not a maritime power. By the time the commissioners were ready to negotiate, the Saxon government had

[76] Alfred von Reumont, *Geschichte Toscanas seit dem Ende des florentinischen Freistaates* (2 vols., Gotha, 1876-1877), II, 116-148.

[77] Commissioners to Favi, June 8, 1785, *Dip. Corresp.*, I, 582-583; "Observations on counter draft," I, *ibid.*, 583-591; Favi to Commissioners, Aug. 26, 1785, *ibid.*, I, 578.

[78] *Journals*, May 7, 1784, XXVI, 361.

[79] Jefferson to Baron de Staël, Oct. 2, 1784, June 12, 1786, *Dip. Corresp.*, I, 511-513, 788-794.

[80] Jefferson to Jay, Oct. 11, 1785, *ibid.*, I, 653-654.

[81] Commissioners to Jay, April 25, 1786, *Dip. Corresp.*, I, 602.

become disgusted at the treatment it had received and was convinced by its agent in America that little profit lay in trade with the United States.[82]

Thus ended the rather pretentious mission—in failure as far as any immediate relief for American trade was concerned. The new policy had not been properly implemented by the adoption of centralized regulation of commerce at home. Even if it had been supported in that way, it is doubtful if great success could have been obtained in a two-year period. The heart of the plan consisted in successful negotiations with powers having American colonies. Americans did not understand the conditions abroad which gave monopoly its grip: vested private interests and considerations of naval power. It was not much easier for a British government to dictate to the West India merchants, or for the French ministry to control the Farmers General than for Congress to enforce its will in Rhode Island. The commissioners made two mistakes which could probably have been avoided. The aversion of most of the governments to negotiating at Paris indicates that better results could perhaps have been obtained by accrediting agents directly to the various courts.[83] A second error lay in the addressing of overtures to all the governments. Toward the end of the mission, Jefferson began to realize this mistake and undertook to avoid the consequences. The result was the development of a new principle in American policy, namely, that because of its inherent nature, American trade was particularly valuable to the nations having American colonies, and that consequently its price was cheapened when yielded on a basis of equality to non-colonial states.

Both Jefferson and Congress saw the danger of tying the country up with treaties conferring no great benefits, and the commission in Europe, instead of seeking them, did all it could to avoid them. But withdrawal was embarrassing, since the United States had made the first advances. The commissioners, in doubt, passed the decision to Congress by dragging

[82] W. E. Lingelbach, "Saxon-American Relations," *AHR*, XVII, 519-524.
[83] The British, Spanish, Portuguese, and Prussian governments refused to negotiate at Paris.

out the negotiations until their powers had expired. It was possible to argue in favor of treaties, even without commercial advantages. Jefferson suggested that in case of war in Europe, additional treaty ports in the north and in the Mediterranean would be desirable.[84] Jay, while opposed to such treaties, recommended renewal of the powers for treaties with those states still willing to negotiate,[85] but Congress took no action in the matter.

After the expiration of the two-year commission for commercial treaties in May 1786, there was no uniform, constructive policy in existence. People still talked of the possibilities of commercial treaties, of retaliation, of national unity, of an American navigation act, but nothing decisive was attempted. American commercial policy must be sought in three isolated negotiations. The English mission of John Adams is of great importance because he kept dinning into the ears of Jay and the members of Congress the necessity for a national government as the remedy for the commercial depression in the United States. In Paris, Jefferson, with the coöperation of a willing French government, labored with some success to limit the British monopoly of American trade by creating in France a market for American produce. In New York, Jay endeavored to seize what appeared to be a magnificent opportunity to stabilize the existing market in Spain, and secure the good will of a government which had demonstrated its great influence over the Barbary pirates in favor of the United States.

EFFORTS TO ESTABLISH CLOSER COMMERCIAL RELATIONS WITH FRANCE

Jefferson's work in France is an important episode in the interesting story of the struggle of France for a share of American trade after the Revolution.[86] With the end of the

---

[84] Jefferson to Jay, Oct. 11, 1785, Jan. 27, 1786, *Dip. Corresp.*, I, 654, 714-715.

[85] Report of Secretary Jay, May 11, 1786, *Dip. Corresp.*, I, 675-676.

[86] In spite of the able chronicling of several of the more important aspects by Nussbaum, this phase of Franco-American relations is very much in need of a thorough and comprehensive investigation.

war, French relations with the United States underwent a change. The new policy was not one of contemptuous indifference or hostility, however. The court was undoubtedly displeased and disgusted with the conduct of the American authorities. But throughout Vergennes' tenure of the ministry for foreign affairs, that policy was correct and cordial, though based upon cool calculation of ultimate French interests.[87] Montmorin, who succeeded Vergennes in 1786, was not so correct or cordial, but he adhered to Vergennes' policy. His statement in 1787 that he felt that the union was on the verge of breaking up and that France had never pretended to make a useful ally out of her protégé, but only desired to withhold the continent from the English is little more than recognition of the facts and a reaffirmation of the hands-off policy.[88] With regard to commerce the government, and Vergennes in particular, did everything in its power to aid the United States —with the object, of course, of enriching France. Vergennes, at least, seems to have been under no illusion with regard to France's immediately replacing Great Britain as America's principal market.[89] In making concessions to the United States, two considerations limited the government; one the desire to favor French marine industries, and the other the necessity to avoid arousing the clamors of private interests which might feel themselves injured by a liberal policy. As early as 1783, the foreign minister had worked out a fairly

[87] He stated that policy rather succinctly in an instruction to Luzerne, July 21, 1783: "After all, we have never based our policy with regard to the United States on their gratitude: that sentiment is extremely rare even among sovereigns, and republics know it not. Therefore, Monsieur, all that we need to do with regard to the Americans is, as you have quite properly observed, to let things follow their natural movement; never to swerve from that noble, frank, and disinterested course to which we have adhered up to the present with regard to the Americans; to observe them carefully in all their proceedings; and, if we cannot direct them according to the great principles which have served as the basis for our alliance with them, to take in time the necessary measures to avoid becoming dupes of their ingratitude and false policy." AAE, CP, EU, XXV.

[88] Montmorin to Otto, Aug. 31, 1787, ibid., XXXII, 350-351.

[89] Vergennes to Luzerne, Dec. 24, 1783, ibid., XXVI.

comprehensive program of measures to be taken in an effort to attract American exports to France.[90]

The first efforts of French merchants in 1783 and 1784 to capture, or rather to retain the American market ended in disaster. The ports were glutted with manufactures. The Americans were unable to buy, or buying, were unable to pay their debts. The French felt that they had been cheated, and lost faith in the honesty of the American merchants with whom they had dealt. They were unfamiliar with American courts, and felt that the bad faith of the Americans, paper money, and American lawyers were responsible for their ruin.[91] The ill success of these first badly planned ventures in competition with the English added to the difficulty of developing a direct trade between the United States and France. The English merchants suffered great losses also, but they were more familiar with the means of collection and were in a position to grant longer credits to their impecunious customers.

From time to time, proposals were made by both French and Americans with a view to overcoming the great advantages of the British. In May 1783, Sir James Jay, brother of John Jay, was in France urging one plausible scheme. According to a view widely held, the chief obstacle to the ex-

[90] In a memoir dated November 20, 1783, Vergennes outlined the measures which his government might take, among them the following: abolition of the duties on the manufacture and export of brandy; reduction or abolition of duties on naval stores, candle grease, hemp, flax, lumber, staves, and potash from the United States; admission of indigo, cotton, and sugar from the United States on the same terms as when imported from the French colonies; reduction of the duties on the produce of the American fisheries; provision for the export of salt to the United States on the same terms as to the French colonies; securing the adoption by the Farmers General of a system of purchasing tobacco which would better serve the interests of navigation and commerce; reduction of the cost of ocean transportation by abolishing the requirement for apprentice seamen on French merchantmen; the establishment of free ports for American trade in France; the undertaking of measures for loosening credit for the advancement of commerce with the United States. AAE, CP, EU, XXVI, 131-132.

[91] Otto to Vergennes, June 30, 1785, Aug. 26, 1785, *ibid.*, XXX, 73-76, 246-248.

pansion of French trade in America was the inability of French merchants to extend long credits. Jay proposed that the French government overcome this by granting subsidies to export houses in France. In addition, it would be advantageous to support *Whig* merchants in the United States, and this could be done by subsidizing them also. Vergennes and Ormesson, the *contrôleur général*, gave him a respectful hearing, and Lafayette urged that his scheme be adopted.[92] Lafayette himself filed a memoir with the Ministry for Foreign Affairs, urging the encouragement of Franco-American commerce, and suggested the opening of the French colonies as one method of drawing American trade to France.[93] In February, 1784, W. Alexander, a Richmond merchant, in a long memoir, advocated a modification of the Jay plan. Alexander believed that many French manufactures: "wines, brandies, fine linens, silks, modes, laces, embroidery, almost everything for ladies' ornament or apparel, paper, confections, liquors" were adapted to the American market. "The causes of the partiality for English goods," he stated, "seems to lie entirely in the return of ancient usages and in the superior capitals and activity of the English merchants." He proposed that the Farmers General advance him 500,000 livres on a contract for the purchase of tobacco. He would use this sum to extend his business in the handling of French manufactures.[94] In May 1785, one Savary de Valcoulon presented a memoir to Vergennes asking a subsidy for a house at Norfolk.[95] The poverty-stricken French government was unprepared, however, to engage in a program of subsidizing private business.[96]

One concession by the French government much talked about, and from which a great deal was apparently expected,

[92] AAE, CP, EU, XXIV, 220-221, 224-225, 415-416 are memoirs by Jay; Vergennes to Ormesson and the latter's reply, May 23, 1783, *ibid.*, 226, 229; Lafayette to Vergennes, June 12, 1783, *ibid.*, 332.

[93] AAE, M et D, EU, II, 100.

[94] Memoir of Alexander and Company, Feb. 10, 1784, *ibid.*, XXVIII, 188-190.

[95] *Ibid.*, XXIX, 249-260.

[96] Vergennes to Luzerne, July 21, 1783, *ibid.*, XXV.

was the establishment of a free port especially for the United States. It was hoped that such a port would become an important market center, where American produce would be exchanged not only for French goods but also for other European and East India goods.[97] The French cities competed vigorously for the privilege of being America's free port, petitions being filed from Port Louis, Marennes, Dunkerque, La Rochelle, L'Orient, and Antibes.[98] In the end, L'Orient was designated.[99] Bayonne was later added, and, of course, American vessels had the privilege of using the other free ports such as Dunkerque and Marseilles.[100] But the free ports turned out to be of little use to American merchants, and Jefferson was quite willing in 1789 to yield the privileges to please Necker, who wished to suppress them to prevent smuggling.[101]

A concession which merchants from the United States found of considerable value was the establishment on Île de France (Mauritius) of an entrepôt for the American East India trade. The request for this privilege seems to have come from the men engaged in the first ventures to China. Introductions to the governor were obtained from Luzerne.[102] The French government was glad to comply with this request, and orders were given in April 1784, that the American vessels be accommodated. Île de France thus became a valuable half-

[97] Vergennes to Ormesson, 1783, AAE, CP, EU, XXV, 301-303. For a statement of the privileges of a free port, see Vergennes to Lafayette, June 29, 1783, Wharton, VI, 509. The city was reputed foreign with regard to France, and the restrictions and prohibitions on foreign trade applied only when goods were to be imported into the interior.

[98] Ibid., XXIII, 7-11, 99-103, 172-174, 205-206; XXIV, 268-269, 367; XXV, 48-51.

[99] AAE, CP, EU, XXV, 165-166, 231-241, 301-303; XXVII, 202-203, 460-463; XXVIII, 27-28, 195. See also Lafayette to the President of Congress, July 20, 1783, Wharton, VI, 579.

[100] Vergennes to Luzerne, Dec. 24, 1783, Wharton, VI, 792; Calonne to Lafayette, Jan. 9, 1783, Wharton, VI, 751-752.

[101] He wrote Jay, May 9, 1789: "I have never been able to see that these free ports were worth one copper to us. To Bayonne our trade never went, and it is leaving L'Orient." Dip. Corresp., II, 288-289.

[102] Luzerne to Vergennes, Jan. 8, 1784, AAE, CP, EU, XXVII.

way station or port of refreshment, and even of trade, for American Indiamen.[103]

The main problem of those interested in turning American trade toward France was the arranging for a profitable exchange of American staples for French produce and manufactures. That was the object in view in the memoir of Vergennes heretofore referred to, and was the principal aim of Jefferson's diplomacy. A great deal of progress was made in the period between Jefferson's arrival in 1784 and the outbreak of the French Revolution, that is, if the liberalizing of governmental trade regulations could have operated to produce the desired result. A great many of Vergennes' propositions were put into force. In 1783, the duties on the export of salt were reduced, and those on brandies abolished, and an investigation was begun into the various port charges to which Americans objected. In 1785, the duties on American whale oil were materially reduced, and a little later the charges on imported ships and ship timbers, potash and pearl ash, beaver skins, and rawhide were suppressed.[104] The concession with regard to whale oil was believed to be particularly valuable to the United States.[105]

The article produced in America which was most in demand in France, and which would have been most useful in arranging a direct trade between France and the United States was tobacco. But since the purchase and sale of tobacco in France was a close monopoly in the hands of the Farmers General, the use of that branch of trade to develop an exchange with the United States depended upon the coöperation of the Farm.[106] In his early minute on the encouragement of trade with America, Vergennes had indicated that he realized the

[103] Castries to Vergennes, April 28, 1784, *ibid.*, 322; Stephen Higginson to John Adams, Jan. 17, 1789, *AHA, AR*, 1896, I, 762-765.
[104] See letter of Vergennes to Franklin, July 21, 1783, AAE, CP, EU, XXV; Vergennes to Jefferson, Nov. 30, 1785, *Dip. Corresp.*, I, 710; Calonne to Jefferson, Oct. 22, 1786, *ibid.*, 827-837.
[105] However, Jefferson informed Montmorin, Nov. 6, 1787, that the original reduction had not stimulated the shipment of whale oil to France. *Ibid.*, II, 112.
[106] F. L. Nussbaum, "American Tobacco and French Politics, 1783-1789," *Pol. Sci. Quart.*, XL, 498-499.

importance of this matter.[107] The best plan for securing the object in view would have been to buy the tobacco at the free ports at the market price. Probably the American merchants would then have been encouraged to take at least a part of the return cargo in French manufactures. But the Farmers General had in view their private profit rather than the economic welfare of the kingdom. They adopted the policy of making use of their power as the largest purchaser of tobacco to force down the price, first by refusing to buy at all immediately after the war, and then by contracting for their supply with a single American house and under such conditions as to enable them to manipulate the market.[108]

Jefferson's function in France was to keep the program of favoring American commerce constantly before the authorities, and to be always on the alert to prevent some irresponsible official from revoking concessions once laboriously obtained. In this work he had the loyal and effective aid of Lafayette. Their alliance with some of the French ministers in an effort to control the tobacco monopoly in the interest of Franco-American trade is an interesting example of their work. Although they were unable to destroy the monopoly, they were able to obtain a small alleviation of it and some encouragement of the free sale of tobacco.[109] Most of the concessions made in favor of American trade were contained in ministerial orders, and were consequently subject to revocation or alteration by similar orders. Late in 1787, Jefferson was able to secure the embodiment of all the concessions in a single decree, which would require an act of the royal council to amend, thus affording the friends of American trade time to mobilize their forces for resistance.[110]

---

[107] AAE, CP, EU, XXVI, 131-132.

[108] Nussbaum, op. cit., 500-504.

[109] This episode is worked out in detail by Professor F. L. Nussbaum in two articles, one published in Pol. Sci. Quart., XL (1923), 497-516, and the other in Jour. Mod. Hist., III (1931), 529-613.

[110] Jefferson to Jay, December 31, 1787, Dip. Corresp., II, 126-129. The letter which was "arrêtized" is in Dip. Corresp., I, 827.

The principal American desire in regard to trade with France, as with Great Britain, was admission to the West Indies. The French government insisted, however, that the colonial trade was on a different footing from the direct trade with France. Probably the most important object in maintaining the restrictive system was the desire to support the navy,[111] but another was to avoid the ill will of private interests, particularly the grain interests of southwestern France.[112] On the other hand, the needs of the colonists, and the probability that the Americans would engage in wholesale smuggling if the attempt were made to maintain a complete monopoly dictated certain liberalizing measures.[113] The islands were, of course, open during the war, but the orders placing the restrictive regulations of 1767 again in force were published in the United States, much to Luzerne's regret, about the same time that the news of the British Order in Council of July 2 was circulating. This added to the currency of the rumor that Britain and France were acting in concert to strangle American commerce.[114]

A decree of August 30, 1784 established the permanent basis for the regulation of the island trade. Although a number of concessions were made to the Americans, the old colonial system was retained in principle. The ports were opened to American shipping, but American flour was prohibited, and Americans could not export sugar, coffee, cotton, or cocoa from the colonies. These arrangements necessarily cramped

[111] Adams to Livingston, July 7, 1783, Wharton, VI, 517-518.

[112] Numerous petitions and memorials opposing alteration of the monopoly are on file in the French Archives. Pierre Texier to Vergennes, July 29, 1783, AAE, CP, EU, XXV, 107-108. Municipal officers of Montauban to Vergennes, Dec. 31, 1783, *ibid.*, XXVI, 267-268; Merchants of Moissac to Vergennes, Jan. 1, 1784, XXVII, 3-6; Vergennes to the Bishop of Rodez, Feb. 2, 1784, *ibid.*, 117; Memoir of the Bordeaux merchants, April 1, 1784, XXVII, 238; cf. Nussbaum, "The French Colonial Arrêt of August 30, 1784" in *South Atlantic Quart.*, XXVII, 65.

[113] See Nussbaum's article, *passim*, and Vergennes to Luzerne, Feb. 15, 1784, AAE, CP, EU, XXVII, 136-137.

[114] See *ante*, p. 53 and note. Luzerne to Vergennes, Nov. 27, and Dec. 1, 1783, AAE, CP, EU, XXVI. For an American protest against these regulations, see letter of John Morgan to the President of Congress, August 23, 1783, Papers of the Continental Congress, no. 63, 177-181.

the trade of the middle states, where flour and bread were the most important staples.[115] To the discontent of the grain-growing states was added that of New England when in 1785 a bounty was placed upon dried cod from the French fishery introduced into the West Indies, and a duty was levied upon that imported by foreigners.[116] Massachusetts and New Hampshire shortly afterward enacted navigation laws, which applied to French shipping as well as British. Their effect, however, was not to incline the French ministry to kinder treatment of the New England fisheries. French merchants protested and the government made firm representations to Jefferson. Jay reported to Congress that the acts were violative of the spirit of the treaty, and were poor returns for the comparative liberality of the French government. The result was that the acts were not enforced.[117]

This attitude of the French government made it very clear that it did not intend to allow its hand to be forced in the matter of commercial favors to the United States. It had refused in the beginning to embody such concessions as it was willing to grant in a treaty in order to keep the threat of their withdrawal always over the heads of the Americans. When the Calonne letter of 1786 was issued as a royal *arrêt*, Montmorin instructed Moustier to make plain to the members of Congress that a decree was not a convention.[118] But the injury to Massachusetts and Pennsylvania resulting from the closing

[115] The decree is summarized by Nussbaum in *South Atlantic Quart.*, XXVII, 69-70.

[116] Rufus King to Jonathan Jackson, April 22, 1786, Burnett, *Letters*, unpublished material; Otto to Vergennes, May 20, 1786, AAE, CP, EU, XXXI.

[117] Castries to Vergennes, Sept. 25, 1785, AAE, CP, EU, XXX, 314; Otto to Vergennes, Oct. 25, 1785, *ibid.*, 369-371; Vergennes to Otto, Dec. 25, 1785, *ibid.*, 461-463; Otto to Vergennes, Dec. 20, 1785, 469-472; Otto to Vergennes, June 23, 1786, *ibid.*, XXXI, 416-417; French merchants to French chargé d'affaires, July 28, 1785, *Dip. Corresp.*, I, 170-173; Report of Secretary Jay on Representations of French merchants, Oct. 7, 1785, *ibid.*, 174-176; Vergennes to Jefferson, Oct. 30, 1785, *ibid.*, 707-708; Jefferson to Vergennes, Nov. 20, 1785, *ibid.*, 708-709. In September 1785, the consideration in the Pennsylvania legislature of a navigation law drew from Otto a representation charging that its enactment would be in violation of the treaty. Otto to Vergennes, Sept. 6, 1785, AAE, CP, EU, XXX, 270-277.

[118] Montmorin to Moustier, Nov. 21, 1788, *ibid.*, XXXIII, 342-345.

of the West India market for fish and flour, caused the resentment toward France to continue. The incident of the navigation acts was seized upon by the American government to renew the pressure for a more favorable commercial treaty with France. In reply to Vergennes' protest, Jefferson proposed that the principle of national treatment of each others' subjects be adopted as the basis of a new treaty.[119]

In the United States, an even more radical proposal was made, namely, to yield to France a practically exclusive position in the commerce of the United States in return for the opening of the West India market and a more favorable reception of American produce in France. The idea may have originated with Jefferson, who in June 1785, suggested to Monroe that the lack of constitutional authority on the part of Congress to regulate commerce could be overcome by placing the desired regulations in treaties with foreign nations.[120] Some months later Rufus King, then the leading delegate from Massachusetts, called on Otto, the French chargé d'affaires, and complained bitterly about the exclusion of fish from the French isles, and expressed regret at the inability of Congress to retaliate such injurious regulations. He went on to declare that he believed Congress would be willing to exclude Great Britain entirely from American commerce if the French government would grant concessions in the French West Indies. In reporting this interview, the chargé added that other delegates, particularly those of Virginia and South Carolina had spoken in the same vein, and that it would probably not be difficult for France to profit from the situation, although the Americans would very likely demand too high a price for the favors granted.[121] In August 1786, Jay, in conversation with Otto, suggested a negotiation on the basis of the levy of extraordinary duties on British trade with the United States, the opening of the French West Indies, the favorable reception of American wood and naval stores, and

[119] Jefferson to Vergennes, Nov. 20, 1785, *Dip. Corresp.*, I, 708-709.
[120] Jefferson to Monroe, June 17, 1785, Jefferson, *Writings* (ed. Ford), IV, 54-59.
[121] Otto to Vergennes, May 20, 1786, AAE, CP, EU, XXXI.

the abolition of the privileges of the French monopolistic companies.[122] Otto naturally considered the time a very favorable one for new commercial arrangements, but the French government could hardly consider a treaty expressly antagonistic toward Great Britain desirable so soon after the conclusion of the hardly won Eden treaty with that Kingdom.[123]

It was not within the power of either the French or American governments to teach American trade the way to France. In spite of the favorable attitude and liberal regulations of the royal administration and the American hostility toward Great Britain, the United States took only 1,800,000 livres value of goods from France in return for French purchases of American produce amounting to 9,600,000 livres. The colonial trade approached a little nearer to a balance, but 11,100,000 livres of imports into the Antilles resulted in an export to the United States of only 6,400,000 livres value. These statistics are the average per year for the two-year period, 1787-1789.[124] The principal American export was tobacco, and little was imported into the United States from France except wines and brandies. Jefferson had expected that the tariff reductions in favor of American whale oil would open a French market for that article, but he declared later that almost none was being sold in France.[125]

The French government had not given up hope in 1789, however, of winning part of American trade away from Great Britain, and methods were still being considered for reviving the interest of French merchants in the American market. The Count de Moustier, the last Old Régime minister to the United States, devoted months to the study of economic conditions in the United States with a view to evolving a workable plan for new commercial conquests. Writing in 1789, he was enthusiastic in pointing out the marvelous opportunities. The

[122] Otto to Vergennes, Aug. 13, 1786, *ibid.*, XXXII, 39-42.

[123] Otto to Vergennes, Sept. 22, 1786, *ibid.*, 50-52. For the Eden treaty, see p. 77 above.

[124] E. Levasseur, *Histoire du commerce de la France*, I, 530-531. The statistics of imports are abnormally large, due to the large purchases of American wheat, flour and rice in 1787-1789. *Dip. Corresp.*, II, 254, 284, 331-332.

[125] Jefferson to Montmorin, Nov. 6, 1787, *Dip. Corresp.*, II, 112.

French merchants, he said, had never known American trade. Their disastrous speculations in 1783 and 1784 had been made without knowledge of the tastes, usages, laws, and language of the people. They had confided their ventures to ignorant and unfaithful agents. The Americans had been cheated as often as they cheated the French. Moreover, the country had undergone a veritable commercial and moral revolution since 1786, of which the adoption of the new constitution was an aspect. New customs and new laws increased the security of commerce. The government and people were disposed to favor France above all other nations. As an initial stimulus, he believed an appeal should be made to the patriotism of the French merchants. Since France was the richer country, she must make the first purchases. To encourage this, associations of merchants should be formed under the auspices of the provincial estates. If the provincial estates were unable to finance the initial enterprises, then the King must undertake it himself. He asked to be permitted to return to France to explain his proposals there.[126] Earlier, he had suggested that Frenchmen could profit from studying the methods of manufacture in Great Britain, for it would be found much easier to change French methods than the tastes of the Americans.[127] Montmorin looked upon his investigations with favor, whether or not he approved the final plan.[128] Moustier's proposals perhaps involved too much paternalism for any large success, but the interest shown in his work, and the encouragement given him, indicate that the French fight for the American trade was not ended. But for the coming of the Revolution and foreign war, new efforts would undoubtedly have been made, with perhaps greater success than before.

THE CONTRIBUTIONS OF JOHN JAY AND JOHN ADAMS

Whatever the influence of Jay upon the general conduct of foreign affairs during the period of his incumbency of the

[126] Moustier to Necker, May 12, 1789, AAE, CP, EU, XXIV, 91-105; Moustier to Montmorin, June 1, July 2, 1789, *ibid.*, 139-146, 217-220.
[127] Moustier to Montmorin, Feb. 8, 1788, *ibid.*, XXXIII, 16-21.
[128] Montmorin to Moustier, June 23, 1788, *ibid.*, 208-213.

office of Secretary for Foreign Affairs, he influenced in slight
degree the commercial foreign policy of Congress. The decision to send the commission to negotiate commercial treaties
was made, and the instructions decided upon before his arrival in the United States. He developed, however, in the
course of his term of office, certain very definite ideas upon
the problem of commercial regulations. He was an intense
nationalist, and favored centralized control of trade. He could
even derive a kind of pleasure from the adverse regulations
of foreign nations, for he believed they would encourage the
growth of national feeling at home.[129] In accordance with his
usual logical scheme of thought, he wished a complete commercial system to be adopted and carried out. For this reason,
he opposed the policy of the commission for negotiating
treaties generally. He objected to most-favored-nation treaties
as interfering with the establishment of a future policy fitting
the needs of the United States.[130]

But he was not averse, failing the establishment of a well-
ordered system, to using whatever means were available to
meet the urgent immediate requirements of the suffering
commercial population of the country. His views coincided
with those of the New England leaders like Rufus King and
Elbridge Gerry.[131] Consequently, he resented the exclusion
of American fish from the British and French West Indies.
In an effort to do something for the New England fishing
industry, he was apparently ready in 1786 to approve a treaty
with France which would obligate the United States to levy
a discriminating duty on British goods and shipping.[132] He
believed a treaty with Portugal one of the most valuable

[129] Jay to Jefferson, June 15, 1785, Dip. Corresp., I, 614-615; Jay to Jefferson, Jan. 19, 1786, ibid., 637-638; Jay to Adams, Nov. 26, 1785, ibid., II,
476-477; Jay to Charles Thomson, April 7, 1784, Jay, Corresp., III, 125.

[130] Report of John Jay on a Treaty with Prussia, March 9, 1786, Dip.
Corresp., I, 598-600; Report of John Jay on a Plan of a Treaty of Amity and
Commerce, May 17, 1785, ibid., 529-531.

[131] See Otto's report to Vergennes that Jay was allied with the New England
group. Otto to Vergennes, May 20, 1786, AAE, CP, EU, XXXI. The central
flour exporting states were vitally interested in the same markets.

[132] See ante, p. 90.

which the United States could conclude, and recommended sending a minister there to complete the negotiation which the Jefferson commission had begun.[133] In the same light should be viewed his attitude in the negotiation with Gardoqui for the settlement of the Mississippi question.

When the government of Spain sent Don Diego Gardoqui to the United States in 1785 to secure the consent of the United States to the closure of the Mississippi and to the adjustment of the southwestern boundary in favor of Spain, Jay felt that he was in a splendid position to obtain some relief for the commercial states, where hard times were driving the people to the verge of revolution.[134] Gardoqui was authorized to offer some very valuable commercial concessions.[135] The proposal to guarantee to American citizens in Spain the same privileges as Spanish subjects was very much belittled by those opposed to yielding on the Mississippi question. They argued that Spanish regulations made no important distinction between Spaniards and foreigners. But they failed to notice the provision that a conventional tariff should be concluded within a one-year period. What Jay had in mind was a reciprocity treaty of the modern type, with specific tariff concessions. Further, the King would buy masts and stores for the navy in the United States, paying specie for them, provided they could be furnished as cheaply as from the

[133] Jay to Congress, May 11, 1786, March 12, 1788, Dip. Corresp., I, 664-675; III, 83-84. King had similar sentiments. King to Gerry, July 6, 1786, King, Correspondence, I, 186-187.

[134] Jefferson believed that the depression in the New England fishing industry was at least partially responsible for Shays's rebellion. Jefferson to Carmichael, Dec. 26, 1786, Dip. Corresp., II, 11-12.

[135] Gardoqui's instructions dated Oct. 2, 1784, are printed in Manuel Conrotte, La intervención de España en la independencia de los Estados Unidos, 270-276. The Spanish government was adamant on the subject of admitting the United States to a trade with her colonies, although that boon continued to be very much desired by American merchants. The latest move to obtain it had been made the preceding year. Robert Morris presented a long memoir to Rendón, the Spanish agent, in which he proposed that Spain enter into contracts with a limited number of American merchants who would be permitted to carry on trade with the colonies. By this method, he argued, the danger of illicit trade by Americans would be reduced to a minimum; but if no trade were permitted, all Spain's resources could not prevent smuggling. Morris' memoir is an enclosure in Rendón to Josef de Galvez, April 20, 1784, AHN, Estado, legajo 3885, exp. 25, docs. 3 and 4.

Baltic countries. Such purchases would undoubtedly aid in stabilizing American currency. But the most important commercial proposition made by Gardoqui was that to help the United States abate the menace of the Barbary pirates and so open the great Mediterranean markets for fish and flour. Charles III had already shown his influence in this regard by aiding in the conclusion of the treaty with Morocco.[136] To the part of the population interested in commerce and to practical statesmen who knew the weakness of the government and country, the treaty could not but have appeal. The clearing of the Mississippi could be accomplished only by war against the third naval power of the world, and a naval war, whatever the results with regard to the Mississippi, would probably cost the hardly won share of the Newfoundland fishery. A treaty on the basis of Jay's propositions would both preserve the fishery, and provide a market for fish and flour.[137]

The gain to be derived from such a treaty with Spain would have been largely, though not entirely, sectional. Producers of wheat, rice, and naval stores south of the Potomac would have profited, but by far the greater returns would have come in the North. American indigo could not compete with the better Spanish article. But southerners were more interested in the price of western lands, and it was on that consideration

---

[136] The original plan of the proposed treaty, and a discussion of the commercial proposals from the Spanish point of view, are in Gardoqui to Florida Blanca, Feb. 1, 1786, AHN, Estado, legajo 3893, apartado No. 3, doc. 7. See also Gardoqui to Jay, May 25, 1786, *Dip. Corresp.*, III, 199-201, in which he renews the negotiation and emphasizes the value of Spanish trade in the United States. The Spanish proposals were first revealed by Jay in his report to Congress, Aug. 3, 1786, *Secret Journals of Congress* (ed. T. B. Wait, 4 vols., Washington, 1821), IV, 44-63. The proposed treaty is summarized in Bemis, *Pinckney's Treaty*, 87-88, and later Spanish proposals, *ibid.*, 116-123. See also A. P. Whitaker, *The Spanish-American Frontier, 1783-1795*, ch. v.

[137] The fear of loss of the fishery is expressed in King's letter to Gerry, previously cited, p. 94. Jay and his chief supporter, King, would have been happy to see the Mississippi remain closed, since it would check the migration of people to the West. "The rage for separations and new states is mischievous; it will, unless checked, scatter our resources, and in every view enfeeble the Union." Jay to John Adams, Oct. 14, 1785, *Dip. Corresp.*, II, 420. "Should there be an uninterrupted use of the Mississippi at this time by the citizens of the U. S., I should consider every emigrant to that country from the Atlantic states as forever lost to the Confederacy." King to Gerry, June 4, 1786, King, *Corresp.*, I, 176.

that the fate of the negotiation turned. The five southern
states formed a solid phalanx of opposition, with Monroe and
Charles Pinckney as the leaders. Monroe was violent, privately charging Jay with bad faith and trickery in trying to
evade his instructions on the Mississippi matter.[138] In a motion which he introduced August 29, he asserted that the
United States would gain nothing from the commercial privileges of the proposed treaty, and criticized the policy of
stipulating reciprocal national treatment because it would prevent the United States from discriminating in favor of its own
commerce. He also denied that Jay had authority to conclude
a commercial treaty under the powers granted him, and that
Congress possessed the power to cede the navigation of the
Mississippi. He proposed that Congress appeal to the government of France to mediate between the United States and
Spain.[139]

Charles Pinckney opposed the treaty more judiciously in a
speech in Congress August 16. He likewise minimized the
advantages to be gained by such a treaty, but stressed particularly the danger to the union for one section to purchase
favors at the expense of another. He believed that the movement for greater power in the central government would
produce results, and that, consequently, Congress ought to
avoid binding itself in commitments of doubtful value. In
conclusion, he reverted to the warning that the yielding with
regard to the Mississippi "may involve us in uneasiness with
each other at a time when harmony is so essential to our true
interests—as it may be the means of souring the states, and
indispose them to grant us those additional powers of government, without which we cannot exist as a nation, and without
which all the treaties you may form must be ineffec-
tual. . . ."[140] The delegates of the seven northern states, those
of Delaware being absent, rallied to Jay, and on August 29 a
resolution was adopted authorizing him to negotiate on the

---

[138] Monroe to Jefferson, July 16, 1786, Monroe, *Writings*, I, 141; Monroe
to Madison, Aug. 10, 1786, *ibid.*, 143; Monroe to Henry, Aug. 12, 1786,
ibid., 144-151.
[139] Monroe, *Writings*, I, lviii-lxxii.
[140] Pinckney's speech is printed in full in *AHR*, X (1905), 817-827.

basis of yielding the use of the Mississippi for a term of years.[141] But the persevering opposition of the five southern states made a treaty impossible. Jay himself admitted "that a treaty disagreeable to one half of the nation had better not be made, for it would be violated."[142] Pinckney's prophecy of a successful movement for a stronger government came to pass, and all could look forward to a better position for the United States in regard to the momentous questions to be settled. On Jay's recommendation the negotiation with Spain was suspended to await the formation of the new government.[143]

With regard to Great Britain, no progress was made during the period under discussion, although the Americans did not cease to try. The commissioners for the negotiation of commercial treaties applied to the Duke of Dorset, the British ambassador at Paris, as to the ministers of other foreign powers.[144] The ambassador reported his government ready to consider proposals, but only in London.[145] On the commissioners expressing their willingness to go to London, Dorset was instructed to inquire "what is the real nature of the powers with which you are invested, whether you are merely commissioned by Congress, or whether you have received separate powers from the respective states."[146] The commissioners were able to avoid giving a reply to that pertinent question because of the arrival of the news of John Adams' appointment as minister to Great Britain.[147]

Adams' appointment as minister, February 24, 1785, did not supersede the commission in the negotiation of a commercial treaty. His instructions on the subject only authorized him to "represent to the British ministry the strong and necessary tendency of their restrictions on our trade to in-

[141] *Secret Journals*, IV, 110.
[142] *Ibid.*, 303.
[143] *Ibid.*, 453-454.
[144] The Commissioners to the Duke of Dorset, Oct. 28, 1784, *Dip. Corresp.*, I, 515-517.
[145] The Duke of Dorset to the Commissioners, Nov. 24, 1784, *Dip. Corresp.*, I, 542.
[146] The Duke of Dorset to the Commissioners, March 26, 1785, *ibid.*, 574-575.
[147] Commissioners to the Duke of Dorset, May 16, 1785, *ibid.*, 575.

capacitate our merchants, in a certain degree to make remittances to theirs."[148] In July 1785, he submitted to Lord Caermarthen a copy of the draft treaty which the commission had prepared, altered so as to provide for national instead of most-favored-nation treatment in each other's ports.[149] Jefferson joined him in London early in 1786 and a reply was sought. The minister objected that the project contained too many articles of a political nature, and asked for a draft purely commercial. This was provided, but it was obvious that there was no desire to treat.[150] Adams kept the subject of commerce before the government as much as he could, but never received any satisfactory reply.[151] The order in council of July 1783 was enacted into a law in 1787.[152] Adams was convinced that they would not negotiate until the United States made it to their interest to do so. The British mission, then, had no effect in interesting the British government in a commercial arrangement. The important work of Adams was of a different nature. Its value lay in his constant urging upon Jay and the delegates in Congress the Adams remedy for the bad situation in which the country found itself; namely, retaliation of high duties, an American navigation act, and a stronger national government. He was a prolific and conscientious correspondent, and few of the numerous long dispatches which he penned in London failed to contain at least a few lines of argument in favor of a commercial war upon the mother country.[153]

[148] *Ibid.*, II, 343.

[149] *Ibid.*, 407-417.

[150] The Commissioners to John Jay, April 25, 1786, *Dip. Corresp.*, I, 600-602.

[151] See his account of a conference with Pitt on the subject, *op. cit.*, II, 455-462.

[152] H. C. Bell, "British Commercial Policy in the West Indies, 1783-1793," *EHR*, XXXI (1916), 440-441.

[153] Adams to Jay, May 3, June 10, June 26, August 6, November 24, 1785, January 4, 1786, *Dip. Corresp.*, I, 487-488, II, 377-388, 385-387, 423, 537, 558-559. It is interesting that Jay, in two reports to Congress, November 11, 1785, and May 8, 1786, advised that certain of Adams' letters be not published, and that no recommendations be made to the states to follow out his recommendations because compliance would result in unsystematic regulations inimical to national interests, and a failure to comply would diminish the small prestige Congress still possessed. *Dip. Corresp.*, II, 533-535, 558.

IV

THE EARLY POLICY OF THE
NATIONAL GOVERNMENT
1789-1796

FOREIGN TRADE AND THE CONSTITUTION

THE COMMERCIAL provisions of the Constitution were the natural sequence of the experience of the Revolutionary and Confederation periods. It is futile to try to estimate the relative weight of the demand for the protection of foreign trade in the movement for the Constitution, but it was unquestionably effective,[1] both in the pre-convention period and in the prelude to ratification. There was slight opposition in the Convention to the general proposition that the federal government should be vested with the power over interstate and foreign trade. Restrictions as to its exercise, however, received strong support. Some of the leading statesmen of the staple states still feared that New England would use the federal power to acquire a monopoly of the carriage of southern produce and that the planter would be obliged to pay tribute in the form of freight. To prevent such a result, Charles Pinckney proposed that a two-thirds majority in Congress be required for the enactment of a navigation law.[2] Delegates from the commercial sections were able to save the privilege of legislation by majority vote upon the subject

[1] P. L. Ford, *Essays on the Constitution*, 72-74, 265, 357-358, 377-378. Charles A. Beard, *Economic Origins of the Constitution* gives evidence upon the subject, pages 40-51, 171-175, 183-187, 294, 296, 300, 302, 309. With regard to individually interested delegates, he states: "Personalty in mercantile, manufacturing, and shipping lines was represented by at least eleven members: Broom, Clymer, Ellsworth, Fitzsimons, Gerry, King, Langdon, McHenry, Mifflin, G. Morris, R. Morris." *Ibid.*, 151.

[2] Charles Warren, *Making of the Constitution*, pp. 574-583.

only by yielding the immediate prohibition of the slave trade and the power to tax exports. Not all southerners, of course, were hostile to favors for commerce. Some doubtless still believed that protection would develop a native merchant and ship-owning class within their boundaries. Others sympathetically recognized the fact that the New England states stood to profit little from the separation from Great Britain, and needed *douceurs* to reconcile them to the sacrifice of a large share of their trade.[3]

Historians customarily emphasize the great power over commerce which was conferred upon the national government in the Constitution. This course is proper as concerns foreign commerce, only when reference is intended to the practically non-existent influence of the preceding government. When compared with the commercial authority of contemporary European governments, that of the United States appears highly defective. The power to levy duties upon exports was abandoned with reluctance by those interested in exerting pressure upon foreign governments to secure relaxations in their commercial systems.[4] For example, the levy of a duty on exports to the West Indies in British vessels would probably have been the most effective means of calling the attention of the British government to the bad policy of the exclusion of American shipping. The want of this weapon was keenly felt on later occasions. Another serious handicap was the requirement of a two-thirds majority in the Senate for the ratification of treaties—a further consequence of planters' fears of the "rapacity" of the trading population, emphasized by the memory of the recent threat of Jay to force the Gardoqui treaty down their throats. This provision, coupled with the general prevalence of the two-party system in American politics, makes practical unanimity necessary for the conclusion of treaties. Hence, experimentation with commercial treaties has been exceedingly difficult. Another deterrent to treaty making has been the frequent insistence by the House of

[3] *Ibid.*
[4] *Ibid.*, 573-574.

Representatives that its assent to commercial regulations in treaties is necessary.[5]

THE CONFLICTING PRINCIPLES OF JEFFERSON AND HAMILTON

By 1789, wholesome realism had, in the minds of informed people, replaced the extravagant dream of a world demand for America's trade. The challenging of Europe to commercial wars was not so widely advocated as it had been immediately after the reimposition of the old restrictive systems. The reason was the return of a considerable degree of prosperity to those sections of the country depending upon foreign trade. By means of economy, skill, and the aid of the encouragements provided by state discriminatory laws, American shipping was beginning to recover a share in the direct trade with Great Britain, while forged papers and the connivance of British officials enabled it to reënter the West India and Mediterranean fields. A series of successful ventures to the Far East encouraged an optimistic outlook toward the future.[6]

The keynote of the new realistic attitude was sounded by Tench Coxe in his *Enquiry into a Commercial System,* published on the eve of the session of the Constitutional Convention at Philadelphia. He paid tribute to the preceding era in these words:

Triumphant over a great enemy, courted by the most powerful nations in the world, it was not in human nature that America should immediately comprehend her new situation—really possessed of the means of future greatness, she anticipated the most distant benefits of the revolution, and considered them as already in her hands. She formed the highest expectations many of which, however, serious experience has taught her to relinquish, and now that the thoughtless adventures and imprudent credits from foreign countries take place no more, and time has been given for cool reflexion, she will see her true situation and need not be discouraged.[7]

[5] For discussions of the constitutional aspects of treaty making, see S. B. Crandall, *Treaties, their Making and Enforcement,* ch. xiii; H. St. G. Tucker, *Limitations on the Treaty-Making Power,* ch. iv; R. E. McClendon, "Origin of the Two-thirds Rule in Senate Action upon Treaties," *AHR,* XXXVI (1931), 768-772.

[6] Channing, *United States,* III, 408-423, 481-482.

[7] Tench Coxe, *An Enquiry into the Principles on which a Commercial System for the United States of America Should be Founded,* 42-45.

For the future, according to Coxe, in place of world-wide trade a few modest resources could be profitably exploited: the fisheries, the coasting trade, the newly opened intercourse with the Far East, Russia, and France. The sources of Coxe's study are perhaps not now to be discovered, but his ideas were judicious and the system recommended bears a remarkable resemblance to that adopted by the new national government.

The country expected, doubtless, that Congress would enact, with more vigorous implementing, the commercial policy of the Continental Congress—a system of harsh regulations for nations refusing concessions, and more liberal treatment for those whose governments favored friendlier commercial relationships. The view was entertained that the people in ratifying the Constitution had given the government a mandate to proceed in that policy.[8] It is significant, therefore, that a new policy was evolved and substantially adopted during the first year of the national government. It was the work, largely, of Alexander Hamilton, although suggestions of the principles are to be found elsewhere. In fact, Hamilton seems to have adopted the new plan only after entering Washington's Cabinet, for his ideas expressed in *The Federalist* seem not to differ greatly from those of the men who worked out the former system.

The leading principles of the new program were equality of treatment for all foreign nations, and avoidance of European commitments. Like the systems of Europe, it was permeated with fiscalism. To Hamilton, the one thing essential to the safety of the nation was the establishment of its financial credit by providing an adequate and dependable revenue. Since the only practicable source of permanent income consisted in duties on imports, that source must be guarded against interruption. For that reason, commercial wars must be avoided and strict neutrality preserved in European affairs. That continued economic subordination to Great Britain must follow was to be regretted; but, after all, that country was

[8] See page 105 below; also *The Federalist*, No. 11, and the references to Beard, *Economic Interpretation* in note 1 above.

the best source of supply and the best market for the United States. As the country grew in strength, the question of resistance might be reëxamined. But the true means of attaining economic independence would be to make reliance upon foreign nations unnecessary through the development of domestic manufactures. The ideal of Hamilton became absolutely clear after the outbreak of the European wars, but his influence is easily traceable in Congress from the beginning. Every sound encouragement within the control of the federal government, the system pledged to the ship-building industry and native merchants. It promised little in the way of an expanded market for agriculture, except the gradual growth of a native industrial population.[9]

The group whose thinking ran along the older lines also had representatives in strategic positions in the new government. Jefferson in the Department of State was in an ideal place to encourage activities of the sort which he had pursued as minister to France, and to initiate experiments in commercial relations with foreign countries. Madison was highly influential in the House of Representatives. There were probably no general principles in the Hamiltonian program which either of these men would have contradicted outright. The necessity of protecting the revenue, the danger in commitments to European nations, the advantages to be derived from the promotion of domestic industry were equally obvious to them. The difference lay chiefly in point of emphasis, and in the evaluation of the circumstances of the United States.

The Jefferson-Madison school believed that a worthwhile degree of economic independence was attainable immediately through the encouragement of other nations to compete with Great Britain in the American trade. In so far as there was a sectional special interest involved in the plan, it was the de-

[9] Hamilton's views on commercial foreign policy are best set forth in *The Federalist*, No. 11; the Report on Manufactures, *ASP, Finance*, I, 128; Hamilton to Jefferson, Jan. 11, Jan. 13, 1791, Alexander Hamilton, *Works* (ed. H. C. Lodge), IV, 345-348; Outline of William Smith's Speech, *ibid.*, 205-224; Speech of William Smith of S. C., in House of Representatives, Jan. 13, 1794, *Debates and Proceedings in the Congress of the United States* (hereafter cited by the binder's title of *Annals*), IV, 174-209.

sire of the producers of the great agricultural staples to avoid a monopoly of the carriage and marketing of their produce by the shipping and merchants of any one nation. Free competition meant lower freight, and the prevention of the piling up of debts with a single group of merchants, as had been the case before the war. A further object was the opening up of larger markets abroad for American produce, and the abolition of the British entrepôt for the exchange of American and Continental produce, by an encouragement of a direct trade with the Continent. Sectional interests were not the only motives, however. Jefferson and his supporters labored just as hard to secure and protect markets for fish and ships as for tobacco, rice, and flour.

Proponents of this program did not expect to gain everything at once, but only to make a beginning with the resources at hand. One great resource was believed to be the indispensability of the American trade to British prosperity—the value being relatively greater for Britain than for the United States because, from the farmer point of view, it was the exchange of food and essential raw materials for luxuries. Another resource was the European situation. As political independence had been secured by playing upon, and making use of the rivalries of the European nations, so Jefferson believed that the British commercial monopoly could be broken in the same way, that if discrimination in favor of the more liberal continental governments did not produce immediate commercial advantages, it would induce Great Britain in protection of her own interest to adopt a more favorable policy toward the United States.[10]

THE COMMERCIAL LEGISLATION OF 1789-1790

Two attempts were made in the first Congress in the establishment of the fiscal system to discriminate against Great

[10] Expressions of his views on commercial policy are to be found throughout Jefferson's writings. The most complete discussions in brief compass are in his report on the fisheries, and on the privileges and restrictions of the commerce of the United States in foreign countries. *ASP, C&N,* I, 8-12, *FR,* I, 300-304. See also W. K. Woolery, *The Relation of Thomas Jefferson to American Foreign Policy, 1783-1793, passim.*

Britain and in favor of France and the other states with which treaties existed. In a resolution for raising a revenue, Madison proposed in April 1789 the levying of a duty upon the tonnage of vessels entering the ports of the United States—one rate for American vessels, a higher rate for those of states having treaties with the United States, and a still higher for those not having treaties.[11] The other proposition was inserted in the bill for laying duties on imports, and proposed a higher duty upon distilled spirits from countries having no treaties than upon those imported from treaty states. A preference for French brandy over British West Indian rum was intended. The supporters of these propositions probably did not expect that the discriminations would be of much more than merely psychological effect. They desired to encourage the French government to persist in its policy of relaxation, and to indicate to Great Britain that the United States possessed both the inclination and the power to resist the monopolistic system.[12]

The proposed legislation met strong opposition, especially from representatives from New York and New England. It was held that the nation was not yet strong enough nor sufficiently united to undertake a commercial war. Domestic manufacturing could not supply the country if imports were interrupted, nor was the merchant fleet large enough to carry off the exports if the British were excluded. Moreover, American commerce was on as good a footing with non-treaty states as with those with which treaties existed. The revenue, it was asserted, would be injured by reprisals abroad, and it would be a bad policy for the United States to show preference as between foreign nations. The best solution of the commercial problem would be to allow the merchants to trade freely wherever they judged best. Madison and his supporters argued that the merchants could not make a free choice until trade could be made to flow in its natural channels, which did not lead to Great Britain. The people, in approving the Constitution, had intended that the commercial power of Congress

[11] *Annals*, I, 103.
[12] *Ibid.*, 201-202, 204-206.

be used to discriminate between friends and unfriendly rivals. The proposed discrimination, they contended, would favor the development of a navy through the encouragement of merchant shipping, and would promote agriculture by improving facilities for export. The representatives from the southern states, in general, supported Madison's propositions, though some did so with reluctance, and a few opposed.[13]

The House of Representatives adopted both propositions: a tonnage schedule of six cents per ton for American ships, thirty cents for those of nations "in alliance," and fifty cents for all others, and a schedule on distilled spirits with a similar distinction. The Senate, however, struck out both provisions.[14] The House offered considerable opposition to the Senate's action, particularly as to the tonnage bill, but in the end concurred rather than risk the loss or prolonged delay of the revenue bills.[15]

Madison was convinced that the principal reason for the refusal of the Senate to support the House measures was lack of confidence in the efficacy of the proposed discriminations and the desire to work out a more far-reaching plan.[16] In conformity with this view, the Senate, on June 17, constituted a committee with Pierce Butler as chairman to report a plan. This committee soon presented a recommendation for an additional tonnage duty on foreign ships loading in the United States with goods consigned to ports closed to American vessels, but added that such a law ought to originate in the House of Representatives, since it would be of the character of a revenue law. In addition, it advised the preparation of a bill imposing similar restraints on the trade of European settlements in America with the United States as the mother countries imposed upon the trade of the United States with those settlements. The Senate adopted the report, and added Ells-

---

[13] *Ibid.*, 108-109, 112, 176, 177, 181-182, 183-186, 186-191, 200-204, 204-206, 234-240, 240-247.

[14] William Maclay, *Journal*, 74-75, 87.

[15] *Annals*, I, 454, 586, 590, 608-610, 615-618.

[16] *Ibid.*, 588, 608; Madison to Monroe, Aug. 9, 1789, Madison, *Writings* (ed. Hunt), V, 415.

worth, King, and Read to the committee, which was to draft
a bill. No results followed the appointment, however.[17] Maclay thought that the argument of the weakness of the House
discrimination, and the appointment of the committee to report a bill were merely pretexts to kill the proposal. He attributed the scheme to New York or British influence among
the members.[18]

The foundations of the commercial system of the federal
government were laid in four laws passed in July and August,
1789; viz., the tariff act, the tonnage act, the act to regulate
the collection of duties, and the act for the registering and
clearing of vessels.[19] The omission of the proposal to tax the
distilled spirits of non-treaty powers higher than those of
"allies," left nothing specifically retaliatory in the tariff act.
However, it was quite possible to intend discrimination without so labeling it. The wines and spirits schedule could well
have been an example. Rum was actually taxed more heavily
than brandy, and Madeira higher than other wines, which
would include all qualities of French wines.[20] But the Hamiltonian principle of making no nominal distinction between
foreigners was strictly adhered to. The policy expressed in this
legislation was obviously a policy of protection of American
industry. The tonnage duty on American vessels was set at
six cents per ton, that on foreign vessels at fifty cents. Even
more effective as an aid to shipping was the ten per cent discount allowed upon the amount of duties assessed, if the goods
were imported in American ships. A monopoly of the coasting trade was established for American shipping, not by prohibiting the participation of foreigners, but by excusing
American vessels of fifty tons or less from the necessity of
entering and clearing,[21] and other coasting vessels from pay-

---

[17] *Annals*, I, 45, 49, 57; *ASP, FR*, I, 6.
[18] Maclay, *Journal*, 94-95.
[19] *Statutes at Large of the U. S.*, I, 24-27, 27-28, 29, 49, 55-65.
[20] Fitzsimons, a friend of France at this time, cited this item as being a
favor to French commerce. *Annals*, I, 201. On the other hand, the protection
of the American distillers was doubtless a consideration.
[21] *Statutes at Large of the U. S.*, I, 94-95.

ing tonnage duties oftener than once a year. Foreign vessels were admitted only at the larger ports and were required to pay the foreign tonnage duty at each entry. Goods from the Far East, when carried in American vessels from beyond the Cape of Good Hope, were rated distinctly lower in the tariff than when imported in foreign vessels or indirectly by way of Europe.

Writers of a nationalistic bent, even some prominent historians, have concluded that the shipping legislation of 1789 produced the great replacement of British by American tonnage in the intercourse with Great Britain, which occurred in 1790.[22] The conclusion seems to be derived from the fact that the increase followed the legislation—a formula of doubtful merit. Other factors deserve consideration. Consul Phineas Bond, always well informed and on the alert for whatever threatened British trade, wrote the Duke of Leeds in 1791 that "the diminution of the number of British vessels employed herein lately is rather to be imputed to the scantiness of the last crop, the little demand for wheat and flour in Europe and the exorbitant rates of insurance occasioned by the prospect of war with Spain than to any check the enterprising spirit of our shipowners may have received by the regulations as they now stand."[23] Data furnished by British merchants engaged in the American trade enabled the Committee of the Privy Council for Trade and Foreign Plantations to conclude in 1791 that the tonnage duty under the acts of 1789 and 1790 was three pence per ton less than the average of the similar duties collected by the several states prior to 1789, and that the discrimination in duties on goods imported in British ships were one and one-half per cent less than the average of those charged by the states.[24] Neither the British government nor British merchants exhibited any great

---

[22] A. T. Mahan, *Sea Power in its Relation to the War of 1812*, I, 80; J. P. Baxter, 3rd, "Our First National Shipping Policy," *U. S. Naval Institute Proc.*, XLVI (1920), 1251-1264.

[23] *AHA, AR*, 1897, 467-468.

[24] *Report on the Commerce and Navigation between His Majesty's Dominions and the Territories Belonging to the United States* (London, 1791), 81-85.

concern with regard to the new American shipping policy.

Renewed efforts were made in both houses of Congress in 1790 to secure the enactment of discriminative commercial laws. In February, a Senate committee was ordered to report a plan for the regulation of trade with the American colonies of European powers.[25] In the House, the matter came up in connection with the consideration of petitions from shipping centers for a higher tonnage duty on foreign vessels than that provided in the act of the preceding year.[26] Madison attempted to secure the exemption from the proposed increase, of states having treaties with the United States. He met considerable opposition, even from some who had supported his similar proposals in 1789.[27] He then proposed progressive increases in the tonnage duties on ships of non-treaty states. This was even more strongly opposed.[28] Eventually he abandoned the idea of distinctive treatment based upon the existence of treaties, and gave his support to what appeared to be a more popular scheme, a strong navigation act. The plan under consideration proposed the closing of United States ports to foreign vessels from ports closed to the vessels of the United States, the prohibition of export in foreign vessels of articles not admitted in foreign ports in American vessels, and the prohibition of the importation in the ships of a foreign country, of articles other than the produce of that country.[29] However, two influences combined to prevent any important change in commercial regulations in 1790. Representatives of the southern states would not permit a higher tonnage duty, and the Administration used its influence to prevent measures likely to irritate the British government, pending the outcome of a diplomatic approach.[30]

[25] *Annals*, I, 947, 950, 958, 965.
[26] *Ibid.*, II, 1557-1559, 1560-1565.
[27] *Ibid.*, 1570-1572.
[28] *Ibid.*, 1573-1581.
[29] *Annals*, II, 1655-1657; Jefferson, *Writings* (ed. Ford), V, 196.
[30] Maclay, *Journal*, 380-381; Madison, *Writings*, V, 196. Perhaps the most important change in the shipping laws was the translation of the ten per cent discount on duties assessed, in favor of American vessels, into a surcharge of ten per cent when the carrier was a foreign ship. *Statutes at Large of the U. S.*, I, 181.

COMMERCE AND THE CRISIS IN
ANGLO-AMERICAN RELATIONS

Before Jefferson arrived to assume his duties as Secretary of State, Washington engaged Gouverneur Morris to sound the British government on its attitude toward a commercial treaty, and particularly with regard to the admission of American vessels to the West India trade. In a series of conferences in April and May, 1790, Morris found the ministry unprepared to make a commercial arrangement satisfactory to the United States, without a political connection derogatory to American independence.[31] This information the President communicated to Congress February 14, 1791.[32] The message was the signal for a revival of the proposals of retaliation. A committee in the House promptly reported a navigation bill, which provided that imports into the United States should be permitted only in American vessels and those of the country producing the articles imported. It was proposed in addition, to levy a special duty of one cent per gallon on rum and twelve and a half cents per gallon on other distilled spirits coming from ports from which American vessels were not allowed to export them.[33] For the moment, it appeared that Jefferson's star was in the ascendant and that his policy of resistance to Great Britain was to become the avowed policy of the United States government.

That a navigation law was not enacted early in 1791 was due to the decision of the British government to send a minister to Philadelphia. On January 19, Hamilton told George Beckwith, the unofficial British agent, that he thought that retaliatory legislation would be passed before Congress adjourned. Letters were received from London the same day announcing the decision of the government to send a regular minister. On the following day, Hamilton assured Beckwith that no adverse legislation would be enacted that session.[34]

---

[31] *ASP, FR*, I, 122-27.

[32] J. D. Richardson, *Messages and Papers of the Presidents*, I, 96.

[33] *ASP, C&N*, I, 8-22.

[34] Beckwith to Grenville, Jan. 19, March 3, 1791, PRO, FO, America 4, XII. See also *Annals*, II, 1969.

The British government had been watchful toward American commercial policy from the beginning of the national government. The legislation of 1789 was studied carefully by the Committee of the Privy Council for Trade and Plantations, and the consuls and other agents in America gave particular attention to commerce. All became thoroughly alarmed at the determined attitude of Congress and the Administration in January and February, 1791, and felt that only immediate action by their government could prevent measures injurious to British trade.[35] The Committee for Trade and Plantations in a lengthy report printed January 28, 1791, held that although the existing regulations need excite no alarm, a negotiation ought to be undertaken with the object of preventing further adverse legislation.[36] The alarming news from America stimulated that body in May to advise the foreign minister that "as little Time as possible should be lost, in taking proper Means for counteracting the Intention of those Members of Congress, whose Interest or Inclination it may be to support any Propositions that may be unfriendly to the Commerce and Navigation of this Country. . . . "[37]

The first draft of instructions for George Hammond, designated for the new post of minister to the United States, was prepared by Lord Hawkesbury, president of the Com-

[35] Bond wrote on January 3 that he thought that, in face of the President's recommendation of December, the restrictive regulations would pass. *AHA, AR*, 1897, 467-469. On March 14, he reported a whole series of events he believed threatening to British trade. *Ibid.*, 474-477. On March 19, Temple lamented "that there is now so great an appearance that a war of Duties, Tonnage, & Restrictions is likely to take place between Great Britain and these states," and on May 23 reported that he was sorry "to inform your Grace that the Secretary of States Party & Politicks gains ground here, and I fear will have influence enough to cause Acts & Resolves, which may be disagreeable to Great Britain, to be passed early in the next session of Congress. PRO, FO, America 4, IX. P. Allaire, the British secret agent in New York City, writing to Sir George Yonge on March 21 declared, "Your House is too conversant with business for me to presume to give my opinion, but if you do not take great care, you will lose the great privilege you now enjoy."*Ibid.*, X.

[36] *Report on the Commerce and Navigation between His Majesty's Dominions and the Territories belonging to the United States of America, January 28, 1791* (London, 1791), 97-99.

[37] Stephen Cottrell to Lord Grenville, May 26, 1791, PRO, FO, America 4, X.

mittee for Trade and Plantations. The part relating to commerce followed the recommendations of that committee as presented in the January report. The willingness of the British government to negotiate was declared, and the basis of mutual most-favored-nation treatment recommended. It would be desirable to obtain from the United States an agreement not to advance import duties beyond the existing level, or, failing that, the acceptance of the rates stipulated in the British treaties with France or Holland. The government expected to continue the existing preferential rates in favor of certain United States produce, but would not bind itself by treaty to do so. The subject of the admission of American vessels to the West Indies should be excluded from the negotiation. Any existing discrimination by the United States in favor of the colonies of any other country must be abandoned. While American tonnage duties equal to those collected in Great Britain would be unobjectionable, a higher rate would lead to retaliation.[38] Hammond's final instructions, dated September 1, 1791, followed the Hawkesbury draft very closely.[39] The suggestion of a conventional tariff and the proposal to exclude the West India trade from the negotiation, however, were omitted. Hammond was not authorized to conclude a treaty, but was required to refer all proposals to London. Thus, after three years of effort, the United States government had succeeded in bringing the British ministry to the point of discussing commerce, but had failed to elicit any indication of a disposition to make concessions.

The policy adopted by Jefferson under the new circumstances was one of firmness. He was not in the least deceived by the British tactics. In fact, he had been able to obtain a full summary of the report of January 28, and consequently was almost as fully apprised of British policy as was Hammond himself.[40] Immediately after the adjournment of Con-

---

[38] Hawkesbury to Grenville, July 4, 1791, PRO, FO, America 4, X.
[39] Ibid.
[40] Bond was able to discover that the Secretary of State knew the contents of the report. Bond to Grenville, Oct. 8, 1791, *AHA, AR,* 1897, 492.

gress in March, he ordered that overtures be made to the
governments of Spain, France, and Portugal for the formation of an informal league whose object should be the forcing
of Great Britain to abandon the navigation laws. The method
would be the simultaneous adoption of the bill reported by
the committee of the House of Representatives in February.
He felt that if the other powers would coöperate with the
United States in this matter, it would "form a remarkable and
memorable epoch in the history of the freedom of the
Ocean."[41] When Hammond arrived, Jefferson with discon-
certing boldness uncovered the fact that the minister possessed no powers for a commercial treaty.[42] He then announced in cabinet meeting that he proposed to submit to
Congress a report on commercial relations, in which he would
be obliged to recommend retaliation against Great Britain.[43]
Hamilton raised the point that the beginning of a commercial
war would in all probability be received in England as a
proof of hostility, and so prevent every chance of securing
the evacuation of the northwest posts, without which the
United States could not hope to free themselves from the
Indian war. Jefferson then agreed to delay the report until
he could find out from Hammond the chances of obtaining
an evacuation of the posts. The protracted negotiation with
Hammond prevented its being presented at that session of
Congress. The Secretary of State seems to have had little
expectation that the recommendation of a navigation act
would be favorably acted upon by Congress.[44]

An entire year of negotiation, during which the commercial problem was subordinated to the other points of
difference[45] between the two countries, produced no results.

[41] Jefferson to Carmichael and Humphreys, March 15, March 17, April 11,
1791. U. S. Dept. of State, Instructions to U. S. Ministers, (hereafter cited as
Instructions), I, 18, 20-21, 28.

[42] ASP, FR, I, 188-190.

[43] Jefferson, Writings (Memorial ed.), 298-300. Hamilton conveyed the impression to Hammond that the agreement to exchange ministers had caused Jefferson to abandon the report. Hammond to Lord Grenville, Jan. 9, 1792, Henry
Adams Transcripts.

[44] Jefferson to Edward Rutledge, Aug. 29, 1791. Writings (ed. Ford), V, 375.

[45] On the American side, these were: the evacuation of the northwest posts, the

The British government adhered to its policy of procrastination. In February 1793, Jefferson again prepared the report on commercial relations for presentation to the House of Representatives. He sent parts of it to the various European ministers in residence, asking their statements as to its accuracy.[46] He then inquired of the House as to whether or not its presentation was desired at that time. A select committee considered the matter and, probably upon the Secretary's advice, decided not to make the call. Hammond believed that the postponement was due to a desire to await the arrival of Genêt, the new French minister, who was expected to bring some attractive propositions from the republican government in Paris.[47] However, the outbreak of war between France and Great Britain, and Genêt's undiplomatic conduct, which caused Washington to request his recall, prevented any favorable developments in Franco-American commercial relations.

Finding his efforts to negotiate a settlement futile, and his policies obstructed by his opponents in the government, Jefferson resigned at the end of the year. One of his final acts as Secretary of State was the presentation, on December 16, of the long postponed report on the situation of American commerce.[48] It constituted a farewell declaration of his policy, which he no longer hoped to see carried into execution. The report is an extraordinary example of the reduction to simplicity of a complicated technical subject. It is no mere digest of foreign customs regulations, but the result of profound study and an uncommon grasp of the relationship of the

---

disputed northwestern boundary, and indemnity for the slaves carried away when the British armies evacuated American ports at the end of the Revolution. Great Britain was concerned about the confiscation of the property of loyalists and the obstacles placed by the states in the way of British creditors in collecting debts owed by Americans.

[46] Jefferson, *Writings* (ed. Ford), VI, 179, 186, 188-189; U. S. Dept. of State, Domestic Letters, V, 50-53; *Annals*, III, 122, 1150-1152.

[47] *Annals*, III, 885, 894; Hammond to Greenville, March 7, 1793, Henry Adams Transcripts.

[48] *ASP, FR*, I, 300-304. For Jefferson's explanation of the method by which he arrived at his conclusions, see his letter to Hammond, Feb. 16, 1793, in U. S. Dept. of State, Domestic Letters, V, 50-53.

United States to European economy. It is far from being the partisan and pro-French document which Hamilton's supporters branded it. Jefferson's purpose was not to show partiality toward any foreign nation, but to seek the advantage of the United States wherever he could find it.[49] He wished to encourage the nations of continental Europe, particularly France, to reorganize their commercial systems so as to afford a competitive market for the United States, and by the same act, as he believed, establish their own commercial prosperity. He proclaimed his allegiance to the doctrine of free trade, but declared that "free commerce and navigation are not to be given in exchange for restrictions and vexations, nor are they likely to produce a relaxation of them."

The situation in which he found American commerce, weighed down by the selfish regulations of foreign governments, suggested certain plain remedies to the Secretary of State. The United States should impose high duties and prohibitions on the produce of nations which imposed high duties and prohibitions on the produce of the United States, levying the higher duties on those goods which the United States could most easily produce or obtain from more friendly countries. One result to be expected from the adoption of this policy would be the migration of foreign capitalists to this country, where they would establish factories. When any nation refused to admit American merchants to any part of its dominions, the United States should refuse to receive its merchants, or, at least, restrict their transactions by law. When United States vessels were restricted to the carriage of the produce of their own country, foreign vessels should be likewise limited in American ports. When a foreign nation refused to admit American produce in American vessels into its dominions, the United States should prohibit its export in foreign vessels. Jefferson also recommended a return to the policy of discrimination in favor of countries having treaties with the United States.

The conditions influencing the consideration of commercial

[49] Gilbert Chinard, *Thomas Jefferson*, 375.

policy in the winter of 1793-1794 differed radically from those of 1790, for example. With a general European war in progress, an American policy of discrimination in favor of the treaty states was certain to be interpreted in Great Britain as favoritism for Britain's enemies. Further, the relations between the United States and Great Britain, from other causes than unfair commercial restrictions, were becoming more tense. To the Indian and frontier problems, over which feeling was increasing, was added the grievance of the rules of maritime warfare enforced by the British navy, and deemed contrary to international law by the United States. Moreover, in the altered European situation, the commercial principles of three years before were hardly applicable. In time of peace, the Continent might make shift partially to replace Great Britain as the American market. This could not be the case while the more advanced industrial sections were disrupted by revolution and foreign war, and Great Britain controlled the channels of communication. Many of the foreign commercial regulations formerly complained of no longer existed. The great danger to American commerce lay not in the municipal regulations of foreign governments, but in their application of what they considered the rights of belligerents. Consequently, the ensuing struggle to carry the retaliative commercial laws in the United States must be considered as made not entirely to establish a desirable commercial system, but partly for political purposes and partly as a measure of general hostility toward Great Britain.

With Jefferson in retirement, Madison remained as leader of the advocates of resistance to Great Britain. On January 3, he introduced a series of resolutions in conformity with Jefferson's recommendations,[50] with an additional resolution proposing the levy of an extra duty on the imports from any country which might injure American trade—in lieu of damages. Madison asserted that he did not propose to go the full length of the declared rates at first, but merely wished Congress to declare a national policy, which could be executed by

[50] *Annals*, IV, 155-158.

degrees as circumstances might require. Hamilton had had ample time to organize an opposition in the House of Representatives. He had been collecting data for the purpose of refuting Jefferson's conclusions ever since the inception of the great report. This material and an outline of a speech was given to William Smith of South Carolina, who was designated to lead the Federalists in the House.[51]

It was Hamilton's strategy to brand Jefferson's report a pro-French document, and then to prove that France was not more favorable to American commerce than Great Britain. The debate became too largely a discussion of the relative merits of the French and British systems, to the neglect of Jefferson's larger principles.[52] Smith cited statistics to show that Great Britain had placed the trade with the United States upon a better basis than with any other country.[53] It was not their legislation, he said, which enabled them to monopolize American commerce, but their enormous superiority over other nations in manufacturing. He admitted that it would be good policy for the United States to diminish dependence upon a single foreign nation, but it would be improper to do it artificially by means of a tax upon the American people for the benefit of other nations. The better method "for counteracting the effects of the spirit of monopoly, which more or less tinctures not the system of Great Britain merely, but that of all Europe" would be "an efficacious system of encouragement to home manufactures." Great Britain could probably win a commercial war. All her allies would look upon the adoption of the proposed resolutions as proof of sympathy for the cause of their enemies. The interests of the United States demanded submission for the present. "Our progress is and will be rapid enough," he declared, "if we do not throw away our advantages. . . . Why should this young

[51] Hamilton, *Works*, IV, 205-221. See also Hamilton to Jefferson, Jan. 1, 1792, *ibid.*, 199-202.
[52] Smith's speech is in *Annals*, IV, 174-208.
[53] Madison, in his able rebuttal, showed that the discriminations in favor of certain American products were obsolete survivals from the colonial relationship and no longer effective. *Annals*, IV, 366-395.

country throw down the gauntlet in favor of free trade against the world? There may be spirit in it but there will certainly not be prudence."

The more violent attitude of the New England merchant class was set forth as follows, by Fisher Ames:

The footing of our exports, under the British system, is better than that of their exports to the United States, under our system. Nay, it is better than the freedom of commerce, which is one of the visions for which our solid prosperity is to be hazarded; for suppose we could batter down the system of prohibitions and restrictions, it would be gaining a loss. . . . It is as plain as figures can make it, that if a state of freedom for our exports is at par, the present system raises them above par. To suppose that we can terrify them by these resolutions to abolish their restrictions, at the same time to maintain in our favor their duties, to exclude other foreigners from their market is too absurd to be refuted. . . . The system before us is a mischief that goes to the root of our prosperity. The merchants will suffer by the schemes and projects of a new theory. Great numbers were ruined by the convulsions of 1775. They are an order of citizens deserving better of government than to be involved in new confusions. It is wrong to make our trade wage war for our politics. It is now scarcely said that it is a thing to be sought for but a weapon to fight with.[54]

It is a peculiar fact that the system which was intended to bring American commerce into its own received almost no support from those states in which the influence of the merchant class was strongest.[55] The initial resolution, which was merely a declaration that the commerce of the United States ought to be set upon a better footing with regard to foreign nations, was carried in the House of Representatives by a vote of fifty-one to forty-six. It was found difficult to bring the others to a vote, and they were postponed.[56] The crisis in relations with Great Britain was becoming so serious that mere commercial regulations, even severe ones, would not meet the need. In the movement for the Jay mission, Madison's resolutions passed from the stage.

[54] *Annals*, IV, 331-336, 346-347.
[55] This situation attracted attention at the time. See *Annals*, IV, 272; Hammond to Grenville, Feb. 22, 1794, Henry Adams Transcripts.
[56] Madison to Jefferson, Madison, *Writings*, VI, 210.

FRANCE AND THE UNITED STATES DRIFT APART

In the background of the anti-English movement, there always existed the idea that commercial connections with France more advantageous than those existing could be worked out. The federal régime opened with apparent high promise of a growing commercial intimacy between the two countries. The Count de Moustier was then finishing his report,[57] which reëvaluated for French merchants and officials the opportunities of American trade. The impression of the favorable royal decrees still prevailed in the United States, and was only partially nullified by continued resentment at the arrangements which obstructed the sale of fish in the French islands.[58] Washington, not yet President, but speaking with the prestige of the outstanding leader in the formation of the Constitution, wrote encouragingly of the forces operating to overcome the advantages hitherto held by the British.[59] Reference has already been made to the popular conception that the commercial power of Congress had been established to enable the government to reward friends and penalize enemies. Americans also expected much from the liberalization of the French government after the beginning of the Revolution.[60]

The first blow at the commercial "alliance" was struck by the United States, when, in the tariff and tonnage laws of 1789, France was placed upon the same plane as Great Britain. It is impossible to judge to what extent the official French attitude toward these acts was determined by regard for the injury they threatened to trade. To a large degree,

[57] See *ante*, p. 91.

[58] Jay to Jefferson, April 24, 1788, Jay, *Correspondence*, III, 326-327.

[59] Washington, *Writings* (ed. W. C. Ford), XI, 306-312.

[60] William Short's enthusiasm for the possibilities of trade with a free France was great. "It is useless for me to call to your mind a consideration of which you undoubtedly feel the full weight—that is, that the shackles of commerce which have hitherto prevented the extending our connections of that kind with France are about to be destroyed, & that the two countries will in future necessarily find their mutual advantage in encouraging those connexions—the manufactures of France are undergoing a sensible change which will adapt them to our choice." Short to the Secretary of State, March 3, 1790. U. S. Dept. of State, Dispatches from U. S. Ministers (hereafter cited as Dispatches), France, I, 121.

the point was seized upon as one, the character of whose decision would determine whether the United States would remain loyal to the political alliance. At any rate, the French shipping interest protested against the legislation, and used it as an excuse for resisting further relaxations. There was ground for asserting that the tonnage duty was in violation of Article V of the treaty of 1778, which excused United States vessels from the payment of a similar French duty—a clause which apparently was included in recognition of the fact that no alien tonnage duty was collected in the United States. At least that was the French thesis.[61]

Jefferson repudiated this interpretation of the treaty. But in a report to Congress, he favored meeting the wishes of the French government if it could be done without enabling other nations having treaties with the United States to claim the same concession without compensation.[62] This last difficulty, he thought, could be overcome by specifying that the concession with regard to tonnage was meant to be compensation for the decrees of 1787-1788. Hamilton approved Jefferson's interpretation of the treaty, but strongly opposed the recommendation. It would produce a bad effect in Great Britain, and set a bad precedent in addition, for French shipping might grow under a free government to a point of ruinous competition with the United States. The tonnage duty was intended to provide an important part of the revenue, and if given up, a substitute ought to be provided. It would be a better policy to embody such concessions in a treaty. The Senate refused to follow out the recommendation of the Secretary of State and adopted a resolution advising the President "to defend the American interpretation in a friendly manner."[63]

The fight in Congress and with Hamilton constituted only one phase of Jefferson's operations in behalf of his commercial

[61] Otto to Jefferson, Dec. 13, 1790, Jan. 8, 1791, *ASP, FR,* 111-112.
[62] Jefferson to Otto, March 29, 1791, *Writings* (Ford), V, 308-313. The report on Otto's application is in *ASP, FR,* I, 109-111.
[63] *Annals,* III, 72-77.

system. He was constantly exerting upon the French government whatever influence he could command to induce it to give him aid. His greatest need was convincing evidence that that government was more favorable in its policy than Great Britain, but the last concessions of consequence to which he was ever able to point, until the outbreak of the Anglo-French war, were the old royalist decrees of 1787-1788. He sent to Paris copies of his report on the fisheries and of the proposed navigation act as suggestions for coöperative action.[64] Finally he explained fully to the French minister just what his difficulties were, and how the French government could help him to overcome them. But however much government officials might wish to coöperate, they were obliged frankly to confess their lack of power to do so.[65]

Political liberalism in France did not mean commercial liberalism, but its opposite. The relaxations of the Old Régime injured, or were believed to have injured, private interests, and earned the hearty resentment of the merchant class. This reaction led to the denouncement by the revolutionary government, of the Eden Treaty of 1786, which marked a long step toward free trade between Great Britain and France. As the Revolution progressed, the movement toward high tariffs and a navigation system modeled on that of Great Britain grew ever stronger.[66]

William Short, Jefferson's successor at Paris, found himself engaged in an unavailing struggle, not to secure new concessions, but to preserve those which Jefferson had obtained, and which the latter considered "the sheet anchor of our connection with France."[67] The contest continued throughout 1790 and the early months of 1791, the American minister being in frequent attendance upon the committee

[64] Jefferson to Short, March 8, 1791, March 15, 1791, Instructions, I, 5, 14-15.

[65] Ternant to Lessart, April 8, 1792, AHA, AR, 1903, II, 108-112. G. Morris to Washington, Jan. 22, 1790, ASP, FR, I, 381. Morris to Jefferson, July 10, 1792, ibid., I, 331-332.

[66] Nussbaum, Commercial Policy in the French Revolution, i (Preface), 47-49; Levasseur, Histoire du Commerce de la France, II, 1-22.

[67] Jefferson to Short, March 15, 1791, Instructions, I, 14-15.

of commerce of the National Assembly. He found the merchants too strong in that body for progress in reciprocal concessions, and one by one most of the privileges conceded before the Revolution were set aside.[68] Jefferson's old alliance of Lafayette and Montmorin, with the aid of Moustier, was unable to stem the tide. The Assembly reëstablished the tobacco monopoly, and levied a discriminating duty which was nearly prohibitive of the transportation of tobacco in United States vessels. In the general tariff, the duties on fish oils and salted provisions were raised for the protection of the French fisheries. The privilege formerly allowed of the naturalization of American-built ships when sold to Frenchmen was withdrawn.[69] The Assembly was no more disposed to meet the wishes of the United States with regard to the West Indies than the Old Régime had been.[70]

Two years of revolution in France had thus succeeded in changing commercial relations for the worse instead of improving them. The two countries were virtually engaged in a commercial war by the end of 1791. Jefferson declared that Congress would adopt retaliatory measures unless the

[68] Short wrote as follows of the hostility felt toward American trade in France: "But you can have no idea of the preventions which exist in the assembly against the commerce of the United States—It procedes from several causes—of which however the principal is that those who are listened to on commercial matters being the deputies of the trading towns who are merchants, have either suffered themselves mediately or immediately, or been witnesses of those who have suffered in their commercial speculations with America—Another reason also is that these same persons see with an evil eye whatever regards the commerce of a people that they fear will sooner or later, lawfully or unlawfully take from them a part of their profits in the West India trade of which they consider the monopoly as their birth right. You may add to this their idea of our preference in favor of every thing English which induce us as they say, to take bills of exchange on London for the articles we sell in their ports, so that all sacrifices made to encourage our commerce become a pure loss." Short to Jefferson, November 6, 1790, Dispatches, France.

[69] See Short's dispatches of the following dates: July 7, Aug. 4, Aug. 22, April 23, June 14, Oct. 3, Oct. 21, Nov. 6, Dec. 23, 1790, Jan. 16, Feb. 18, Feb. 22, Feb. 25, March 12, April 25, May 3, June 10, July 20, 1791, Dispatches, France, I, II. See also, G. Morris to Washington, March 9, 1791, ASP, FR, I, 385-386; Jefferson to Short, July 28, Aug. 29, 1791, Instructions, 74-77, 90-91; Jefferson to Joseph Fenwick, U. S. consul at Bordeaux, Aug. 30, 1791, Jefferson, Writings (ed. Ford), V, 380.

[70] Ternant to Lessart, April 8, 1792, AHA, AR, 1903, II, 108-112; G. Morris to Washington, Sept. 30, 1791, ASP, FR, I, 388-389.

law discriminating against United States ships in the tobacco trade was repealed.[71] On June 2, 1791, the Assembly adopted a resolution recommending the negotiation of a new treaty with the United States,[72] but the executive took no measures to carry out the recommendation. The first actual proposal for a new treaty came from the United States, and surprisingly, not from Jefferson but from the Secretary of the Treasury.

Hamilton's object in undertaking a commercial negotiation with France at this time does not appear with clearness. Jefferson afterwards concluded that it was a plot to lead him into a discussion with Hammond and perhaps a British treaty surrendering the contentions for which he proposed to hold out. In October 1791, Hamilton had a long interview with Ternant, the French minister, in the course of which he stressed the importance of the West India trade to the United States and expressed the wish for a new treaty, holding out the hope that the United States would meet the French government's wishes with regard to the American tonnage duty. Ternant was noncommittal, only remarking that he thought the old treaty should be executed (referring to the tonnage act) before a new one should be undertaken.[73] The Secretary of the Treasury then proposed to Washington and Jefferson that the latter arrange articles with Ternant to be referred to the French government for consideration. Jefferson objected because Ternant had no instructions, and the result would be to reveal the American ultimatum without in any way committing the French government. But because the President thought the thing worth trying, Jefferson drew up a project for the mutual exchange of the privileges of natives, and proposing a conventional tariff with the existing tariff of the United States as the basis. Hamilton objected to the low rate of duties, and drew up a much higher schedule. He then

---

[71] Jefferson to Short, July 28, 1791, Aug. 29, 1791, Instructions, I, 74-77, 90-91.

[72] Short to Jefferson, June 6, 1791, June 10, 1791, Dispatches, France, II.

[73] Ternant to Montmorin, Oct. 9, 24, 1791, *AHA*, *AR*, 1903, II, 57-59, 62.

proposed that a similar negotiation be undertaken with Hammond, a procedure which the Secretary of State refused to undertake. The matter was then allowed to drop.[74]

Jefferson continued during the early months of 1792 to exert pressure upon the French government to enter into a negotiation or to repeal the unfavorable legislation of 1791. He informed both Short and Morris that the United States was awaiting proposals in accordance with the expressions of the decree of June 2, 1791.[75] In April, the necessity for increased revenues to prosecute the Indian war offered an opportunity for readjusting the duties on wines more to the satisfaction of French interests. In an instruction to Morris, Jefferson painted this as a considerable concession to France, which would increase the market for lower grade French wines. In the same instruction, he pointed out that "it will be impossible to defer longer than the next session of Congress some counter regulations for the protection of our navigation and commerce."[76] In a conference of April 8, the Secretary discussed the subject of a new treaty at some length with Ternant, and informed him how desirable it was that he be enabled to present the French case favorably in the report which he expected to submit at the next session of Congress. He warned him that continuation of unfavorable regulations could only redound to the advantage of England and the English party in the United States. He then expounded to the minister his favorite idea of a mutual naturalization treaty, which would at the same time open the French West Indies

[74] Jefferson's account of this matter in the "Anas" is in *Writings* (Memorial ed.), I, 296-297; the treaty project, with Hamilton's schedule of duties is in the *Writings* (Ford ed.), V, 397-400.

Hamilton apparently made some use of the proposed negotiation as a sort of bait to Hammond. Hammond to Grenville, Dec. 19, 1791, Henry Adams Transcripts.

[75] Jefferson to Short, Jan. 5, 1792, and to Morris, March 10, 1792, Instructions, I, 111; Jefferson, *Writings* (ed. Ford), V, 450.

[76] Jefferson to Morris, April 28, 1792, Instructions, I, 140. The wines schedule is discussed in the same instruction and in Ternant to Lessart, April 4, April 8, April 22, 1792, *AHA, AR*, 1903, II, 104-105, 108-112, 117-119. The law is in *Statutes at Large*, I, 259-263. It placed French wines in a relatively more favorable position in the American market than Portuguese wines.

to United States produce and shipping and give French vessels a favored status in American ports.[77] The continued prodding produced no effect, however. The minister for foreign affairs told Morris in July that his disposition was favorable, but that his tenure of office was too precarious to justify him in the formation of long time policies.[78]

The overthrow of the monarchy ended all immediate hope of a commercial treaty,[79] though Jefferson still urged Morris to press upon any *de facto* government the necessity of the abolition of the obnoxious restrictions upon American trade.[80] The outbreak of war between France and Great Britain, at the same time that it multiplied the problems and dangers of the United States, again brought the subject of a mutual naturalization treaty into prominence. One of the first acts of the Convention after the beginning of war was to adopt a decree placing American vessels and produce upon the same footing as French vessels and produce, and directing the executive to open a negotiation with the United States to obtain reciprocal concessions. Genêt conveyed a copy of this decree to Jefferson and proposed to open negotiations.[81] The Genêt controversy and recall prevented the serious consideration of commercial matters. In fact, the Administration was hesitant about meeting the new proposition for fear that, if the royalists should regain control in France, the treaty would prove embarrassing. However, Jefferson secured Washington's approval of an instruction to Morris to urge the renewal of Genêt's instructions to his successor.[82] Monroe, on his succeeding Morris as American representative in France in 1794, was forbidden by Secretary Randolph to discuss the subject of a treaty, and was advised that any negotiation on Franco-

[77] Ternant to Lessart, April 8, 1792, *AHA, AR*, 1903, II, 108-112.
[78] Morris to Jefferson, July 10, 1792, *ASP, FR*, I, 331-332.
[79] Washington to Morris, Oct. 20, 1792, Washington, *Writings* (ed. Ford), XII, 203.
[80] Jefferson to Morris, Oct. 20, 1792, Instructions, I, 215-216.
[81] The decree on the American trade is in *ASP, FR*, I, 147.
[82] Jefferson's account of the discussion in the Cabinet is in *Writings* (Memorial ed.), I, 393-397. See also Jefferson to G. Morris, Aug. 23, 1793; Jefferson to the President, Aug. 22, 1793, *Writings* (ed. Ford), VI, 395-396.

American trade must take place in the United States. It was not until the Jay treaty was completed and before the federal government that a French minister, Adet, was instructed to treat, and he was not supplied with powers to conclude.[83] The last hopes for a treaty ended, of course, with the *rapprochement* between the United States and Great Britain, but the subject continued to live for some time in the recriminations passed between the French and the American governments.

THE RAPPROCHEMENT BETWEEN GREAT BRITAIN
AND THE UNITED STATES

The general character of any Anglo-American commercial arrangement had been to a considerable degree predetermined before John Jay departed upon his extraordinary mission to stave off war with Great Britain. The British government had understood since the time of Beckwith's mission that Hamilton and his followers would be content with the existing status of commerce provided American vessels of limited tonnage were admitted to the West Indies under such restrictions as would preserve the British monopoly of the carriage of their island produce to Europe. The extension of the list of articles of American produce admitted to a market in the British dominions was a very secondary object of Hamiltonian policy. The insistence of Great Britain upon an equivalent for any concessions in her islands, if any concession whatever were considered, was a matter of common knowledge. On the eve of Jay's departure, Hamilton suggested the abolition of the tonnage duty on British vessels as such an equivalent.[84] That the British commercial interest was concerned at the threat in the United States to discriminate in favor of other nations, and fearful that the existing taxes on British shipping and manufactures would be in-

[83] E. Randolph to Monroe, June 10, 1794, *ASP, FR*, I, 668. Note relative to a new treaty of commerce between France and the United States, 25 Brumaire, an 3, AAE, CP, EU, XL, 216-217. See also correspondence of Adet and Edmund Randolph, *ASP, FR*, VI, 68-69, I, 640-642, and Adet's reports to the Committee of Public Safety, July 3, and July 17, 1795, *AHA, AR*, 1903, II, 741-744, 745-748.

[84] Hamilton to Jay, April 23, 1794, Hamilton, *Works*, V, 117-119.

creased, is clearly shown in the report of the Committee for Trade in 1791.

In the official instructions to Jay,[85] the commercial agreement was made a matter of secondary importance; or rather, as the negotiation was outlined in the instructions, the commercial settlement was to be reserved as a testament of renewed amity, after the critical questions of neutral rights and treaty violations had been satisfactorily adjusted. The Secretary of State, Randolph, appended a long list of suggestions for a commercial treaty, including the suppression of the most-favored-nation formula, equality of treatment of American and British ships in the East Indies, and the admission of wheat, fish, salt meats, and other American staples into the British dominions upon the same footing as the admission of British manufactures into the United States. However, it was expected that few of these could be obtained. The Hamiltonian minimum on the West India trade was to be a *sine qua non* of any commercial treaty. If the carrying trade were not yielded, "it would not be expedient to do anything more than to digest with the British ministry the articles of such a treaty as they appear willing to accede to. . . ." The tenor of this document indicates that the Administration was prepared to surrender its power of attack upon British commerce only upon the evacuation of the northwest posts, the satisfaction of its demands with regard to neutral commerce, and at least a limited admission to the West Indies.

After a period of general discussion with Lord Grenville, of the differences between the two countries, Jay presented his first written proposal on August 6.[86] It is evident that Grenville had made clear in the previous discussion the minimum price for which his government would open the West Indies by treaty. Jay's project proposed the admission of American vessels of not over one hundred tons to the direct trade between the West Indies and the United States, on the condition that the United States would prohibit the export

[85] This instruction is in *ASP, FR,* I, 473-474.
[86] *ASP, FR,* I, 486-487.

in American vessels of West India produce, except sea stores and rum, either from the British islands or the United States to any other part of the world. In the remainder of the British Empire, except within the jurisdiction of the chartered companies, and in the United States, there was to be an exchange of the privileges of natives. In both the West Indies and other parts of the Empire, the British government was to be free to countervail the American tonnage duty. A conventional tariff establishing reciprocal rates of customs duties was to be prepared and attached to the treaty as soon as convenient. Lord Grenville's counter-project of August 30[87] reduced the tonnage of American vessels to be admitted to the West Indies to seventy, and required the prohibition of exports of West India produce from the United States in any vessel whatever. General most-favored-nation treatment was substituted for Jay's proposed national treatment, and it was stipulated that all alien duties on shipping should be abolished. Among Grenville's propositions were also stipulations that neither country should add new prohibitions of imports to those already in existence, and that goods for the Indian trade should be admitted free of duty across the northern boundary.

These were apparently the only propositions of a commercial nature which received serious attention during the negotiation. It is true that on September 30 Jay submitted a draft in which he included a number of other stipulations, but this was done apparently as a mere maneuver, for Jay could have had little hope of securing their acceptance, and he was not bound by his instructions to insist on them.[88] The American envoy was able during the remaining weeks of the negotiation to obtain two alterations in Grenville's terms, which he considered advantageous to the United States. He refused to

---

[87] *Ibid.*, 489-490.

[88] S. F. Bemis attaches great importance to this project. See his *Jay's Treaty*, 243-246. The project is printed in full, *ibid.*, 286-314. Jay sought to introduce the most-favored-nation clause in the conditional form, and to secure the free admission of masts, ship timbers, staves, boards, plank, and spars into British territories, reduction of the duties on rice and whale oil, and abolition of the export duty on salt from Turk's Island.

assent to the abolition of alien duties on shipping, and accepted instead an authorization for the British government to equalize by levying duties similar to those collected in the United States on tonnage and on goods imported in foreign vessels. This was a concession of doubtful value, although Grenville's proposition lacked reciprocity since it excepted the duties for the support of British lighthouses from the settlement. Jay also refused to assent to the proposition to admit goods for the Indian trade duty free.[89] His insistence here may have prevented the establishment of a channel for a free trade in British manufactures among the western settlers. Otherwise, the main provisions of the Grenville articles of August 30 were written into the final treaty.[90]

The warfare of speech and pamphlet which was pursued in the United States after the contents of the Jay Treaty became known probably brought out few considered opinions on the worth of its commercial clauses. Opponents of ratification attacked all clauses which appeared to offer an opportunity for effective criticism, while advocates defended all parts of the treaty except the West Indies article, which found few friends. Partisan political feeling dictated support or opposition in most cases, and flavored the statements of speakers and writers. Proponents of the treaty were hard pressed to find commercial advantages, but find them they did. Much was said of the value of the British North American market for East India goods from the United States, and of the importance of American access to the fur trade on the British side of the boundary. The stipulation for admission to British India was also placed in the light of a great boon. Opponents pointed out that the India article established fewer privileges for American trade than actually existed by virtue of British regulations, for American shipping was admitted to the trade between India and China, and, it was said, to the Indian coasting trade, both of which were outside the terms of the treaty. Nor could the opposition find any reciprocity in the opening

[89] Jay to Randolph, Oct. 29, 1794, *ASP, FR,* I, 500.
[90] Miller, *Treaties,* II, 245-274.

of the North American provinces, since the Indian trade of
the whole of the United States was yielded in exchange for
that of a single British colony, while the poverty-stricken and
scanty population of the northern settlements would offer
only a small market for luxuries from the Far East. The
reservation in the treaty of the right of Great Britain to match
the American alien duties was also violently attacked as de-
troying the chief bulwark of the American shipping industry.
The omission of the conditional clause from the article stipulating most-favored-nation treatment[91] was also condemned,
because it would effectively prevent the United States from
making commercial bargains with other nations.[92]

The ratification of the Jay Treaty by the Senate, June 24,
1795, marked the indubitable triumph of Hamilton's commercial policy and terminated for the duration of the treaty
all opportunities for extensive experimentation in the regulation of foreign trade. The effect of the controversy during
the first six years of the national government, and the measures taken by that government had a more far-reaching effect, however, than the term of that treaty. The arguments of
the great leaders not only furnished the texts for future gen-
erations of contenders, but provided the source of many of
the main principles of commercial treaties and regulations
down to the present day. Federalist policy received a particularly weighty and permanently influential pronouncement
in Washington's Farewell Address:[93]

But even our commercial policy should hold an equal and impartial
hand;—neither seeking nor granting exclusive favours or preferences;
—consulting the natural course of things;—diffusing and diversifying

[91] In compliance with instructions, Jay avoided the use of "the most-favored-
nation clause" in the treaty. Most-favored-nation treatment, is however, stipulated in the 15th article, which uses the terms "all other nations" and "any other
nation" instead of the conventional term.

[92] A large number of the pamphlets and speeches written and delivered by
opponents and supporters of the treaty were collected and published by Mathew
Carey, in the three volumes of his *American Remembrancer*, printed at Philadelphia, 1795-1796.

[93] Published September 17, 1796. Washington, *Writings* (ed. W. C. Ford),
XIII, 318-319.

by gentle means the streams of commerce, but forcing nothing; establishing with Powers so disposed—in order to give trade a stable course, to define the rights of our Merchants, and to enable the Government to support them—Conventional rules of intercourse, the best that present circumstances and mutual opinion will permit; but temporary, and liable to be from time to time abandoned or varied, as experience and circumstances shall dictate; constantly keeping in view that 'tis folly in one nation to look for disinterested favours from another,—that it must pay with a portion of its independence for whatever it may accept under that character. . . .

SPAIN, PORTUGAL, AND THE NETHERLANDS

Although most of the commercial problems for the national government arose in relations with Great Britain and France, commerce with other nations was also an important object of policy. That obstinate adherent to extreme mercantilism, Spain, gave ground for little hope of ever relaxing the exclusive system, particularly in the American colonies.[94] But patient American statesmen remained almost continuously in an attitude of expectancy that that highly desirable event might happen. The creation of a special commission in 1792 to renew the discussion of the difficult Mississippi navigation problem gave the government an opportunity to review the facts and possibilities of an advantageous commercial arrangement with Spain. The memory of the furor aroused by the proposed Jay-Gardoqui commercial treaty would probably have prevented the United States from including commerce among the subjects to be arranged with Spain, had the Spanish government not insisted upon it. Hamilton was of the opinion that advantages might be obtained.[95]

In a report to the President on the proposed negotiation,[96] Jefferson recommended that commerce be included in the

[94] During the years 1793-1795, while at war with France, Spain permitted a restricted trade in provisions between the United States and Cuba. A number of consulates were set up in American ports, the business of which was to issue permits to trade to American merchants. Nichols, "Trade Relations," *HAHR*, XIII (1933), 289-313.

[95] Hamilton to Jefferson, March, 1792, Hamilton, *Works* (ed. 1904), IV, 361-362.

[96] The report, dated March 7, 1792, is in *ASP, FR*, I, 134-135.

discussions, since the Spanish government desired it. However, he had little expectation that a satisfactory basis for an arrangement could be found. He was opposed to the proposition made by Gardoqui in the previous negotiation, that each country grant the subjects of the other the privileges of natives, because Spain would not include her colonies in such a plan. He proposed the French treaty of 1778 as a model. Although there was little chance of success, he wished the envoys to try to obtain free ports in the colonies, particularly at Havana. The right to cut logwood in the Bay of Campeche would also be desirable. A treaty "making special agreements on every special subject of commerce, and of settling a tariff or duty to be paid on each side on every particular article" would require minute information which could not be furnished the envoys. Consequently it would be best to avoid that type of treaty unless some extraordinary advantage, such as admission to the colonial trade, should be offered. He wished them to ask the removal of a recent increase of the duty on grain and flour. Carmichael and Short, the men appointed to the Spanish mission, never progressed in the negotiation to the point of discussing commercial articles. They were put off upon one pretext or another, and eventually the Spanish government intimated a desire that they be replaced by a more pretentious representative.[97]

Thomas Pinckney, the new envoy sent in 1795, inherited the instructions of Carmichael and Short. Pickering, who soon assumed the Secretaryship of State, did not immediately feel qualified to replace them. Short, feeling the pulse of events at the Spanish court, was quick to sense the possibilities for the United States in the change of Spanish policy which resulted in withdrawal from the alliance against France, and in the effect upon the Spanish government of the almost parallel *rapprochement* between Great Britain and the United States. He repeatedly urged Pickering to instruct Pinckney on commerce, and declared that the great opportunity then

[97] Short to Secretary of State, May 7, June 1, June 2, Sept. 22, 1795, Dispatches, Spain, II; Pickering to Short, Aug. 31, 1795, Instructions, III, 32-37.

existing to obtain concessions might never occur again. Pickering, in September, advised Pinckney to secure as wide a commerce as possible. He particularly desired the admission of American food products, manufactures, and East India goods into the Spanish colonies. The exchange of these goods for specie or bullion would be a great stimulus to the East India trade, and provide the resources so necessary to the American banks. Spanish warships had recently warned American whaling ships out of the Pacific. That practice ought to be stopped, and a port designated, such as Juan Fernandez, where whalers might refit and secure refreshment. But however important these things might be, no effort to secure them must be permitted to delay the prompt settlement of the boundary and Mississippi questions.[98]

In a treaty project submitted to the Prince of the Peace, August 20, Pinckney included articles for general most-favored-nation treatment, and specific provision for free ports in the American colonies, the Canaries, and the East Indies, to which Americans might carry and sell American produce and from which they might export native merchandise, paying no higher duties on goods or vessels than those paid by Spanish subjects in the United States.[99] The Prince of the Peace refused to include commercial articles, pointing out that certain circumstances in the European situation made it distinctly contrary to Spanish interests to grant concessions. Pinckney also learned that the Spanish government wished to reserve any commercial concessions which it might feel free to make, as the price of an alliance with the United States, which would guarantee the American colonies.[100]

A commercial treaty with Portugal, or at least an arrange-

[98] Pickering to Pinckney, Sept. 23, 1795, Instructions, III, 51-55.
[99] Enclosure in Pinckney to Secretary of State, Oct. 1, 1795, Dispatches, Spain, VI.
[100] Pinckney to Secretary of State, Oct. 28, Dec. 18, 1795, Dispatches, Spain, VI. After the rejection of his general commercial articles, Pinckney offered a separate article, which proposed that commissioners be named to negotiate a treaty of commerce, and that, until their work was completed, each country should enjoy most-favored-nation privileges in the dominions of the other. This also was rejected. This article is printed in Bemis, *Pinckney's Treaty*, 388.

ment for the admission of flour from the United States, was one purpose in the dispatch of a minister, David Humphreys, to that country in 1791.[101] Luis Pinto de Souza, with whom Jefferson and Adams had negotiated in London the unacceptable treaty under the commission of 1784, had been promoted to the post of foreign minister at Lisbon; and this fact doubtless encouraged Jefferson to hope that the prohibition of flour might be abolished. However, Humphreys found the Portuguese government unyielding in the matter, giving him, after many evasions, in March 1793, the positive statement that it did not consider it to the interest of its subjects to admit American flour.[102] Jefferson's proposition for a league against the British navigation laws was disposed of by referring it to a procrastinating Board of Commerce.[103] In fact, the Humphreys mission was of slight value to American trade. Minor services were performed in the making of representations against a proposed treaty between Portugal and Naples which would have made the latter kingdom the sole source of the Portuguese grain supply, and in securing the withdrawal of a regulation which forbade vessels arriving with grain in a Portuguese port from proceeding elsewhere in search of a better market.[104]

The Netherlands always stood next to France in the minds of those Americans who expected the continental European nations to rival Great Britain in trade with the United States. In instructing Short as American representative there in 1792, Jefferson recommended "as the most important of your charges, the patronage of our commerce and the extension of its privileges, both in the United Netherlands and their colonies, but most especially the latter."[105]

[101] *ASP, FR*, I, 127-128.
[102] Humphreys to the Secretary of State, Jan. 25, March 19, 1793, Dispatches, Portugal, I, 271-278, 297-303; Pinto to Humphreys, March 20, 1793, enc. in Humphreys to Secretary of State, March 24, 1793, *ibid.*, 306-308.
[103] Humphreys to Secretary of State, July 21, 1791, Dispatches, Portugal, I, 115-116. See *ante*, p. 113.
[104] Same to same, Sept. 9, Oct. 31, 1792, *ibid.*, 241-242, 243-244. Secretary of State to Humphreys, March 22, 1793, Instructions, I, 257-258.
[105] Jefferson to Short, Jan. 23, 1792, Instructions, I, 116.

When John Quincy Adams succeeded Short in 1794, Randolph urged him to keep particular watch over the operations of the articles of the existing treaty; and particularly to collect and forward data on the details of American trade in that quarter of Europe, in order that the government might be prepared to act to protect or extend it.[106] Adams set industriously to work to collect information, and secured the coöperation of the American consuls in the Netherlands and Germany.[107] However, the disturbances following the outbreak of war and the French invasion of Holland threw obstacles in the way of these pursuits and created commercial problems of an altogether different character.

[106] J. Q. Adams, *Works* (ed. W. C. Ford), 199-200.
[107] Adams to Secretary of State, Nov. 24, 1794, April 2, May 5, 1795, Dispatches, Netherlands, I, 39-42, 141-143, 172-173.

V

WAR AND PEACE
1796-1815

THE NINETEEN years embraced in the period here discussed deserve common treatment, not because they
measure the development of a definite policy or of related
principles or events, but because they are largely sterile as
far as the growth of reciprocity policies is concerned. It was
a period of marked changes, of crisis succeeding crisis; but
none of them arose from direct commercial relationships,
and reciprocity in trade became a subject to be attended to
only as an incident to more vitally pressing matters. Whatever of interest the period contains lies in striking isolated
episodes, in the influence of personalities, in suggestions of
policies which never reached maturity, of the slow confirma-
tion through passage of time of previously established routine
principles. This state of affairs is easily accounted for. The
background of European war conditioned all international
relations. Commerce throve without regulation when it
could be protected from spoliation by the belligerents.

The political revolution of 1800, which swept Jefferson
and his friends into power, might have been expected to
produce a revival of some of the ideas which Democratic-
Republican leaders had championed prior to the Jay Treaty.
Although Jefferson's fundamental conceptions had probably
not altered,[1] conditions both in the United States and in

[1] Jefferson wrote Thomas Pinckney in 1797 as follows: "War is not the best
engine for us to resort to, nature had given us one *in our commerce*, which if
properly managed, will be a better instrument for obliging the interested nations of Europe to treat us with justice. If the commercial regulations had been
adopted which our legislature were at one time proposing, we should at this

Europe had so changed as to render the former program impracticable. The treaty of 1794 was an almost insuperable obstacle, though some Americans felt that its terms left room for a fight for the West India trade. Jefferson admitted in 1798 that southern votes could no longer be rallied to support an energetic commercial policy. He no longer favored close relations with France.[2] It required the enthusiastic romanticism of a Joel Barlow to conceive of Napoleonic France as a disinterested ally and champion of American trade in a commercial contest with Great Britain. The general policy of the Jefferson and Madison administrations, like that of John Adams, was to avoid, with rare exceptions, commercial negotiations and to await European peace and a knowledge of the peace treaties and existing commercial conditions before determining upon a policy.

THE LAST YEARS OF FEDERALIST RULE

One of the first tasks of the United States government after the settlement of 1794-1795 with Great Bretain was the readjustment of relations with France. There was an underlying commercial problem of importance—the question as to whether or not the American tonnage acts of 1789-1790 were in violation of the treaty of 1778—but it contributed little to the seriousness of the Franco-American dispute which ensued. The real quarrel developed from the American government's determination to remain strictly neutral with regard to the European conflict, and from its acquiescence in the rules of maritime warfare which permitted Great Britain to destroy the trade, extremely important from the French standpoint, between American ports, the French colonies, and France. When Charles C. Pinckney was sent as

moment have been standing on such an eminence of safety and respect as ages can never recover. But having wandered from that, our object should now be to get back, with as little loss as possible, and when peace shall be restored to the world, endeavor so to form our commercial regulations that justice from other nations shall be their mechanical result." *Writings* (ed. Ford), VII, 129.

[2] Jefferson to Hugh Williamson, Feb. 11, 1798, *ibid.*, VII, 200-201; Jefferson to Gerry, June 21, 1797, *ibid.*, 149-150.

minister to France in 1796 for the purpose of reconciling the French government to the Jay Treaty, which that government charged was in conflict with the Franco-American treaties, Secretary Pickering instructed him to announce the readiness of his government to enter a commercial negotiation. His primary duty was to collect information, and, if possible, draw the negotiation to the United States.[3] The French government refused to receive Pinckney, and the incipient negotiation ended in recriminations as to who was responsible for its death. In a pamphlet in the form of a diplomatic note, the French minister to the United States, Adet, charged that the administration had evaded the various offers made by France to negotiate a new commercial treaty. Pickering answered with the assertion that, as compared with the disposition of the French governments, the United States had evinced an eagerness to enter a negotiation.[4]

Relations between the two countries constantly grew worse as the century drew to a close, until by 1798 an actual, though unrecognized, state of war existed. President Adams in 1797 sent John Marshall and Elbridge Gerry to join Pinckney in a renewed attempt to restore cordiality. In the meantime, French warships and privateers began to attack American commerce. The commissioners were not officially received in France, but certain agents of the government (known in the United States as "X," "Y," and "Z," because they were so designated in the published correspondence) approached them with offers of a satisfactory treaty provided the United States would make a loan to France and would pay heavy bribes to certain French officials and agents. The proposition was indignantly spurned, and the American government began to organize an army and commission war vessels in preparation for hostilities. By act of Congress, all the subsisting treaties with France were abrogated. A number of naval actions occurred in the Caribbean. In the end, how-

[3] Pickering to C. C. Pinckney, September 14, 1796, Instructions, III, 249, 253-255.
[4] Adet to Pickering, Nov. 15, 1796; Pickering to C. C. Pinckney, Jan. 16, 1797, *ASP, FR*, I, 568-569, 583.

ever, the French government realized that it could gain
nothing by war with the United States, and agreed to receive
a minister. In February 1799, Adams appointed a new commission consisting of Oliver Ellsworth, William R. Davie,
and William Vans Murray. On arrival in France, the envoys
found that Bonaparte had risen to the position of supreme
power, and he was for peace. Although the French government refused to pay an indemnity for past commercial
spoliations, it agreed to refrain from further attacks and
acquiesced in the abrogation of the troublesome former
treaties.The crisis was liquidated in the Convention of 1800.

Pickering had opportunities to express his commercial
policy toward France in his instructions for the mission of
1797, which terminated in the "XYZ affair," and for the
Ellsworth-Davie-Murray mission.[5] The French interpretation of the treaty of 1778, which would have made the
American tonnage act as applied to French vessels illegal,
was firmly denied. The United States, the Secretary held,
was under no obligation to do more than place French vessels
upon the footing of those of the most-favored-nation. "But
the introduction of a principle of discrimination between the
vessels of different foreign nations," he added, "and in dero-
gation of the powers of Congress to raise revenue by uniform
duties on any objects whatever, cannot be hazarded." The
placing of French vessels in American ports upon the same
footing as those of the United States could not be considered.
Thus, the Federalist Secretary of State, in unequivocal
language, repudiated Jefferson's old plan for the exchange
of the privileges of citizens with France. It was the Jay
Treaty, rather than Pickering's statement, however, which
delivered the deathblow to that proposition. He wished an
attempt made to obtain the admission of a greater number
of articles of American produce to the French West Indies,
and the right to export from the colonies all articles of their
produce, at least to the extent of the value of the imported
cargo. In 1799, he thought that favors for American trade

[5] *ASP, FR,* II, 156, 303.

in the colonies might be asked as compensation for the depredations of the French privateers on American vessels in the
Caribbean. No compensation could be offered for freer
admission to the colonial trade, however. For the regulation
of the direct trade with France, an arrangement very similar
to that in the Jay Treaty was recommended. Davie, Ellsworth, and Murray made a valiant effort to obtain some
concession with regard to the islands, but were unsuccessful.[6]
The treaty of 1800 simply stipulated that each nation should
place the other upon the footing of the most-favored-nation.
The conditional clause was not included.[7]

Following the ratification of the Jay Treaty, there remained to settle with Great Britain certain questions left
unsettled by that instrument or brought into being by it.
Among the most important of these was the question of the
West India trade, left in the air by the Senate's rejection of
the twelfth article. In an instruction dated March 5, 1796,
which was not sent, Pickering stated that the principal objections to the twelfth article were the prohibition of the
export of articles commonly produced in the West Indies,
including cotton, even though grown in a non-British colony
or in the United States, and the limitation on American ships
in the trade to seventy tons. "If the two leading objections . . .
cannot be removed," he stated, "the further negociations must
be abandoned; for the United States will not relinquish their
right of exporting in their own vessels any article of their
own produce, or of the produce of other countries, for the
sake of the proposed restricted commerce with the West India
possessions of Great Britain." He would agree to no greater
restriction than an embargo on the reëxportation of the produce of the British islands only, when imported in American
vessels.

Pickering declared that there was little reason for anxiety
about the West India trade at the moment. He believed that
conditions at the end of the European war would make it
necessary for France, the Netherlands, and Great Britain

[6] *ASP, FR*, II, 320-322.
[7] Miller, *Treaties*, II, 457-487.

to throw their colonies open to the United States without restriction. His confidence in this view was so great that he ordered that no agreement lasting longer than two years beyond the end of the war should be made, unless complete freedom of commerce could be obtained. A limitation of the trade to vessels of less than eighty-five tons could not be accepted. He wished the negotiators to try to add beef, pork, butter, lard, hams, and fish to the list of articles admitted to the colonies from the United States. It would also be advantageous to secure the right for American vessels to trade to Nova Scotia and Newfoundland, between the United States and which there had been, prior to the Revolution, a profitable exchange of provisions for fish. The trade was now confined to British vessels, and was consequently much interrupted by French privateers.[8]

The letter of March 5 was enclosed as a memorandum for information in a corrected instruction to Rufus King dated June 8. The Administration had by this time reached the conclusion that the stipulation that the United States should not export West India produce imported from the British colonies was too great a price to pay for the proposed limited admission to the islands. Once such a restriction should be admitted into a treaty with Great Britain, a precedent would be set, the benefit of which could be claimed by France and other colonial powers. The only restriction to which the United States could submit, under the new decision, would be the limitation of exports from the islands in each vessel to the value of the same vessel's incoming cargo.[9] Grenville promised King to take the subject of the colony trade up with the cabinet, but no serious discussion of the subject with the American minister was attempted.[10] The ministry was doubtless well satisfied with the action of the United States which

[8] The instruction of March 5 was addressed to Thomas Pinckney. Instructions III, 154-161.

[9] Instructions, III, 146-154. Other commercial matters confided to King's care were the settlement of the regulations for American vessels trading between Montreal and Quebec, the question as to whether or not goods from India unladen in the United States could be reëxported to Europe, and securing the right to trade between British territories in India and other Asiatic countries.

[10] King to the Secretary of State, Sept. 8, 1796, Dispatches, Great Britain, VI.

guaranteed most-favored-nation treatment for British commerce while leaving the West India regulations untouched.

The spirit in which the commercial articles of the Jay Treaty might be enforced in Great Britain was a matter of major interest to the United States. The ministry presented the necessary bills to Parliament in May 1797. King, the United States minister, immediately made a study of the proposed legislation, and endeavored to secure regulations more favorable to the United States. Under Article XV of the treaty, Great Britain reserved the right to impose on American vessels a tonnage duty equal to that levied on British vessels in the United States, and a duty "adequate to countervail" the American additional duty of ten per cent on the duties on imports in British vessels. The proposed legislation provided for a tonnage duty of two shillings per ton on American vessels. This did not equal the similar American duty, but only the difference between the duties on British and on American vessels. Since British import duties varied according to origin of imports and the vessels in which they were carried, the copying of the American provision for a ten per cent additional duty was not feasible, and a rather complicated schedule was adopted. For example, on imports of bar and pig iron, pot and pearl ash, and naval stores, the extra duty was calculated on the duties collected on those articles when imported from British colonies. On the other hand, the extra duties on staves and whale oil were based on the duties collected on those articles from foreign countries. An arbitrary extra duty of one shilling six pence per hundredweight was levied on tobacco in American vessels. This was considerably less than a ten per cent surcharge on duties collected under the British plantation rates. The proposed legislation provided for American trade with India substantially in the language of the treaty.[11]

King attempted to obtain an interpretation of Article XV, which would have permitted American vessels to import

---

[11] The acts, which do not differ in any important respect from the bills first shown King, are in *ASP, FR*, II, 103-107.

goods into Great Britain from any part of the world—an interpretation which would have been equivalent to a major alteration of the Navigation Laws. He was principally concerned, however, with the provisions for countervailing the American discriminating duties. He complained that the methods proposed for matching the ten per cent discrimination were complex and obscure as compared with the simple provision of the American law. He called attention to the fact that the British light duties, or charges on shipping collected for the maintenance of lighthouses, were at least equal to the American tonnage duty, and argued that an additional duty could not with justice be added to them. He criticized the section relating to trade with India because of his belief that it was intended to limit American trade to the letter of the treaty, whereas it had been the custom to extend additional favors to friendly nations, including the United States. He was especially interested in securing the right for American vessels to carry goods from Europe to Indian ports.[12]

At a conference in July 1797, Lord Grenville read to King the answer prepared by the Board of Trade to the latter's criticisms. It was denied that permission had been given for American vessels to import from any place whatever, since the negotiators could not have intended nullifying the Navigation Laws without so stating in unequivocal terms. The mode of levying the countervailing duties was shown to be necessary in the existing state of the customs regulations. The answer emphasized the tendency to favor American commerce above that of other nations, and the fact that the proposed retaliation did not reach the height permitted by the treaty. The government refused emphatically to consider the light duties as capable of being applied to the countervailing object. They were not collected as part of the public revenues, as were the American tonnage duties, and were for the most part the property of private corporations. A more favorable reply was given to the representation regarding the India article. The object of the legislation,

[12] King to the Secretary of State, June 12, 1797, ASP, FR, II, 109-111.

it was declared, was to establish legally the right stipulated in the treaty, and not to deny to the United States favors beyond those stipulated, which might be conferred upon other nations. Within a short time King was able to report that a British court had held that American vessels might legally trade from Europe to India.[13]

The American minister gathered from the tenor of the answer to his objections that no favorable alterations were to be expected. He made some further unavailing complaints to Grenville, particularly against the proposed tonnage act. He also requested that the countervailing duty on fish oils be scaled down in the same way as that on tobacco. The foreign minister refused to consider any alleviations, and asserted that fish oils could not be placed in the same category with tobacco, because Great Britain and the United States were rivals in the fisheries. King advised his government that it possessed a remedy for the unfair tonnage duties in its power to enact a special duty for the support of lighthouses, which could not be considered in violation of the treaty of 1794.[14] The British bills for executing the treaty and for regulating trade with India were passed July 4, 1797.[15]

This legislation gave rise to considerable dissatisfaction in the United States. Jefferson and his friends adopted the attitude that the acts of Parliament constituted convincing evidence of the wickedness of the policy which had produced the Jay Treaty. The British countervailing duties, in the opinion of merchants consulted by him, would end the competition of American shipping in the trade with Great Britain. America's pro-British policy had confirmed the French government in its adherence to the discriminating duty on tobacco in American vessels, and that duty, especially if extended to other articles, would drive the shipping of the United States from that trade.[16] However, others than

---

[13] King to the Secretary of State, July 4, 1797, *ASP, FR*, II, 111-114; Dec. 28, 1797, Dispatches, Great Britain, VI.

[14] King to the Secretary of State, July 4, 1797, *ASP, FR*, II, 111-114.

[15] The acts are in *ASP, FR*, II, 103-107.

[16] Jefferson to Horatio Gates, and to James Madison, Feb. 21 and Feb. 22, 1798, Jefferson, *Writings* (ed. Ford), VI, 204-205, 206-207.

Jeffersonians were dissatisfied. William Bingham, writing to King in April 1798, declared that the laws had excited a sensation of no friendly tendency. The East India trade was now on a worse footing than formerly, since all neutrals had in the past been free to carry from India to Europe. The equalization of tonnage duties, plus double light money paid by American vessels, would place United States shipping in a very unfavorable position, while the additional ten per cent of the duties payable on American produce would be prohibitive of American shipping wherever British duties were higher than American. A circumstance giving further advantage to Great Britain was the fact that the shipments of exports from the United States required greater tonnage, because consisting of bulky raw materials, than the imports from Great Britain.[17] Discontent with the commercial relations between the two countries was increased because of certain British war taxes, particularly advances in the tonnage duties and additional import duties on American produce. An especial grievance was the export duty known as the convoy duty, levied ostensibly to pay the expense of convoying shipping, the rates of which were heavier on cargoes going to America than on those bound to European ports. King's representations against these met with no success.[18]

While King was dealing with the subjects of greatest interest, commercially, to the United States, relations with other countries required attention. Early in 1797, the Prussian and Swedish governments, through their consuls general in the United States, proposed renewal of their old treaties which were approaching the date of expiration.[19] Partly for the purpose of renewing these treaties and partly because an able observer was wanted in northern Europe, John Quincy Adams was ordered to Berlin. The United States

[17] William Bingham to Rufus King, April 2, 1798, R. King, *Writings* (ed. C. R. King), II, 299-300. Bingham was a prominent merchant and banker of Philadelphia.

[18] King to the Secretary of State, March 17, June 1, 1798, Dispatches, Great Britain, VI.

[19] Pickering to C. G. Paleski, March 4, 1797, and to Richard Soderstrom, May 4, 1797, U. S. Dept. of State, Domestic Letters, X, 4-5, 40.

desired amendments which would permit the subjection of Prussian and Swedish vessels to a general embargo, and certain alterations in the clauses regarding neutral rights. In the Jay Treaty, the principle of "free ships, free goods," had been abandoned, as had that of the strict limitation of the list of contraband to munitions and implements of war. Both principles were included in the old Swedish and Prussian treaties. In view of the fact that war with France seemed unavoidable, and that the principles had not been adopted by the great maritime powers, Pickering wished to secure release from these restrictions on naval warfare. The instructions contained nothing on commercial reciprocity.[20] The Adams administration was indifferent as to whether or not renewals could be effected.[21] In July 1799, a new treaty was concluded with Prussia, with the same provisions regarding peace-time commerce as the former one, but without the former guarantees as to neutral trade.[22] The renewal with Sweden was delayed for some time, and then that government indicated that it did not wish to continue the negotiation. It had lost interest in an American treaty because of the change in policy with regard to maritime law.[23]

The controversy with France in the closing years of the century caused the United States to be temporarily courted by France's European enemies. A commercial treaty was proposed in each case as the instrument of friendship, though other provisions than those regulating mutual exchange of goods were undoubtedly the principal motives. The Russian ambassador at London, Woronzoff, suggested a commercial negotiation to King in the fall of 1798.[24] President Adams promptly appointed King plenipotentiary

[20] Pickering to Adams, July 15, 1797, Instructions, IV, 106-108.
[21] Pickering to Adams, Nov. 7, 1798, June 3, 1799, *ibid.*, IV, 361, V, 146-147.
[22] Miller, *Treaties*, II, 433-456.
[23] Pickering to J. Q. Adams, March 17, 1798, *ASP, FR*, II, 251; Adams to Pickering, Oct. 1, 31, 1798, and July 29, 1799, Dispatches, Prussia; J. Q. Adams, *Works*, II, 369-370.
[24] King to Secretary of State, Nov. 10, 1798, King, *Correspondence*, II, 462-463.

to carry on the discussions at London.[25] Pickering's instructions stressed the point of securing most-favored-nation treatment for American trade in Russia, and expressed the wish that King would use the Russo-British treaty of 1797 as a model, with the object of obtaining all the privileges of the British.[26] King was obliged to inform his chief that the dispatch of full powers and instructions was premature. The willingness of the Czar to negotiate had depended upon American hostility toward France, and since a negotiation had been begun with the latter power, that with Russia had best be postponed.[27] At about the same time as the Russian proposal, Lord Grenville told King that the British government would use its good offices to aid the United States in negotiating a commercial treaty with the Ottoman Empire.[28] William Smith, the minister to Portugal, was designated for that negotiation.[29] Proceedings in this quarter did not reach the stage of detailed instructions. Smith's mission was soon suspended, and although King and Smith maintained an interest in the matter, nothing further was done.[30]

David Humphreys was transferred from Lisbon to Spain in 1796. He was advised to be on the lookout for an opportunity to extend American trade to the Spanish colonies.[31] In November 1797, the Spanish government opened to neutrals all the Atlantic ports of her American colonies. The reason, however, was not the pressure by the American government, but the isolation of the colonies by the British navy. The ports were ordered closed again in April 1799, but trade continued under the old system of permitting the

[25] Richardson, *Messages and Papers*, I, 282.
[26] Pickering to King, May 22, 1799, Instructions, V, 136-141. The Russo-British treaty of 1797 was a most-favored-nation treaty, which contained no special concessions to Great Britain. G. F. de Martens, *Recueil de traités* (2nd ed., Göttingen, 1817-1835), VI, 357-367.
[27] King to the Secretary of State, March 16, June 5, 1799, King, *Correspondence*, II, 568, III, 29-30.
[28] King to the Secretary of State, Nov. 10, 1798, *ibid.*, II, 462-463.
[29] Pickering to Smith, Feb. 11, Feb. 13, 1799, Instructions, V, 67-70, 72-73.
[30] Pickering to King, May 29, 1799, Instructions, V, 143-144; King to Secretary of State, June 5, 1799, Dispatches, Great Britain, VIII.
[31] Pickering to Humphreys, Feb. 17, 1797, Instructions, IV, 8.

governors to admit neutral vessels at discretion.[32] William Smith, who succeeded Humphreys in Portugal, was directed to continue to press for the admission of American flour, and to secure information about Brazil, particularly with regard to the possibilities of a direct trade between the United States and that colony.[33] The minister was able to report in a short time that the prohibition of flour had been removed.[34] Local conditions, and not Smith's representations, were doubtless responsible for this relaxation. He awaited "an auspicious moment" to take up the matter of the Brazils, but it never came. The government, very much occupied with European affairs, adhered to a policy of polite evasion.[35] Pickering was not much interested in the Portuguese foreign minister's references to a treaty, unless it should permit an intercourse with Brazil.[36] Jefferson, on assuming the Presidency, recalled Smith, and terminated the American mission to Lisbon.[37]

In 1796 the government of the Netherlands proposed to Pickering, through its minister to the United States, a revision of the old commercial treaty. The Secretary of State was very cautious, and desired to know what alterations were desired, in order that the authorization of the Senate to a negotiation might be obtained. John Quincy Adams, then minister to the Netherlands, undertook to find out what changes were desired, but was never able to bring the subject into serious discussion.[38] William Vans Murray, succeeding

[32] Humphreys to the Secretary of State, Nov. 21, 24, 1797, April 19, May 17, 1799, Dispatches, Spain, IV. The trade to Cuba, Porto Rico, and South America, which was of considerable volume, continued, subject to annoying interruptions and hindered by arbitrary regulations, high duties, and spoliation by privateers, until Spanish control ceased with the overthrow of the Bourbon monarchy by Napoleon in 1808. See Nichols, "Trade Relations," *HAHR*, XIII (1933) 289-313.

[33] Pickering to William Smith, July 15, 1797, Instructions, IV, 86-87.

[34] Smith to the Secretary of State, Oct. 9, 1797, Dispatches, Portugal, V.

[35] Smith to the Secretary of State, Feb. 27, 1798, June 23, Nov. 10, 1798, June 18, Aug. 5, 1799, Jan. 21, 1800, Dispatches, Portugal, V.

[36] Pickering to Smith, March 22, 1800, Instructions, V, 312.

[37] Madison to Smith, June 1, 1801, U. S. Dept. of State, Dispatches to Consuls, I, 47-48; Smith to the Secretary of State, Aug. 16, 1801, Dispatches, Portugal, V.

[38] Pickering to J. Q. Adams, Sept. 28, 1796, Instructions, III, 265-266; Adams to the Secretary of State, Dec. 13, 1796, Dispatches, Netherlands, II.

Adams, was authorized to draw up a treaty, which was to be sent home for consideration before being signed. The United States, the Secretary stated, would be interested in a freer commerce with the Dutch colonies.[39] No negotiation was undertaken.

EARLY DEMOCRATIC-REPUBLICAN POLICIES

Although the first year of Democratic-Republican control of the government coincided with the return of peace in Europe and its consequent removal of the advantages possessed in time of war by American trade, no revolutionary plans with regard to commercial policy were revealed. The President referred to the subject in his first annual message to Congress in the following terms: "We cannot, indeed, but all feel an anxious solicitude for the new difficulties under which our carrying trade will soon be placed. How far it can be relieved, otherwise than by time, is a subject of important consideration."[40] A Federalist executive could hardly have been less vehement.

One of the difficulties for which great solicitude was felt was the heavy duty levied in France upon tobacco in American ships. Madison ordered the new minister, Robert R. Livingston, to lose no time in suggesting that the duty be removed, and in calling to the attention of the French government any other "regulations unduly favoring the French commerce at the expense of ours."[41] Livingston reported that every maritime power in Europe could be depended upon to try to diminish the commerce of the United States. "France has already excluded us from her African Colonies," he wrote. "Her premiums will exclude our oil; and her heavy duties upon tobacco in foreign bottoms will prevent our carrying that article for ourselves. She refuses to naturalize our ships; so that a very large capital in that article, will sink in our hands." He recommended that his government institute a policy of retaliation. "Let the United

[39] Pickering to William Vans Murray, April 6, 1797, Instructions, IV, 27-28.
[40] Richardson, *Messages and Papers*, I, 331.
[41] Madison to R. R. Livingston, Dec. 18, 1801, Instructions, VI, 13-14.

States impose a duty upon specific articles of her (*sic*) own produce, exported in foreign bottoms, equivalent to the difference of the duty paid in Europe on such articles when imported in American or national vessels," he advised. "This will secure us the carriage of our own articles; first, because we can carry cheaper; and second, because this duty, being paid in advance, imposes a greater burden than one that is paid out of the sale of the produce."[42] Livingston had apparently forgotten the provision of the Constitution which forbade export duties, but understood very clearly what tactics were best adapted for securing more impartial treatment for American shipping.

The American minister found that the prevailing sentiment among the advisers of the First Consul were all for a policy of imitating British restrictions upon the commerce of other nations as a means of building up a great navy. In an effort to alter this point of view he prepared a memorial on Franco-American commercial relations and circulated it among members of the court. In this pamphlet, he contended that France could never overcome the British lead in naval power by methods of restriction and colonization. She could receive little help from Spain and Holland, now in decline as maritime powers. A better method would be to encourage the navy of the United States. With thirty ships of the line, the United States could keep half the British navy in American waters. That fleet, if American commerce were properly encouraged, could be developed in twenty years. Even without a navy, the United States could aid France by doing her carrying and supplying raw materials in time of war. The plan which he suggested was a treaty of commerce which would admit the vessels of each into the ports of the other with only a six per cent duty on the value of the articles imported and the same tonnage duty as that paid by natives. The United States would undertake not to import into the French colonies anything except the produce of France and

[42] Livingston to the Secretary of State, Jan. 13, 1802, Dispatches, France, VIII.

the United States. One effect favorable to France of such an arrangement would be the prevention of twenty-five thousand seamen, then manning American vessels, going into the British merchant service. The way would also be opened for the sale of large quantities of French produce in the United States. In conference with Talleyrand, Livingston broached some of these ideas, but found that minister cold to them. He concluded that Talleyrand was decidedly unfriendly to the United States.[43]

A year later, the French government had not altered its navigation laws, nor had the United States resorted to retaliation. Madison instructed Livingston to renew his complaints, declaring that there was no doubt that France's restrictions "will and can be counteracted by the United States if not corrected by herself." He stated that the United States government was willing to enter into a negotiation taking up the whole subject of commerce. But the President "prefers for the discussions this place to Paris, for the double reason that the requisite commercial information could be more readily gained here than there, and that a French negotiator might here be more easily and fully impressed with the importance of our commerce to France, than could be done at Paris."[44] It is evident that there was little enthusiasm at Washington for a commercial treaty with Napoleon. This had further decreased by October 1803, when Madison wrote the minister that "your suggestion as to a commercial arrangement of a general nature with France, at the present juncture, has received the attention of the President; but he has not decided that any instructions should be given you to institute negotiations for that purpose. . . .[45]

The Louisiana Purchase treaty of 1803, though not a commercial treaty, contains commercial articles which are of interest for two reasons. One of them, which established

[43] Livingston to the Secretary of State, March 24, 1802, Dispatches, France, VIII. The memorial is an enclosure in this dispatch.

[44] Madison to R. R. Livingston, Feb. 23, 1803, Instructions, VI, 80.

[45] Madison to Livingston, Oct. 6, 1803, Instructions, VI, 146.

the commercial privileges of the most favored nation for France "forever" in the ceded territory, formed the basis of a long drawn-out dispute between the French and American governments after 1814—a dispute which will be discussed in a later chapter. This treaty also contains one of the few examples of a grant by the United States of commercial privileges for a non-commercial equivalent, namely, territory. Napoleon insisted on extraordinary privileges for French and Spanish commerce as part of the purchase price of the colony. In a treaty project which he prepared to guide his agents, French citizens and Spanish subjects were to enjoy in perpetuity the privileges of entrepôt at New Orleans which were conceded to the United States by Spain in the treaty of 1795—privileges which no other nation might obtain. Similar places of deposit were to be established near the mouths of the Red, Arkansas, Missouri, and Ohio rivers. French and Spanish ships and merchandise were to be guaranteed forever the same privileges allowed to the shipping and merchandise of the United States.[46] Madison, in his instructions for the purchase of New Orleans, had authorized special commercial privileges at that place to compensate Napoleon for the loss of the principal port of the colony intended to supply provisions for his West Indian sugar islands.[47] Livingston and Monroe, therefore, agreed to important commercial articles, although the plan of the First Consul was drastically modified. It was stipulated that French or Spanish ships, loaded only with the produce of the European dominions of either the respective countries or their colonies and coming directly from those places, should be admitted during a twelve-year period at New Orleans or other port of entry in the ceded territory, on the same conditions as American ships arriving from the same ports. No other nation should be admitted to the same privileges during that period. After the expiration of twelve years, the

[46] "Projet d'une convention secrète avec les Etats-Unis d'Amérique," *Correspondance de Napoléon I*[er] (32 vols., Paris 1858-1869), VIII, 365-367.

[47] Madison to Livingston and Monroe, March 2, 1803, Instructions, VI, 81-96.

ships of France should be treated forever upon the footing of the most-favored-nation in the legal ports of entry of the ceded area. The Act of Congress for executing the treaty was so drawn as to reduce to a minimum the privileges of French vessels during the stipulated twelve-year period. Instead of a general provision giving French and Spanish vessels and merchandise the same footing as those of the United States, New Orleans was made the only port of entry for foreign vessels, and American vessels from France and Spain and their colonies were limited to that port.[48]

The initial policy of the Jefferson administration was to proceed in a conciliatory and matter-of-fact way to try to protect the vastly expanded American merchant marine from the effects of suddenly restored peace, and the discriminations of the European nations, the effect of which had been largely nullified by war conditions in the preceding period. The principal danger was thought to lie in the British laws for counteracting the American discriminating duties, although the French restrictions previously referred to, and those of other powers were not forgotten. As usual in such cases, a twofold policy of diplomacy and legislation was decided upon. The legislative policy was in no sense threatening, as it had been from 1789 to 1794, though there was always the warning that retaliation would be resorted to if necessary. As proof of his desire for cordial relations with Great Britain, Jefferson retained the Federalist incumbent, Rufus King, as minister at London until 1803.

The diplomatic effort can best be described first because its history carries with it a clear delineation of the existing situation. Madison's instruction to King on the subject followed immediately after Jefferson's message of December 1801.[49] The Secretary declared that the British countervailing duties "must inevitably banish American vessels from all share in

<hr>

[48] Miller, *Treaties*, II, 498-511; *Statutes at Large of the U. S.*, II, 251-254. Max Farrand, "The Commercial Privileges of the Treaty of 1803," *AHR*, VII (1902), 494-499, treats this subject in its constitutional aspects.
[49] Madison to King, Dec. 10, 22, 1801, *ASP, FR*, II, 497, Dec. 22, 1801, Madison, *Writings*, VI, 441-448.

the direct trade with any part of the British dominions, as fast
as British vessels can enter into competition." He had already
been informed of one American shipowner using British vessels in preference to his own, and of numerous cases of loss
by those employing American vessels. Three remedies suggested themselves. One, the levy of a special tonnage duty
specifically for the support of lighthouses was objectionable
because, if the duties were made high enough to relieve
American shipping, they would probably be construed by the
British government as in violation of the treaty, which forbade the United States government to increase its discriminating taxes. An agreement to repeal the American discriminating duties if Great Britain would repeal hers would be
exceptionable, since it would confer a gratuitous favor upon
other nations not parties to the arrangement. A third and
preferable remedy would be a revision of the British legislation so as to provide for the levy of a ten per cent duty on
goods exported in American vessels. Such an export duty
would be an exact equivalent of the American tax. Instead of
using the American tariff as a basis for their ten per cent discriminatory duties, the British had used their own rates,
which were more than ten times as high as the American. No
sound rules of treaty interpretation could authorize this procedure. A factor which increased the unfairness of the system
was the fact that ten times as much tonnage was required to
convey the American produce to Great Britain as was required
for carrying the British manufactures to the United States.

For once American commercial diplomacy was highly successful, although Madison's first choice of a plan was not
adopted. No attempt was made by the British government
to defend the duties against King's charges of inequality.
The ministry found the suggested remedy of a tax on exports
in American vessels unacceptable, and substituted for it a
program of mutual repeal.[50] Within little more than a month

[50] The repeal was intended to apply only to the discriminating tax on imports
in the vessels of the respective countries. The United States did not raise the question of the repeal of discriminating tonnage duties at this time.

after King, in accordance with Madison's order, had made his representations, a bill was rushed through Parliament and received the royal assent. The American minister was assured of the government's readiness to issue immediately an order in council remitting the duties on tobacco, the shipping season for which had arrived.[51] The execution of the act and the issue of the order were now unfortunately held up by events in the United States.

The legislative program got under way contemporaneously with the diplomatic effort. It was not strongly pressed by the Administration, but Congress was allowed to develop its own ideas. December 14, 1801, Samuel Smith introduced in the House of Representatives a resolution for the repeal of the discriminating tonnage and import duties, the repeal to take effect with regard to any nation only when the President should receive proof that that nation had removed its similar regulations.[52] Congress was unable to imitate the commendable speed of Parliament. Madison wrote King April 7, 1802:

For a considerable time past the proposition on the subject made in Congress by General Smith, has slept on the table. He did not wish to press it against a mercantile current that appeared to set against it. There is reason to believe that owing to ignorance and Jealousy, this current has not even yet entirely ceased. . . .[53]

A month later he reported that the opposition to the measure was so great that its supporters had decided not to press it further during the current session.[54] King found that he could accomplish nothing more in London. The government there had been prepared to issue an order removing the duties on tobacco in American vessels, but the minister could hardly ask its issuance in the face of the attitude of Congress.[55]

The President apparently intended to dismiss the subject

[51] King to Madison, Feb. 5, 1802, *ASP, FR*, II, 497-498; King to Nicholas Vansittart, Feb. 12, 1802, King, *Correspondence*, IV, 68-69; King to Madison, Feb. 13, Feb. 18, April 7, 1802, *ibid.*, 69-70, 72, 99.

[52] *Annals*, XI, 325.

[53] Instructions, VI, 30-31.

[54] Madison to King, May 1, 1802, Instructions, VI, 37.

[55] King to the Secretary of State, June 20, 1802, King, *Correspondence*, IV, 141-142.

with a mere colorless reference in his annual message in December 1802. At Gallatin's suggestion, however, he commended the British government for its "spirit of justice and friendly accommodation," but left it to the wisdom of Congress to determine whether the British principle "would produce a due equality."[56] The House Committee of Commerce and Manufactures made a report January 10, 1803, in which the whole subject of discriminating duties was examined, but with emphasis upon the condition resulting from the British duties. It found in general that the American duties tended to give American shipping a monopoly of the import of goods into the United States, but that the British duties had the effect of driving American shipping from the carriage of American produce to Europe. Attempts to remedy the situation by increasing the rates could be expected to produce augmentations abroad, and end in a useless commercial war. The committee recommended the relinquishment of the duties "so far as they relate to goods, wares, and merchandise, the growth, produce, or manufacture of the nation, to which the ship by whom the same are imported may belong," in favor of such foreign nation as would remove its duties injurious to the interests of the United States.[57]

The opposition of the representatives of the commercial districts continued.[58] The Chamber of Commerce and the "mechanics" of New York City, the Chamber of Commerce of Philadelphia, and the merchants of Newburyport filed firm protests against giving up the protective duties. One strong and perhaps valid objection to repeal was connected with the relation of the duties to the British West India trade. The discrimination acted as a check upon the profitable triangular voyage which a British vessel might make from Europe to the United States and then to the West Indies, or to the West Indies and then to the United States, in which American shipping could not compete. The merchants of

[56] Gallatin, *Works* (ed. Adams), 105; Richardson, *Messages and Papers*, I, 343.
[57] *ASP, C&N*, I, 503-504.
[58] *Annals*, XII, 415, 423.

Norfolk, for example, favored retention only of the duties on vessels coming from ports closed to the vessels of the United States.[59] It soon appeared that favorable action on the committee report was impossible, and on February 12 Smith himself agreed to drop the subject.[60] The rupture of the Peace of Amiens ended the matter as a pressing question. In an act approved March 27, 1804, Congress imposed fifty cents per ton for light money on foreign vessels, thus countervailing the British lighthouse dues, which were in addition to the two shilling extra tonnage duty. At that date there was no danger of a complaint of treaty violation, since the commercial articles of the Jay Treaty had expired October 1, 1803.[61]

The question of the colonial trade was not urged with any great emphasis by the United States during the period of peace. King mentioned the West India trade to Lord Hawkesbury in August 1802, and received the reply that the ministry was too much occupied with other important matters to give proper attention to the subject. He said that much would depend upon the situation of Santo Domingo and other foreign colonies.[62] In January 1803, King presented a note on the subject, in which he pointed out that, if the West India trade were opened, the United States must have an equal share in its regulation. If the United States should be forced to adopt restrictions similar to the British, American shipping would have the longest leg of the voyage by way of the foreign island entrepôts. The United States government would be willing to accept adjustment either by legislation or by treaty, but would prefer the latter. It would be willing to consent to a requirement that the return cargoes of American vessels should be carried directly to the United States, and that "they should moreover be purchased, as well as limited, by the proceeds of cargoes imported in American

[59] *Annals*, XII, 20, 28, 30, 423, 449; *ASP, C&N*, I, 508-509.
[60] *Annals*, XII, 517.
[61] *Annals*, XIII, 799-801; *Statutes at Large of the U. S.*, II, 299-300; Madison to Monroe, March 5, 1804, Instructions, VI, 206-207.
[62] *ASP, FR*, II, 501-502.

vessels."[63] The renewal of the war also terminated this discussion. The trade with the North American colonies received attention as result of the complaint of the Treasury Department that British traders, under cover of that clause of the Jay Treaty regarding the common use of portages in the northwest, were smuggling goods beyond the Mississippi and to the American settlements near the boundary, thus defrauding the revenue and competing unfairly with American merchants. The British government made no difficulty about acquiescing in the American interpretation of the treaty, viz., that it permitted British goods free of duty in so far only as necessary to carry them around obstructions in the waters of the common boundary.[64]

The British customhouse regulations were revised during the period of peace, and the commerce of the United States was made to suffer to some extent as a result of it. A particular cause of protest was the continuation of the convoy duties first levied during the war, i.e., export duties on British manufactures, which were higher on exports to the United States than those to Continental Europe. King entered a complaint on the ground that the duties were in violation of the treaty of 1794—a course approved by Madison. The British government refused to view the matter in the same light. The expiration of the commercial articles soon after the enactment of the duties made it not worth while to press the issue on that ground, although the American government continued to insist that the discrimination was a breach of equality.[65] A further increase of the import duty on American whale oil was the subject of an unavailing protest by King.[66]

It is noteworthy that all these protests and discussions of subjects relating to direct commercial relationships lacked

[63] *ASP, FR*, II, 503.
[64] Madison to King, July 20, 1802, Instructions, VI, 48-49; Gore to Hawkesbury, Sept. 22, 1802, Gore to the Secretary of State, Oct. 6, 1802, *ASP, FR*, II, 588.
[65] *ASP, FR*, II, 500-501; Madison to King, July 23, 1802, and to Monroe, March 5, 1804, Instructions, VI, 50-51, 206-207.
[66] *ASP, FR*, II, 503.

firmness on the part of the United States. No desire for treaty regulations to replace the expiring articles of the Jay Treaty was expressed. Anglo-American relations under the first Democratic-Republican administration were cordial and as free from serious friction as during Federalist rule.[67] After the renewal of the European war, the policy of Jefferson and Madison was to avoid commitments until peace should be restored. The return of tranquility, they expected, would leave the United States in an excellent bargaining position, particularly with regard to the American colonies of European powers. In reply to the suggestion of the renewal of the treaty of 1794, Monroe told Lord Harrowby in 1804 that the object of American diplomacy was "for the present only to remove certain topics which produced irritation in the intercourse, such as the impressment of seamen, and in our commerce with other Powers, parties to the present war. . . ."[68]

Questions continued to arise, of course, in reciprocal commercial relations, but they were not pressed with any great vigor by the United States. The convoy duties remained a grievance. Samuel Smith, always on the lookout for the advantage of the shipping interest, moved resolutions in the Senate with the object of retaliation. Madison sent them to Monroe, hoping they might serve to influence the British government.[69] Although it was claimed that these duties were levied in violation of the treaty, no refunds were ever claimed. In 1805, the treaty could no longer be urged against the taxes, but Monroe was ordered to make representations "drawn from justice, friendship, and sound policy." The pretext offered by the British that a higher tax on shipping bound for America was justifiable because of the greater distance and consequent cost of convoying, was untenable from the American point of view. Exports to the United States were usually made as American property in American vessels, and a British convoy would subject them to capture by Britain's

[67] Madison to Monroe, March 5, 1804, *ibid.*, III, 90.
[68] Monroe to Madison, Aug. 7, 1804, *ASP, FR*, III, 94.
[69] Madison to Monroe, March 6, 1805, Instructions, VI, 275-276.

enemies. Although Madison tried to make use of Smith's resolutions in London, there is no evidence that the Administration gave any support to them in Congress. Smith asked Gallatin for an opinion on his program, which consisted in the prohibition of the import of enumerated British manufactures. The Secretary of the Treasury was very cool toward it. In his opinion there would be great difficulty in selecting the articles to which to apply the prohibition, "for the less of an English article we consume, the less will the prohibition affect them; and the more we consume of it, the more will the prohibition affect our own finances." Inasmuch as a prohibition of British manufactures was the strongest measure of retaliation the United States could employ, it would perhaps be best, he thought, to reserve it for more important grievances than the export duty.[70]

The West India trade also received passing notice in 1805, due to a change of policy of the British government in that area. A series of proclamations by the provincial governors excluded American vessels, whereas it was the usual policy to admit them in time of war, and also prohibited certain American articles, particularly fish, in British vessels. Jacob Crowninshield of Massachusetts in the House of Representatives proposed in retaliation complete non-intercourse with any colonies, the entry to which was denied to American vessels.[71] Madison transmitted this proposal to Monroe in the hope that it might lend support to arguments and war-time exigencies in inducing a return to former policies.[72] Monroe found the British government not amenable to persuasion on this or any other commercial subject. "On a review of the conduct of this government towards the United States from the commencement of the war," he wrote October 18, 1805, "I am inclined to think that the delay which has been so studiously sought in all these concerns is the part of a system,

[70] Gallatin to Samuel Smith, July 17, 1805, Gallatin, *Works* (ed. H. Adams), I, 236-237.
[71] *Annals*, XV, 451-453.
[72] Madison to Monroe, March 6, 1805, Instructions, VI, 276-277.

and that it is intended, as circumstances favor, to subject our commerce at present and hereafter to every restraint in their power. It is certain that the greatest jealousy is entertained of our present and increasing prosperity. . . ."[73]

THE PERIOD OF INCREASING FRICTION IN
ANGLO-AMERICAN RELATIONS

Ever since the outbreak of war between Great Britain and France in 1793, British interference with neutral trade, and the impressment of American seamen by British naval officers had been causes of serious complaint by the United States. Under the régime of the Jay Treaty, however, the British government had been somewhat benevolent in enforcing its despotic maritime regulations, and was often courteous and prompt in redressing grievances. In consequence of the relative free trade allowed between the French and Spanish colonies in America, and Europe, via the United States, which British courts usually held legal provided the cargoes were unloaded and passed through the United States customhouses, American commerce grew apace. Merchant tonnage more than doubled between 1793 and 1805. Beginning in 1804, however, Great Britain, driven by the increased bitterness of the mortal conflict with Napoleon, proceeded to develop policies calculated to draw as much of this trade as possible into British channels, to the profit of the hard-pressed treasury, British maritime industry, and the navy. Regulations were adopted permitting the carriage of the produce of the enemy colonies in America, even in enemy ships, into British colonial ports, whence it could be carried in British shipping to England. British subjects were licensed to trade with the enemy in neutral vessels. Then, in May 1805, in the historic case of the American ship *Essex*, the Lords Commissioners of Appeal in Prize Causes held that touching at an American port did not neutralize a cargo from an enemy port when the intended final destination was another enemy

[73] Monroe to Madison, Oct. 18, 1805, Dispatches, Great Britain, XII.

port. In consequence of this decision, scores of American vessels engaged in such indirect trade were seized and condemned. British cruisers off New York became so active in searching vessels that the port was, in effect, blockaded for long periods. These attacks on the American carrying trade were accompanied by increased abuses in the practice of impressing seamen from American merchant vessels, marking the determination of the government to regain for naval service as many as possible of the British seamen who had been drawn by high wages and more humane treatment into the American merchant marine. Since there was little inducement for naval officers to be extremely conscientious in attempting to distinguish between British subjects and American citizens, hundreds of the latter were forced to serve on British warships.[74]

Although difficulties between the two countries at this time were affected only slightly by questions arising from direct commercial relationships, the American plans for resistance, just as in 1793-1794, assumed the character of commercial retaliation. This was in conformity with Jefferson's deep-seated conviction that the ability of the United States to cut off vital trade with Europe constituted a weapon of sufficient power to enforce a general redress of grievances by European governments, particularly Great Britain.[75] In addition to the proposals of Crowninshield and Smith already referred to, Joseph Clay of Pennsylvania introduced resolutions for the prohibition of intercourse with colonial ports not permanently open to United States ships, and also prohibit-

[74] The various acts of European nations which injured American commerce from 1793 to 1812, are conveniently listed in Anna C. Clauder, *American Commerce as Affected by the Wars of the French Revolution and Napoleon*, 9-14. W. E. Lingelbach, "England and Neutral Trade," *Military Historian and Economist*, II, 153-178, authoritatively traces the history of British policy with regard to neutrals. The subject of impressment is fully treated in J. F. Zimmerman, *Impressment of American Seamen*, chs. IV-V. See also Henry Adams, *History of the United States During the Administrations of Jefferson and Madison*, III, 44-53, 91-96, 143.

[75] L. M. Sears, *Jefferson and the Embargo*, chs. I-II, contains a thorough exposition of Jefferson's pacifistic philosophy and his policy of commercial boycott as the chief support of his diplomacy.

ing foreign vessels from importing goods not the produce of the country of registry.[76] A little later, Smith presented resolutions which led to the introduction of a bill containing a provision similar to the last clause of Clay's proposal.[77] Both these plans threatened heavy blows upon British navigation. The outcome of this pronounced sentiment for retaliation was not the enactment of a navigation law, but the Non-importation Act of April 18, 1806, which was intended to bar the importation of specified British manufactures. The actual employment of this weapon was postponed pending the outcome of a negotiation upon which it was decided to enter.[78]

The discouraging situation which induced Monroe to pen his gloomy dispatch of October 18, 1805, was soon changed for the better. William Pitt, whom Americans held responsible for Great Britain's hostile attitude toward the United States, died in January 1806. His government was succeeded by a Whig cabinet, with Charles James Fox, a man of liberal views on commercial affairs and an old friend of America, as Foreign Secretary. In April 1806, in a conversation with Monroe, Fox voluntarily mentioned the desirability of a reciprocal arrangement with regard to the West India trade, and displayed a disposition to settle the other questions at issue. Almost simultaneously, the American government reached the decision to send a special envoy to assist Monroe, the choice falling upon William Pinkney of Maryland.[79]

The regulation of reciprocal trade was incidental to the other objects in this negotiation. The West India trade was not emphasized to the extent even of making it the *sine qua non* of a commercial arrangement, as had been the case in the instructions for the Jay Treaty. The principal demands of the American government were three: the abolition of

[76] *Annals*, XV, 442.
[77] *Ibid.*, 90, 163, 189.
[78] *Statutes at Large of the U. S.*, II, 379-381, 411. For the Congressional history of the Non-importation Act, see Adams, *History of the U. S.*, III, 146-155, 165-175.
[79] *ASP, FR*, III, 117; Adams, *History of the U. S.*, III, 165-170, 399-400.

impressment; the restoration of neutral trade to its status prior to the *Essex* decision; and the payment of an indemnity for the illegal maritime seizures. Once these demands were acquiesced in, the envoys were authorized to agree to the repeal of the Non-importation Act, and to concert general commercial provisions. The basis of the most-favored-nation would be acceptable to the United States; but the article should be framed so as to end the discrimination against the United States in the convoy duties, to extend to all the possessions of Great Britain, and to admit American vessels to the privileges recently granted to enemy vessels in the West Indies. All alien duties on vessel and cargo might be abolished, or a maximum of alien duty might be fixed. In the latter case, all port charges, including the British private light dues, must be included in the maximum. To obviate the unfavorable features of the British discriminating duties on merchandise, the instructions required that if such duty were permitted by treaty, it should be calculated on the value of the cargo, and not on the amount of duties payable. It was believed that if the discrimination were made a percentage of the value of the cargo rather than of the relatively high imposts levied by Great Britain, the American vessels would be better able to compete in the eastward voyage, which gave employment to far the greater part of the tonnage in Anglo-American trade.

The envoys were charged to exercise great care in framing a most-favored-nation article so as to avoid prejudicing the right of the United States to regulate trade with ports closed to American vessels. Since their trade conferred little benefit upon the British colonies in the East Indies, they probably would have no right to expect greater privileges than those of other nations.

But, as relates to the West Indies and the North American colonies it must be a permanent object of the United States to have the intercourse with them made as free as that with Europe. The relative situation of the United States and those colonies, and particularly those wants which we can alone supply, must necessarily produce that effect at some no very distant period. And it should not be voluntarily retarded, either by abandoning by treaty the strong hold which our right of stopping the intercourse gives us, or by accepting any temporary or trifling privilege, the exercise of which would diminish the probability of soon obtaining a perfectly free trade.

The only limitation on the West India trade which could be agreed to would be the restriction of exports in American vessels to not more than half the value of the incoming cargo of American produce. Eight years or less would be the desirable term for such a treaty.[80]

The government considered it improbable that trade by sea in American vessels with the North American colonies could be obtained, but no provision short of complete reciprocity could be considered satisfactory. An additional instruction of May 30 expressed the desire to suppress the permanent provision in the treaty of 1794 which gave to each party the right to trade with the Indians of the other. It was contended that there was no reciprocity in the arrangement for the United States, for it was unsafe for American traders to venture among the British Indians on account of the hostile attitude of the British Northwest Company. On the American side, quarrels occurred between the rival traders, and the tendency of the British was to influence the Indians against the government of the United States.[81]

Although apparently of the best of intentions, Fox found himself, as in 1782, opposed by interested parties in his plan for a more liberal commercial system; and his government was too weak to force the issue. The death of the Foreign Secretary in September 1806 undoubtedly made the path of the American envoys more difficult. They learned September

---

[80] The instructions are in *ASP, FR*, III, 123. That Gallatin was influential in their preparation, if not their author, is indicated by the draft, very similar to the final dispatch, addressed to Jefferson, in Gallatin, *Works*, I, 284-288. See also an additional instruction dated Feb. 3, 1807, confirming the earlier ones and advising specifically the omission of an article on the West Indies unless the minimum previously described were obtained. Instructions, VI, 381-382.

[81] *ASP, FR*, III, 126. See also Madison to Monroe and Pinkney, June 11, 1806, *ibid.*, 128.

11, 1806, in a conference with Lords Auckland and Holland, the commissioners appointed to treat with them, that no clause which they could accept would be offered on the West India problem. The British plentipotentiaries intimated that any arrangement must contain a limitation upon tonnage as in the suppressed West India article of the treaty of 1794, and in addition a stipulation that the United States would levy a duty upon West India goods, sufficient to check their export to Europe—not only British produce but the produce of *all* West India colonies.[82]

As a commercial treaty, the instrument which Monroe and Pinkney signed December 31, 1806, contained a few articles more favorable to the United States than were in the treaty of 1794. It was doubtless an improvement over the complete absence from the Jay Treaty, after the rejection of the twelfth, of an article on the West India trade, to reserve the right of the United States to retaliate the British restrictions in that quarter. The provisions with regard to discriminating duties were also preferable to the former arrangement. The extra duties on merchandise were abolished. The right of each country to countervail the tonnage duty of the other was recorded in place of Jay's agreement that the British might countervail the existing American duty, which the United States was bound not to advance. The East India trade was, in the language of the treaty, placed on a worse footing than formerly, inasmuch as the carriage of goods in American vessels directly from Europe to India was prohibited, whereas it had been permitted under the Jay Treaty. However, the most-favored-nation clause was made to cover the East India trade, and the United States could have claimed the favor had it been continued to other powers. The commissioners were unable to secure the inclusion of the British light duties in the tonnage rate, and they also failed to secure the abolition of the discriminating features of the convoy duties.[83]

[82] Monroe and Pinkney to the Secretary of State, Sept. 11, 1806, *ASP, FR*, III, 134.
[83] The treaty is in *ASP, FR*, III, 147-151. See also Monroe's and Pinkney's report of Jan. 3, 1807, *ibid.*, 142-147.

After the conclusion of the general treaty, a negotiation was entered upon for the purpose of settling the northern boundary of Louisiana, and intercourse with the North American colonies. In this negotiation, the British insisted upon admission to the Indian trade in Louisiana and upon a clause ending the American practice of charging ad valorem duties upon imports across the land boundary according to their value in Canada instead of in Europe, as intended in the Jay Treaty. They also demanded exemption from the requirement of a license for their Indian traders—or rather the exaction of a fee for licenses. A vague article was offered by the British for fixing as soon as possible regulations for a legalized trade in vessels of either party between the United States and a port or ports in the North American colonies. The envoys reported that they had been shown a proposed act providing a fairly satisfactory system, but that a roundabout way was being followed to evade criticism at home.[84]

In commenting on the proposed articles, Madison declared that the United States would not consent to any extension of privileges for the British in the Indian trade, nor to British subjects going with their goods through United States territory to the Mississippi without payment of duties, nor to the admission of British Indian traders into the country beyond the Mississippi. He had no objections to the stipulation making the method of evaluating goods imported by land or inland navigation the same as when imported to the Atlantic ports from Europe, nor to an agreement that licenses and passes should be freely granted under the same regulations to the traders of both nations. He expressed a readiness to consent to the arrangement proposed by the British for the establishment of a port to which American vessels would be admitted in the North American colonies.[85] This supplemental treaty fell with the general treaty and the return of the Tories to power in England.

It is improbable that any of the purely commercial articles

[84] See the proposed supplemental articles and the report of the commissioners thereon, April 25, 1807. *ASP, FR*, III, 163, 165.

[85] Madison to Monroe and Pinkney, July 30, 1807, *ASP, FR*, III, 185-186.

had much influence in persuading the President to withhold the treaty of December 31, 1806, from the Senate. The failure to settle the impressment and neutral rights controversies more than justified his course. In his comments on the treaty, Madison strongly criticized the East India article because it denied to American vessels the indirect trade, but he was willing to omit the article altogether and depend upon the most-favored-nation clause and British self-interest to give the United States an acceptable place in that commerce. He saw fit to press further only an extension of the privilege accorded American vessels to refresh at St. Helena, to include also the Cape of Good Hope. The President, he stated, did not wish to make the abolition of the convoy duties a *sine qua non*, but wished another effort made to obtain it.[86] Monroe and Pinkney proposed to George Canning, who succeeded Fox in the Foreign Office, a revision of the treaty to include these suggestions of Madison, and also the conditional form of the most-favored-nation clause. Canning refused, however, to continue the negotiation on the old basis, and the new propositions were not considered.[87]

Commercial reciprocity did not again become an important subject in the relations of the United States and Great Britain until the War of 1812 had been fought to settle their major differences. In the intervening years American commerce became the prey alternately of the serpent of the sea and the ogre of the land. Fox's paper blockade of French ports provided the excuse for Napoleon's Berlin Decree (November 1806), establishing a less than paper blockade of the British Isles. The King in Council replied by first forbidding to neutrals the coasting trade of France and her allies, and then (November 1807), by ordering neutral ships bound for the Continent to pay tribute at a British port. The Emperor retaliated by directing that all vessels submitting to the British orders should be seized and condemned as British property (December 1807). The peace-loving Jefferson, rather than

[86] Madison to Monroe and Pinkney, May 20, 1807, *ibid.*, 166.
[87] Monroe and Pinkney to Canning, July 24, 1807; Canning to Monroe and Pinkney, Oct. 22, 1807, *ASP, FR*, III, 194-196, 198-199.

resort to arms, followed Washington's example in somewhat similar circumstances in 1794 and had recourse to the strongest non-military weapon at the command of the federal government, an embargo of all foreign trade (December 1807). When this extreme measure appeared to be driving New England to secession, it was replaced (March 1809) by laws barring intercourse with Great Britain and France only.

Since Great Britain was the better able to enforce her regulations effectively upon American trade, American resentment was largely concentrated on that nation. The continued impressment of American seamen, extended even to national vessels in the Chesapeake outrage of 1807, increased feeling to the inflammable point. A settlement of the principal issues by the conciliatory David M. Erskine at Washington in 1809 was repudiated by Canning, with the result of further embittering relations. The non-intercourse legislation, found unenforceable, was repealed in 1810, with the promise of revival against either of the principal belligerents if the other would repeal its objectionable ordinances. In the latter proposition, Napoleon saw an opportunity to trick the United States into war against Great Britain, and announced the repeal of his decrees as applied to the United States. Madison then revived non-intercourse against Great Britain. At last, having endured every possible indignity, the President, supported by an aroused national feeling, and, in the West, by a craving for the conquest of Canada, in June 1812 led his country into a war for "free trade and sailors' rights."

THE RISE OF THE LATIN AMERICAN PROBLEM

The overthrow of the Bourbon Monarchy in Spain by Napoleon in 1808 was fraught with unusual significance for the commercial development of the Western Hemisphere. Jefferson and his Cabinet promptly determined that the immediate interest of the United States was to prevent the Spanish dominions in America from passing under the political or commercial domination of France or Great Britain.[88]

[88] Jefferson's Cabinet Memorandum, printed in Henry Adams, *History of the U. S.*, IV, 340-341.

The first result of the changed situation in the Peninsula was injurious to the commerce of the United States. As long as Spain was an independent ally of Napoleon, American merchants and shipping practically monopolized the sea-borne trade of the Spanish colonies. Upon the French conquest of Spain, however, the colonial ports were thrown open to Great Britain, and the competition of the latter proved a very serious handicap to American trade.[89] Though deeply interested, the American government attempted no very active commercial policy in the Spanish areas. In 1810, after the independence movement had begun in South America, Madison sent Joel R. Poinsett and Robert K. Lowry as commercial agents to Buenos Aires and Venezuela respectively. In 1812, Alexander Scott was appointed United States agent at Caracas. These agents were ordered to explain to the colonial leaders the advantages of commercial relations with the United States, to encourage the adoption of liberal and stable commercial regulations, and to transmit information on the commerce of the regions in which they were to reside.[90] Their functions were primarily those of observers.

In Portuguese America, however, Jefferson and Madison made a serious effort to turn the flank of the British commercial advance in the New World. The plan originated with Henry Hill of Connecticut, formerly United States commercial agent in Cuba and Jamaica.[91] Hill believed that the removal of the Portuguese Court to America offered the United States an excellent opportunity to loosen Portugal from its dependence upon Great Britain, hinder the British from developing in Brazil a market for manufactures and a source of raw materials to rival the United States, and to develop a rich market for provisions and East India goods

---

[89] Nichols, "Trade Relations" in *HAHR*, XIII, 308-313.

[90] W. R. Manning, *The Diplomatic Correspondence of the U. S., Concerning the Independence of the Latin American Nations*, I, 6-7, 9, 14-16, 1151; C. L. Chandler, *Inter-American Acquaintances*, 38-39.

[91] Hill's work as agent in the Caribbean area is discussed in Nichols, "Trade Relations," *HAHR*, XIII, 307-309. As reward for his work in Brazil, he was made consul at San Salvador.

for American merchants.[92] Hill was immediately sent to Rio de Janeiro, to congratulate the Prince Regent, Dom John, on his arrival in America and to sound the dispositions of the government as to its probable commercial system in its new surroundings. The envoy was cordially received, and assured that the intentions of the court were most liberal, and that the commerce of the United States would be placed upon the footing of the most-favored-nation in Brazil. Hill explained to Madison that the general tariff was twenty-four per cent upon the value of imports, except "wines and other liqueurs" which paid forty-eight per cent; that diamonds, gold dust, and "Brazillette wood" were subject to a crown monopoly; and that coffee, tobacco, and cotton were taxed lightly on exportation.[93]

In August, 1809, Madison sent a regular minister, Thomas Sumter, to Rio de Janeiro. The President was not anxious to rush into a negotiation, however, and, if one developed, he wished to draw it to Washington. Sumter's principal duty was to collect information, and to obtain for the United States, in accordance with the promise made to Hill, all the advantages enjoyed by Great Britain in Brazilian ports.[94] He soon learned that a commercial treaty with Great Britain had been concluded, and this tended to delay the consideration of relations with the United States. His first information was that there was nothing in the new treaty to prevent the United States securing similar terms. The minister for foreign affairs expressed interest in the subject of a commercial convention with the United States, especially when Sumter pointed out to him that it would mean an expanded market for Brazilian sugar. In general, however, little enthusiasm for a connection with the United States was shown. Court opinion held all neutrals as, in a sense, enemies. Sumter was

[92] Hill to Madison, Feb. 17, Feb. 19, 1808; Hill to Senator S. L. Mitchill, Feb. 19, 1808, U. S. Dept. of State, Consular Dispatches, San Salvador, I.
[93] Hill to Rodrigo de Souza Coutinho, Sept. 2, Oct. 6, 1808; Souza Coutinho to Hill, Oct. 4, 1808; Hill to Madison, Oct. 12, 1808, Dispatches, San Salvador, I.
[94] Robert Smith to Sumter, Aug. 1, 1809, Instructions, VII, 50-54.

convinced that if his country were to go to war with Napoleon, British influence in Rio de Janeiro would be neutralized, and the United States could then mature with the Portuguese government "an American system which might last as such beyond ages against all enemies."[95]

The publication of the completed Anglo-Portuguese treaty showed how slight the influence of the United States was in Brazil. Numerous advantages accrued to Great Britain, perhaps the most valuable of which was the right to import British manufactures at an ad valorem duty of only fifteen per cent.[96] Sumter immediately laid claim to equal privileges under the promise of most-favored-nation treatment made to Hill in 1808. In this treaty, for the first time, the United States government found itself confronted, to its disadvantage, with the most-favored-nation clause in the conditional form. The Count of Linhares, the Portuguese foreign minister, explained that the favors conferred by the treaty upon Great Britain had been granted in return for other favors granted Portugal, and that no other nation could pretend to them without giving an equivalent.[97]

After learning of the situation, Secretary Robert Smith advised Sumter to continue his efforts. He believed that when the Braganza family had become somewhat more Americanized, it would feel less dependent upon the British navy. The Prince might then see that Great Britain had yielded very little in return for the many advantages conceded by Portugal. It would be useful for the American minister to suggest the superior advantages of a free trade between

[95] Sumter to the Secretary of State, July 23, Sept. 3, 1810, Dispatches, Brazil, I. A vexatious restriction was applied to American vessels in Brazil in the form of a quarantine, enforced only with regard to the United States. Sumter thought the hostile influence of the Spanish and British ambassadors was responsible. He learned from the minister of foreign affairs that the law was general, but that American vessels were being carefully inspected because of a report that French emissaries were collected in the United States to carry Jacobinism to South America. Sumter to the Secretary of State, Sept. 3, Oct. 2, 1810, Dispatches, Brazil, I.

[96] G. F. de Martens, *Supplément au recueil des principaux traités*, VII, 194-214.

[97] Sumter to Secretary of State, Nov. 8, and enclosure, Count of Linhares to Sumter, Oct. 30, 1810, Dispatches, Brazil, I.

Brazil and the United States. Among these advantages would be assistance in the marketing of Brazilian sugar. Although the British treaty provided, as a concession to Brazil, that Brazilian products, such as sugar, which were denied a market in Great Britain, might be warehoused in British ports pending reëxport to other countries, it could not be expected that the government and merchants would encourage the sale of such articles in competition with exports of the similar products of British colonies. The United States, on the other hand, could supply its own needs and those of Continental Europe with Brazilian sugar, and by carrying it in American vessels directly to market, eliminate the warehouse and other charges incidental to reëxporation from Great Britain. The same would be true of coffee and other Brazilian articles competing with the produce of the British West Indies. Furthermore, the ventures of American merchants in the Far Eastern trade could be turned to the profit of Brazil; and the growing manufactures of the United States would probably soon provide a surplus for the supply of other countries, including Portuguese America. By admitting freely American trade, the government would enable native merchants to compete with the British, who had hitherto monopolized Portuguese commerce.[98]

Sumter advised his superior that nothing worth while could be done for American trade until the matters in controversy between the United States and Great Britain had been disposed of, and the allies of the latter advised as to what attitude to take toward the United States. An increase in the friction between the United States and Napoleon would improve his position at Rio de Janeiro.[99] However, Madison was not disposed to yield American neutrality in return for a favorable commercial treaty. The attempt to overcome British influence upon the Portuguese government in Brazil was no more successful than the previous attempts in Lisbon.

[98] Robert Smith to Sumter, Nov. 12, 1810, Instructions, VIII, 128-131.
[99] Sumter to the Secretary of State, Jan. 11, August 8, Nov. 26, 1811, Dispatches, Brazil, I.

RECIPROCITY IN RELATIONS WITH NAPOLEON

Although the American government did not neglect exertions to place its trade with France upon a favorable basis, it was extremely cautious in entering into negotiations for a treaty with the Emperor. Reasons doubtless lay in the effect such negotiations would have upon relations with Great Britain, the desire to await a general peace before settling commercial relations, and the unsatisfactory general relations with Napoleon. In 1802, Livingston called the attention of the French government to the proposed reciprocity act then before Congress, with the object of securing the adherence of France in the event of its passage. He also contemplated the discussion of a general treaty, but gave up the idea on learning that Talleyrand was averse to the subject.[100]

In 1805, when the Emperor had need of every resource to fill his military chest, his ministers signified to John Armstrong, successor to Livingston, that their master would open the colonial trade freely to the United States in return for an equivalent in the form of a sum of money. Madison took the proposal seriously, though perhaps Armstrong did not.[101]

The objections to such an arrangement (he wrote) are considered by the President as insuperable. If made in time of war, it would beget discontents in Great Britain who would suspect or pretend that the arrangement was a cover for a subsidy; and with the more plausibility, as during the war, nearly the same privileges are allowed without purchase. The precedent, in the next place would be a novel and a noxious one. Add that our trade with the French Colonies, in time of war, being more important to France than to the United States, there is as much reason why she should buy it of us in time of war, as that we should buy it of her in time of peace. Finally, the reciprocity of advantages in the Trade at all times, makes it the real interest of France as of other nations to lay it open to us at all times.

The treaty of 1800 expired in 1809, the United States showing little interest in its renewal. A proposal to renew it

[100] Livingston to the Minister of Foreign Affairs, March 12, 1802, Dispatches, France, VIII.

[101] Armstrong to Madison, Feb. 14, 1805, Dispatches, France, X; Madison to Armstrong, June 6, 1805, Instructions, VI, 304.

made in 1810 by the French government produced no results.[102] In 1810 Robert Smith made one slight effort to enlist French aid in his general scheme of defense against the British war to destroy American commerce. He instructed Armstrong to bring to the notice of the French government the opening of great commercial opportunities in the Spanish and Portuguese colonies as a result of recent developments. A British monopoly of their trade furnished a market for British manufactures, and also enabled that country to establish a political ascendancy over them.

To counteract the tendency of such an exclusive trade (he wrote) nothing could at this time be more effectual than the opening of all the channels of a free commercial communication between the United States, France and her Allies. By such freedom of admission and the abolition of all vexatious restrictions, France and the Nations connected with her would, thro' the medium of American enterprise and navigation, obtain a vent for a large portion of their produce and manufactures which in no other way can find a market in the ports of Spanish and Portuguese America.[103]

In other words, Smith believed he had found a way for coöperation between the American ideal of free trade and Napoleon's Continental System. Napoleon apparently felt that the possibility of forcing the United States into war with Great Britain was more promising.

The putative repeal of the Berlin and Milan decrees in 1810 did not place American commerce with France on any acceptable footing. Only the method of injuring it was changed. On the same day as the notification of the repeal of the decrees, an exorbitant schedule of duties was put in effect. Another regulation forced American vessels to export the value of the imported cargo in French produce, two-thirds of it in silks. Certain vessels were admitted with specified articles when licensed by a French consul—an exercise of authority by foreign consuls which the United States govern-

---

[102] Armstrong to Smith, Feb. 2, Feb. 10, 1810 with enclosure from Champagny, duc de Cadore, and Jan. 28, 1810, Dispatches, France, XI; Smith to Armstrong, June 20, 1810, Instructions, VII, 101-102.

[103] R. Smith to Armstrong, Nov. 1, 1810, Instructions, VII, 121-122.

ment declared it could not continue to permit. The frequent changes in customhouse and commercial regulations discouraged merchants from undertaking trade.[104]

In sending Joel Barlow as minister to France in 1811, the objects of the Administration were to secure release of sequestered vessels, indemnity for those illegally seized and disposed of or destroyed, and the removal of the restrictions which were effectively preventing American trade with European territories under the control of France. His instructions did not contemplate the negotiation of a commercial treaty.[105] Barlow's poetic imagination and enthusiasm were not, however, to be bounded by the prosaic direction of Monroe and Madison, whose many diplomatic reverses had at length taught them that America could expect little in the way of favors from Europe. The minister immediately proposed the settlement of the commercial questions by treaty "on principles of reciprocity, both with respect to the rate of duties . . . and the facility of buying and selling, entering and departing." His memorial in support of his demands contains strong remainders of those of the commercial diplomats during the American Revolution. He envisaged a Europe united under Napoleon, which would afford unprecedented opportunities for American commerce.[106]

He found the Imperial Court sympathetic, and his enthusiasm grew. In a note of December 1811, Bassano, the minister for foreign affairs, informed him that no difficulty would be encountered in settling all the questions pending if the United States would only make their flag respected by Great Britain.[107] Imperial diplomacy was working well. This answer

---

[104] Smith to Armstrong, Nov. 8, 1811, Instructions, VII, 127-128; *ASP, FR*, III, 400-404, 508-509; J. Russell to Monroe, July 13, 1811, Dispatches, France, XII; Monroe to Barlow, July 26, 1811, Instructions, VII, 158-161; Barlow to the Duke of Bassano, Nov. 10, 1811, Dispatches, France, XIII; Monroe to Barlow, Nov. 21, 1811, Instructions, VII, 172. The new commercial system put into effect by Napoleon in 1810 and following years, after the failure of the Continental System, is treated thoroughly by Frank E. Melvin, *Napoleon's Navigation System*, chaps. IV-X.

[105] Monroe to Barlow, July 26, 1811, Instructions, VII, 158-161.

[106] Barlow to Bassano, November 10, 1811, Dispatches, France, XIII.

[107] Bassano to Barlow, Dec. 27, 1811; Barlow to the Secretary of State, Dec. 31, 1811, Dispatches, France, XIII.

perhaps prevented the United States from declaring war upon France at the same time as upon Great Britain.[108] Barlow attempted to secure a signed declaration of the new policy of the Emperor toward America, and took to Bassano a prepared statement for the purpose. "It is not proper for me to sign this declaration," he was told, "but you may notify it to your government, word for word, as if it were signed; for the principles are adopted, and from this day forward they will be in operation." Barlow immediately applied to the Secretary of State for instructions for a commercial treaty— particularly on two points which he favored: mutual national treatment for vessels, and a conventional tariff providing for a reduction of duties on both sides.[109]

Too eager to await the instructions, however, he proceeded to hold conferences with Bassano, and on January 17 sent him a treaty project. Sixteen of the thirty-one articles of this project were copied with little variation from the treaty of 1800. "Several others," as described by Barlow, "are merely regulatory, and some few have adopted principles not found in that treaty; among which there may be one or two that are strangers to all treaties and will be new in the law of nations." An article provided for the mutual naturalization of vessels, extending even to the privilege of carrying articles from a third country, and mutual admission to the coasting trade. No distinction was to be made between native-built vessels and those built in the other country. Customs duties on native produce were in no case to exceed twenty per cent ad valorem, and only one per cent was to be collected on goods reëxported within a year. East India goods were to be admitted at thirty per cent. The provisions of the treaty were to extend to the French colonies and to the Kingdom of Italy as well as to France proper. The project provided for the postponement of the subject of indemnity for spoliations, perhaps the most important subject from the American standpoint, to a future negotiation. The minister was in great hopes of completing the negotiation in record time, but his discussions were retarded,

[108] Monroe to Barlow, June 16, 1812, Instructions, VII, 207-210.
[109] Barlow to the Secretary of State, Dec. 31, 1811, Dispatches, France, XIII.

according to his own report, by the preoccupation of the government with preparations for the invasion of Russia.[110]

Barlow's letters describing his proposals aroused considerable misgiving at Washington. Monroe wrote him that it was not advisable to conclude a commercial treaty, especially if it did not contain due provision for the American claims for spoliations. The provisions of mutual national treatment were "on the whole thought more proper for future consideration than immediate adoption." As to the proposed conventional tariff, the Secretary declared that, however desirable the reduction of the French duties might be, the government could not bind the United States to any given rate, since public exigencies might make it necessary to augment the revenue.[111] The President himself drafted an instruction to point out to Barlow that there was good reason to suspect Napoleon's good faith in his sudden change of policy toward the United States.[112] The arrival of the treaty project in April increased the apprehension of Monroe and Madison. Without delay Monroe wrote the minister that the project contained objectionable matter which might prevent the ratification of a treaty based upon it. "A formal treaty," he added, "was not contemplated by your instructions. The objects contemplated by them were 1st the admission of our productions into France on beneficial terms. 2nd security for our neutral and national rights on the high seas, and 3rdly provision for the Rambouillet and other spoliations; and these objects it was expected might be obtained by Decrees or Acts of the French government adopted separately and independently by itself."[113]

The unfavorable reception accorded at home to his plan of

[110] Barlow to the Secretary of State, Jan. 28, 1812, and to Bassano, Jan. 17, 1812, Dispatches, France, XIII; Barlow to Monroe, Feb. 8, March 3, March 15, 1812, Dispatches, France, XIII; Bassano's report "A Sa Majesté" Feb. 27, 1812, AAE, CP, EU, LXIX.

[111] Monroe to Barlow, Feb. 23, 1812, Instructions, VII, 191-192.

[112] Madison to Barlow, Feb. 24, 1812, Madison, *Writings* (ed. Hunt), VII, 177-181.

[113] Monroe to Barlow, April 23, 1812, Instructions, VII, 200-204. See also Madison to Jefferson, April 24, 1812, Madison, *Writings*, VIII, 189.

treaty-making did not end Barlow's efforts, although it had the effect of drawing his ideas more nearly within the bounds set by previous American policy. Thenceforward, he made indemnity for spoliations a *sine qua non* of a treaty. The Emperor's intention was to maneuver the United States into war with Great Britain, and he was therefore willing to go the length of discussing indemnity in order to amuse and deceive Barlow and his government. A plenipotentiary, the Duke d'Alberg, was designated to carry on the negotiation. Delay followed delay until the United States was safely at war. From that point onward there were a few indications of a serious effort to reach an understanding. After the two negotiators had, in October 1812, succeeded in agreeing in general upon a commercial treaty and a claims convention, Barlow was summoned to the Imperial court at Vilna for the announced purpose of finally concluding the treaty. The treaty was not concluded, however, possibly because of the military difficulties of the Emperor. Barlow's death on his return journey from Vilna terminated the negotiation.[114]

The treaty project, in the stage at which it was left, contained no startling innovations, having been modeled very closely upon the Franco-American treaty of 1800. The principal commercial advantages from the American point of view were: (1) provision for the adequate warning of merchants before changes should be made in commercial regulations; (2) liberal arrangements for the transit through France to other countries, storage, and reëxport of American staples; (3) allowance of one year in which to pay duties in France, after the importation of goods; (4) the adoption of the conditional form of the most-favored-nation clause. The Emperor's

[114] Barlow to Monroe, May 22; Barlow to the Duke d'Alberg, June 5; Bassano to Barlow, May 10, Oct. 11; Barlow to Bassano, Oct. 25, 1812, Dispatches, France, XIII; *ASP, FR*, III, 514-515; Barlow to Monroe, Oct. 20, Nov. 23; Barlow to Bassano, Oct. 25, 1812, Dispatches, France, XIII. The French papers dealing with the negotiation are in AAE, CP, EU, LXIX. Of especial significance are the following: Bassano to the Emperor, April 17; Bassano to Serurier, April 24; Bassano to D'Alberg, May 10; D'Alberg to Bassano, May 28, June 12, June 24; Bassano to D'Alberg, July 11, Aug. 10, Sept. 28; Bassano to the Emperor, Oct. 15, 1812.

ministers insisted on the retention of the regulation that vessels importing goods into France must export French produce to the value of the incoming cargo. They also demanded that that clause of the Louisiana Purchase treaty which provided that French vessels should enjoy national treatment for twelve years in the ports of the ceded territory should be rehabilitated and made to date from the conclusion of the next general peace. In justification of this claim, it was asserted that the continuous state of war had prevented France from enjoying the benefits of the original stipulation. Barlow was unwilling to go further with this article than to agree to refer it to his government.[115]

RUSSO-AMERICAN RELATIONS

One additional attempted negotiation during this period deserves mention—that with Russia. In 1804 Livingston discussed the possibilities of commerce between the United States and the Czar's dominions with the Russian chargé at Paris, Pierre d'Oubril, paying attention particularly to the subject of opening the Black Sea to American vessels. The desirability of a negotiation was suggested to Madison.[116] The United States government showed little interest in a treaty, however, until threatening relations with the western European powers in 1808 made the possession of a powerful friend on the Continent a factor of importance. Madison appointed William Short first United States Minister to Russia in 1808, but

[115] The latest copy of the commercial treaty project is in AAE, CP, EU, LXIX, 325-335, accompanying D'Alberg to Bassano, Oct. 20, 1812. An earlier draft of the commercial and claims convention project is *ibid.*, 272-311.

After Barlow's death, the American government remained in ignorance of the exact nature of the project upon which the minister had been working. Monroe wrote of the treaties in 1813: "Of these [the treaties] no copy has been received, nor can a precise idea be formed from any light otherwise communicated to this department." Monroe to Crawford, May 29, 1813, Instructions, VII, 285-291. Crawford was able to find nothing dealing with the treaties in the legation archives in Paris. He stated that he obtained a copy of the plan of indemnity "from a person belonging to the office of Exterior Relations," but he apparently did not obtain a copy of the commercial treaty. Crawford to Monroe, Aug. 15, 1813. Dispatches, France, XIV.

[116] Livingston to Madison, April 14, 1804, Livingston to Russian chargé d'affaires, April 7, 1804, Dispatches, France, IX.

when the Senate failed to confirm the appointment, it was transferred to John Quincy Adams. Commercial regulations were not an important purpose in the mission, though Adams was authorized to discuss them, and instructions for a treaty were promised.[117]

Adams found the Imperial foreign minister favorable toward a treaty, and advised in September 1810 that full powers be sent him.[118] Smith authorized him to enter the negotiation in February 1811, and sent him a treaty plan. "It is preferred," the Secretary wrote, "that on all subjects peculiarly connected with the commerce of the two Countries, they should be placed, with respect to the intercourse of their citizens and subjects respectively, on the footing of the most favored nation; rather than that a specification of particulars connected therewith should be made in the Treaty. A preference is given to that form, as, for the present at least, best suited to a commercial arrangement." He desired the conditional form of the most-favored-nation clause written into the treaty.[119] Adams encountered no obstacle in the disposition of the Russian government with regard to commercial regulations. However, Russia was, at the time, on the point of forming an alliance with Great Britain against Napoleon, while the United States was on the verge of war with Great Britain. The commercial negotiation was postponed, while the Czar undertook to assist in settling the quarrel between his two English-speaking friends.[120]

[117] Madison to Short, Sept. 8, 1808; R. Smith to John Quincy Adams, July 20, 1809, Instructions, VII, 12, 47.

[118] Adams, *Works*, III, 496.

[119] R. Smith to Adams, Feb., 1811, Instructions, VII, 149-151.

[120] J. Q. Adams, *Memoirs*, II, 271-272; Adams to Monroe, June 9, 1811, J. Q. Adams, *Works*, IV, 162-165, 170-174.

VI

LIBERALITY AND NATIONAL SPIRIT IN COMMERCIAL RELATIONS
1815-1829[1]

A NEW ERA IN COMMERCIAL POLICY

THE PEACE OF 1815 opened a new era in the development of the commercial policy of the United States. The government was never in a more favorable position, from the standpoint of both the foreign and the domestic situation, to carry out an energetic policy. The boundless self-confidence which was to characterize the American people during the remainder of the century was manifested in foreign relations in such episodes as the Florida controversy, the Monroe Doctrine, and certain incidents in the execution of reciprocity policy. During the first few years after Ghent, a vigorous national patriotism surviving the war forced sectionalism and factional politics into the background. A prolonged intermission in Europe's wars had begun, and the United States entered upon a period when foreign influence, both cultural and political, was extremely slight. Since all the old commercial treaties had lapsed, the government was free to develop a new commercial policy if it so desired.

American internal conditions affecting foreign commercial policy had undergone some significant changes within the last decade. Embargo, non-intercourse, and war had brought about an immense development of domestic manufacturing, and industry sought tariff protection when the principal causes of expansion were removed. Agriculture, stimulated by war-time

---

[1] "On a still broader scale, you will remark in reference to the policy pursued towards foreign nations a well tempered combination of liberality and national spirit." John Quincy Adams, *Writings*, VI, 341.

prices, had also been greatly extended. In 1815 the demand for war supplies ceased, and European corn laws and food tariffs were soon reimposed. As a result, the Hamiltonian policy of encouraging domestic manufactures in order to establish economic freedom won the support of a considerable section of the farming areas of the middle and western states. The view was held that since Europe refused to purchase American provisions, the proper retaliatory measure was to keep out European manufactures and build up a manufacturing industry in the United States, whose operatives would provide an increased market for farm produce. The protectionist might well have been grateful to the mercantilist for affording a plausible argument by means of which to rally the farmer to the support of the American System. Foreign markets for produce were not entirely forgotten, but were attended to only incidentally, or when the subject was raised by a foreign government. From the Peace of Ghent to the advent of Andrew Jackson, commercial foreign policy was directed almost exclusively to the protection and extension of the activities of merchant shipping.

Two men of unusual ability exerted the dominant influence in the conduct of foreign relations in the decade and a half following the peace. John Quincy Adams, first as Secretary of State under Monroe and then as President, gave continuity and a very definite character to commercial foreign policy. On his return from London in 1817, he made his own the program already adopted by Congress in the Reciprocity Act of 1815 and adhered to it with dogged persistence throughout his connection with the executive department. His policy of "all or none," as Gallatin named it, won some successes, but contributed to his supreme humiliation in the election of 1828. Even Adams did not hesitate to declare that Albert Gallatin was indispensable in commercial negotiation. Four of the most important commercial negotiations of the period fell to his lot. Although not one was completely successful, he contributed as much as anyone else to the successes which were achieved, by providing the basic work upon which settlements were finally reached. He brought to his task an unequaled knowledge of American finance and economic conditions, a mind adapted to the settlement of complicated technical problems, and an insight into European methods of thought and business which probably no other American possessed. He did not always agree with Adams, particularly in the "all or none" policy, nor did he look with favor upon Adams' antagonistic attitude toward European countries.

ABOLITION OF DISCRIMINATION IN THE DIRECT TRADE

In 1815 the shipping industry required a type of assistance different from that which had appeared desirable when the first national shipping policy was adopted in 1789. It was no longer an infant industry depending upon a closely guarded home market, but was able to maintain a respectable competition for the carrying trade of the world. Discriminating duties were of little advantage to either the shipowner or the revenue when no great number of foreign ships appeared in American ports, and when the duties furnished the incentive for the maintenance of similar regulations by foreign governments. The foreign duties were usually much more effective, since a vastly greater amount of tonnage was required to carry the bulky American produce to Europe than to bring finished goods to the United States. Under these circumstances, the best protective measure appeared to be to secure the removal of foreign restrictions by yielding in exchange the American discriminating duties. Great caution was exercised, however, in putting this policy into effect. Complete freedom from restrictions was first rigidly limited to vessels carrying the produce of the country to which they belonged. It was then grudgingly extended to permit the vessels of the north European maritime states to carry for the adjacent interior countries. After considerable delay, the policy of complete free trade for the carrier was offered to every nation which would reciprocate it.

The first step taken to place the government in a position to attack the obstacles to trade in the form of foreign restrictions was the adoption of the Reciprocity Act of March 3,

1815. It was among the first important laws passed after the conclusion of peace. On February 18, Senator Smith of Maryland proposed again the amended plan which he had advocated in 1802, namely, the abolition of the discriminating tonnage duties and customs surcharge on the produce of the country of the vessel's registry, in favor of any nation that would agree to repeal its similar discriminations. Smith recalled to his colleagues that the British discriminating duties, since the war insurance rates no longer served to counteract them, were a very serious handicap to American shipping. Other European states also had their discriminations. An attempt to remedy the situation by increasing the American rates would only encourage like increases abroad. The resistance which the proposal had encountered when offered fourteen years previously was not repeated. The Senate promptly and unanimously passed the bill which a committee under Smith's leadership prepared, and no significant opposition was encountered in the lower house.[2] Although the act of 1815 contemplated the extension of reciprocity by means of executive proclamation on receipt of proof of the non-existence of discriminating duties in the ports of a foreign nation, there was nothing to prevent the principle being applied by treaty. Both methods were employed frequently in the ensuing years. The bid for foreign nations to accept reciprocity arrangements was the more attractive because the war-time tariff law of 1812, which levied on foreign vessels a duty of one dollar and fifty cents per ton in addition to the regular charge of one dollar per ton for tonnage duty and light money, was continued in force until 1817.[3]

As the competition of Great Britain, aided by her effective duties on produce in American bottoms, had been foremost in the minds of Smith and his supporters in framing the act, so Great Britain was the first nation asked to accept a reciprocal arrangement. The American government on this occasion did not think proper to rewrite its commercial policy

[2] *Annals*, XXVIII, 263-266, 1210; *Statutes at Large of the U. S.*, III, 224.
[3] *Statutes at Large*, II, 768-769, III, 253, 344.

toward Great Britain. The commissioners were simply provided with the instructions issued to Monroe and Pinkney in 1806, the act of March 3, 1815, being added.[4] After the conclusion of the treaty of peace, December 24, 1814, Gallatin and Clay proceeded to London, where they began conferences with the British commissioners (Robinson, Goulburn, and William Adams). John Quincy Adams joined them there after the principal features of the negotiation had been determined. They found the British government reluctant to enter a commercial negotiation. Adams thought it agreed to do so only to avoid the discourtesy of a refusal.[5]

The treaty which was concluded July 3, 1815, except for an article relating to commerce with India, and a reservation of the rights of each country with regard to the regulation of colonial trade, merely provided for the regulation of the direct trade between the United States and the British possessions in Europe. The article regulating the trade with Great Britain proper was the best which had ever been offered the United States. All discriminating duties, including the extra lighthouse charges, were abolished. The article was so worded as to admit the American contention concerning the convoy duties, which had been heavier on shipments to America than to the Continent. Without using the customary form of the most-favored-nation clause, each nation guaranteed that the other in respect to all import and export duties on merchandise and to all prohibitions of imports should be placed on an equality with all other nations. With regard to shipping, each government agreed to place the vessels of the other on a footing of equality with its own, as far as duties and charges were concerned, except that equalization of duties on the cargo should apply only to articles of the growth, produce, or manufacture of the country of the vessel's flag.[6]

[4] Monroe to Adams, March 13, 1815, J. Q. Adams, *Writings*, V, 288; Gallatin to Monroe, Nov. 25, 1815, Gallatin, *Writings*, I, 680-682.

[5] Adams to Jonathan Russell, Oct. 10, 1815, Adams, *Writings*, V, 413-416; Gallatin to Madison, Sept. 4, 1815, Gallatin, *Writings*, I, 650.

[6] Miller, *Treaties*, II, 595-599. One slight inequality was still permitted. The British commissioners insisted on reserving the right to regulate or diminish

This treaty might be fitly called Gallatin's treaty, for he was almost entirely responsible for its conclusion. He was convinced of the importance of equalizing shipping duties by treaty, and of securing British recognition of the right to retaliate the regulations of the colonial trade. He also believed that without a treaty stipulation, the United States would soon be excluded from Indian ports. Clay supported him on the equalization of duties, but cared nothing about the India trade, of which he disapproved because it drained specie from the United States. Adams was altogether opposed to the treaty, and declared that he appended his signature only out of respect for Clay and Gallatin. He believed that the articles contained nothing in the way of a favor to the United States for which Great Britain's own interest did not furnish a sufficient guarantee, and that the American government sacrificed prestige in appearing eager for a treaty.[7]

The treaty of 1815 remained the legal basis of commercial relations between the United States and the British dominions in Europe throughout the period. It was never seriously endangered by the bitter fight with regard to the West India trade, nor by the other controversies between the two countries. Its tendencies favorable to the United States were bolstered by the Navigation Act of March 1, 1817, which, copying a provision of the British navigation laws, prohibited

---

the drawback on reëxport of American goods to a third country in American vessels. The reservation was made reciprocal.

[7] For the disagreement among the American commissioners, see Adams to Jonathan Russell, Oct. 10, 1815, and Dec. 14, 1815, Adams, *Writings*, V, 413-416, 441-442; Adams, *Memoirs*, III, 208-209, 210-212, 219, 225-226, 227-228, 243. In 1817, Adams was still skeptical as to whether or not the treaty deserved to be continued in force. Adams to Rush, Nov. 6, 1817, Adams, *Writings*, VI, 233-246. By 1818, however, the progress made by American shipping in driving the British from the direct trade had apparently reconciled him to the convention. This was after the new navigation law had destroyed the triangular intercourse, however. See his note of a conference with King, Nov. 25, 1818, *Memoirs*, IV, 181.

The other most important documents dealing with the negotiation are Gallatin to Madison, Sept. 4, 1815, Gallatin, *Writings*, I, 650; Gallatin to Monroe, Nov. 25, 1815, *ibid.*, 662-665; Gallatin to Clay, Jan. 4, 1816, *ibid.*, 680-682; Clay and Gallatin to the Secretary of State, May 18, 1815, and enclosures, *ASP, FR*, IV, 9-18.

entirely the importation into the United States of non-British produce in British vessels.[8] Previously, it had been admitted on the payment of the usual discriminating duties. The new legislation gave American vessels a pronounced advantage over their British competitors in the direct trade with Great Britain, since they were not obliged to select their cargoes with a view to the avoidance of the discriminating duty. By eliminating British competition, it may have also aided to some extent the direct trade in American ships with all those countries which produced goods for the American market, and thus helped to reduce the importance of Great Britain as an entrepôt for world trade with the United States. The full advantage of the regulations was not gained immediately because of the peculiar relationship of the direct trade to the British West India trade, which was monopolized by British shipping. The measures taken by the United States to protect itself against the consequences of this relationship will be discussed hereafter. The treaty of 1815 was renewed for ten years without important discussion in 1818. In 1827 it was agreed to continue it indefinitely.[9] At this time it was suggested by Gallatin, the American representative, that the limitation of freedom from discrimination to the produce only of Great Britain and the United States be given up. The British government was unwilling to adopt the principle in its full extent, and anything less was unacceptable to the United States.[10]

Prior to the passage of the reciprocity act, the government of the Netherlands proposed to Monroe the renewal of the old treaty of 1782, with the addition of an article, among others, abolishing all discriminating duties.[11] Monroe dis-

---

[8] *Statutes at Large of the U. S.*, III, 352. A proviso of this act stipulated that its provisions should apply to the navigation of such nations only as had adopted similar laws. As interpreted by the Treasury Department, it applied only to the navigation of Great Britain, and the Kingdom of Norway and Sweden. Mayo, *Synopsis of the Commercial and Revenue System*, 45-46.

[9] Miller, *Treaties*, II, 660, III, 315-317.

[10] Clay to Gallatin, Oct. 31, 1826, Feb. 24, 1827, Instructions to U. S. Ministers, XI; Gallatin to Clay, Dec. 31, 1826, Dispatches, Great Britain, XXXIII.

[11] For the background of this proposal, see Peter Hoekstra, *Thirty-seven Years of Holland-American Relations*, 111-112, 115-117; J. C. Westermann, *The Netherlands and the United States*, 109-140.

played no eagerness to accept the offer. To Eustis, the United States minister to the Netherlands, he explained his reasons for being cool with regard to the proffered treaty. The Netherlands could give no equivalent for abolition because her imports into the United States would bear no comparison with the great bulk of American exports to that kingdom; consequently there could be no motive in an arrangement except as part of a general system with the powers of Europe. He held that the equalization of duties was one of the inducements which the United States could offer for opening the colonies of European powers. "It seems, therefore, to be our interest," he wrote, "to reserve it in the first instance especially for that purpose, to be taken advantage of more particularly with Great Britain and France, whose system is a system of monopoly."[12]

Having been rebuffed with regard to the immediate negotiation of a treaty, the Netherlands government attempted to secure the benefit of the reciprocity act by executive proclamation. By a decree of May 27, the King granted to American vessels the same treatment accorded those of European nations. Monroe pointed out that this regulation did not meet the requirements of the American act because it did not guarantee to United States vessels the treatment of natives and because it applied only to the Dutch possessions in Europe. Ten Cate, the chargé d'affaires of the Netherlands, tried to interpret the decree to satisfy Monroe, but unsuccessfully.[13] Late in 1816, the two governments came to the conclusion that the best chance for an arrangement lay in the negotiation of a general treaty.[14]

For the negotiation, which it was decided to conduct in the Netherlands, Gallatin was sent from Paris to join the regular

[12] Changuion to Monroe, Feb. 24, 1815, Notes from Netherlands Legation, I; Monroe to Changuion, March 23, 1815, April 12, 1815, Notes to Foreign Legations, II; Monroe to William Eustis, May 9, 1815, Instructions, VII.

[13] Monroe to Lechleitner, Jan. 17, 1816, Notes to For. Leg., II, 120-121. Ten Cate to Monroe, Apr. 4, 1816, Sept. 16, 1816, Oct. 10, 1816, Jan. 10, 1817, Notes from Netherlands Leg., I. For a discussion of the Dutch commercial regulations after 1814, see Westermann, op. cit., 172-183.

[14] Eustis to Monroe, Oct. 18, 1816, Dispatches, Netherlands, V; Monroe to Eustis, Nov. 12, 1816, Instructions, VIII, 128.

minister, William Eustis. Their instructions, which were prepared by Rush, temporarily Secretary of State, did not require the commissioners to insist upon the extension of reciprocity to the colonies, although they were urged to secure that concession if possible. They were to use the recent convention with Great Britain as a model. These instructions confirmed the policy of consenting to the separation of colonial trade from European trade in making reciprocity arrangements. The reciprocity act of 1815 did not provide for such separation; hence the necessity for a treaty with the Netherlands.[15]

The conferences at The Hague, which Gallatin and Eustis entered upon with high hopes of success, in August 1817, ended a month later with the conferees disagreeing on three major points: colonial trade, equalization of duties, and neutral rights. The American envoys proposed the mutual abolition of alien duties on tonnage and merchandise, regardless of the origin of the latter, but insisted that the arrangement be applied to the Dutch colonies as well as to the Netherlands proper. The government of the Netherlands still adhered to mercantilistic doctrines, however, and its commissioners would agree to no greater privileges for American ships in the colonies than those of the most-favored-nation. Even for the latter concession they demanded an equivalent, such as the reduction of the American duties on gin and cheese. Gallatin and Eustis then refused to agree to the removal of discriminating duties on any produce in Dutch vessels except that of the Netherlands in Europe. Since a large part of Dutch commerce consisted in exporting goods originating in Germany and Switzerland, equalization on native produce only would have been of little value, and the offer was declined. The Dutch government also refused to agree to the renewal of those articles of the treaty of 1782 which provided that a neutral flag should neutralize the cargo.[16]

[15] Ten Cate to the Secretary of State, Oct. 28, 1817 and marginal notes by Rush and Monroe, Notes from Netherlands Leg., I; Rush to Gallatin and Eustis, April 22, 1817, Instructions, VIII, 139.

[16] Eustis and Gallatin to Adams, Sept. 22, 1817, with enclosed protocols of the conferences, particularly of the second, third, fourth, and sixth, and the

THE FIRST EXTENSION OF THE RECIPROCITY PRINCIPLE

Immediately after the failure of the negotiation, the Netherlands government reimposed its foreign tonnage duty on American vessels, which had been repealed preparatory to the discussions.[17] The United States government, although much annoyed at the failure of the proposed treaty,[18] felt that American shipping stood to lose rather than gain by the continuance of the duties, and decided to yield the ground taken by the commissioners. In fact, Crawford proposed to offer complete reciprocity without any limitations whatever to all countries which would reciprocate it, and drafted a bill for the purpose.[19] He gave up the idea, however, and agreed to the plan set forth by Adams in a report submitted to Congress March 19, 1818. In this report Adams pointed out that the United States could not join the Dutch in equalization of duties on merchandise regardless of origin without breaking down the system with regard to other nations. On the other hand,

. . . the revocation of the discriminating duties upon merchandise imported in vessels of the Netherlands would be of little avail if limited to articles the produce or manufacture of that country, the principal part of whose exportations consists of the produce or manufacture of others.

Without offering a specific solution of the problem of the discriminating duties on merchandise, he recommended the enactment of a law repealing the tonnage duties on Dutch vessels.[20]

---

notes of Eustis and Gallatin to the Dutch plenipotentiaries, Sept. 8 and Sept. 9, 1817; Goldberg and Van der Kemp to Eustis and Gallatin, Sept. 13, 1817; Dispatches, Netherlands, V; Gallatin and Eustis to the Dutch Commissioners, Sept. 18, 1817; Gallatin and Eustis to J. Q. Adams, Sept. 22, 1817, Gallatin to Eustis, Oct. 9, 1817, Gallatin, *Writings*, II, 41-46, 47-51; Westermann, 271-292.

[17] Ten Cate to Adams, Feb. 13, 1818, Notes from Netherlands Leg., I; Eustis to Adams, March 7, 1818, Dispatches, Netherlands, V.

[18] Gallatin to Adams, July 31, 1818, Dispatches, France, XVII; Adams to A. H. Everett, Aug. 10, 1818, and July 25, 1821, Adams, *Writings*, VI, 415-425, VII, 126-127.

[19] Adams, *Memoirs*, IV, 61-62.

[20] *ASP, FR*, IV, 172-173.

The first extension of the reciprocity policy was then evolved in Congress. An act approved April 20, 1818, provided for the repeal of the extra tonnage duty on Dutch vessels, and then, going further, repealed the discriminating duty on merchandise in Dutch vessels in so far as it applied to

... the produce or manufactures of the territories in Europe, of the King of the Netherlands, and such produce and manufactures as can only be or most usually are first shipped from a port or place in the kingdom aforesaid.[21]

The Netherlands government accepted the new act, and again repealed its discriminating duties.[22]

Reciprocity was found to be highly favorable to American shipping; but the Dutch marine failed to regain its former high place in the world of navigation. Statistics from Dutch sources showed that 234 American vessels from the United States entered Dutch ports in 1823-1824 as compared with two under the Dutch flag; and that 162 Americans cleared for the United States and only seventeen Dutch. The government of the Netherlands in 1822 took measures to give encouragement to their weak shipping interest. A law was passed providing for the restoration of ten per cent of the duties payable upon merchandise, when import or export was made in Dutch ships. Certain further encouragements were offered on the carriage of specific articles.[23]

The American chargé d'affaires, A. H. Everett, immediately protested against the impositions as being palpable violations of the reciprocity arrangement of 1818.[24] The minister for foreign affairs gave the amazing explanation that the new regulations were not intended to be discriminatory, but merely

---

[21] *Statutes at Large of the U. S.*, III, 464. For the version of Ten Cate, the minister of the Netherlands, of his lobbying activities in support of this bill, see Hoekstra, *Holland-American Relations*, 141-142; also Westermann, 313.

[22] Quabeck to Adams, Nov. 3, 1818, Notes from the Netherlands Leg., I; Gallatin to Adams, July 31, 1818, with enclosed memorandum from Appleton, Dispatches, France, XVIII.

[23] Everett to Adams, March 17, 1823, *ASP, FR*, V, 590-591.

[24] Everett to Nagell, March 7, Nov. 11, 1823, *ASP, FR*, V, 591, 594-595.

an encouragement to shipbuilding.[25] Adams strongly supported his agent, asserting that the United States could make
no distinction between discriminating duties and bounties or
drawbacks on shipbuilding.[26] The controversy continued for
several years, the United States holding out the threat of
withdrawing the concession made to Dutch vessels.[27]

In January 1824, an act of Congress was approved, which
continued the reciprocity policy, and extended the principle
of the act of 1818 to Prussia, the Hanseatic cities of Hamburg and Bremen, Sardinia, Russia, and the Dukedom of
Oldenburg, as well as to the Netherlands. The President was
authorized to revoke the privilege with regard to any nation
which withdrew the equivalent. This threat failed to move
the Dutch government.[28] In December 1825 Secretary Clay
took the matter into his own hands, and firmly demanded
of Chevalier Huygens, the Dutch minister at Washington,
an official statement of the intentions of his government,
preparatory to invoking the act authorizing the President to
reimpose the extra duties.[29]

The Dutch government, though very weak in technical
arguments to sustain the policy followed, felt the real strength
in its position, and boldly declared its intention to add further
discrimination should the United States alter the existing situation. The United States government found itself in a position where retaliation promised little help. If the old duties
were renewed, they would be collected on only a few Dutch
ships. An increase of duty in the Netherlands would apply
to scores of American vessels. Adams, now President, decided
to follow the prudent course. While Clay continued to hold
the Dutch government responsible for a clear violation of the
arrangement, Adams referred the whole subject without

[25] Nagell to Everett, May 27, 1823, *ASP, FR*, V, 593.
[26] Instructions, X, 95.
[27] Everett to Adams, Nov. 10, 1823, with enclosure, *ASP, FR*, V, 590-596;
Everett to Baron de Nagell, Nov. 5, 1823, Dispatches, Netherlands, VII.
[28] *Statutes at Large of the U. S.*, IV, 2-3; *ASP, FR*, V, 597-598.
[29] Clay to Chevalier Huygens, Dec. 10, 1825, Notes to For. Leg., III, 240-
241, Dec. 24, 1825, 246-247; Huygens to Clay, Dec. 12, 1825, Notes from
Netherlands Leg., I.

recommendation to Congress.[30] The Adams administration expired without any action having been taken.

The United States found in the kingdom of Sweden and Norway a government disposed to go even farther than itself in liberalizing its commercial system, though progress was slow at first. Commercial relations between the two countries were important because the United States was the principal foreign market for Swedish iron. It was to the interest of American shipping to obtain the carriage of that heavy commodity. At the opening of the era of peace, however, the Swedish system threatened to make intercourse with the United States next to impossible. Import and export duties and port charges were in most cases from forty to sixty per cent higher on American vessels and their cargoes than on those of Norway and Sweden. In addition, a navigation act similar to that of Great Britain offered serious impediments to trade.[31] Supported by the Crown Prince, Bernadotte, liberal ideas prevailed more and more in the following years, however.

As in the case of the Netherlands, Monroe delayed making a decision with regard to a negotiation on account, as he said, of doubt as to the reaction of Europe in general to the reciprocity policy and the necessity of acting with caution. At length in May 1816, he authorized Russell to proceed in negotiating a treaty in Sweden.[32] The principal purpose of the two governments in the negotiation was to remove the discriminating duties in the direct trade, and as the policy of each in regard thereto was known, Russell encountered no diffi-

[30] Hughes to Clay, July 11, 1826, April 15, 1827, Dispatches, Netherlands, VIII; Adams, *Memoirs*, VII, 161; Clay to Huygens, Oct. 25, 1826, Notes to Foreign Leg., III, 299-304; Huygens to Clay, Nov. 11, 1826, Notes from Netherlands Leg., I; Clay to Hughes, Dec. 12, 1826, Instructions, XI, 219; Hughes to Clay, Oct. 21, Nov. 28, 1827, Dispatches, Netherlands, VIII; *ASP, FR*, V, 590-598, VI, 374-382; Richardson, II, 352-353.

[31] Jonathan Russell to Monroe, July 15, 1815, Dispatches, Sweden, I.

[32] Russell to Monroe, April 29, 1816, Dispatches, Sweden, I; Monroe to Jonathan Russell, May 20, 1816, Instructions, VIII, 57; Kantzou to Monroe, July 13, 1816, Notes from Swedish Leg., I; Monroe to Kantzou, July 23, 1816, Notes to For. Leg., II, 156-157.

culty on that score. However, the Swedish government wished to go further than mere reciprocity in the direct trade, though unwilling at this time to remove all restrictions based upon the origin of goods. American vessels had had since 1798, by Swedish law, the privilege of importing West India goods into Gothenburg with only a ten per cent increase upon the duties paid by Swedish vessels. The Swedish government proposed, and Russell agreed to articles providing that American vessels continue to be admitted to Swedish ports on those terms, and that in return the United States agree to admit Swedish vessels with all products of "countries surrounding the Baltic Sea or bordering thereon," with only the additional charge of ten per cent.[33] When the treaty came up for ratification, the Senate refused to approve the articles mentioned, though ratifying the remainder. American sentiment was distinctly opposed to making compromises with countries having navigation laws; and Congress, a few weeks later, passed the navigation act of 1817, which forbade the importation in Swedish vessels of any except Swedish produce. The Swedish government offered no objection to ratifying the treaty with the objectionable provisions deleted.[34]

FRANCO-AMERICAN DISPUTES AND THE TREATY OF 1822

The restored Bourbon government in France had no sooner become firmly settled than it began to adopt measures to rebuild the French shipping industry, which had been nearly annihilated during the wars. The customs tariffs of 1816 and 1817 established two sets of duties, the lower for French ships, the higher for foreign.[35] The situation was rendered

[33] Russell to Monroe, April 29, Aug. 13, Sept. 5, 1816, Dispatches, Sweden, I.

[34] *Senate Exec. Jour.*, III, 65; Rush to Kantzou, March 11, 1817, Instructions, VIII; Russell to Adams, Jan. 26, 1818, Dispatches, Sweden, I; R. King to C. Gore, Jan. 30, 1817, King, *Corresp.*, VI, 48-49; Miller, *Treaties*, II, 601-616.

[35] *ASP, C&N*, II, 257-280. It is to be noted also that the French system of discrimination was quite different from the American. In the United States there was collected a small tonnage duty or duty based upon the capacity of the ship, and in addition a surcharge upon the sum total of the duties accrued upon the cargo. The French laws, however, charged two distinct and separate rates of impost on goods in foreign and in native vessels.

more unfavorable, as far as American shipping was concerned, by special charges collected by a class of officials known as ship brokers (*courtiers interprètes conducteurs de navires*), who were granted by law the monopoly of dealing between ships' officers and the customs officials, and by the practice of the government in enforcing stringent quarantine regulations on all United States vessels whenever epidemic disease might prevail in any part of the country. The regulations caused little difficulty to American navigation for several years because there were very few French vessels at sea. By 1819, however, the French merchant marine had recuperated to such an extent that Americans began to find themselves forced out of competition.

Gallatin was reminded by Monroe, at the beginning of his mission as minister to France in 1816, of the unfavorable character of the regulations, and was instructed to attempt to induce the French government to adopt the principle of the American reciprocity act both as to the European dominions and the colonies. Another instruction a month later emphasized the necessity of securing reciprocity in the colonies, and expressed the determination not to allow French shipping to monopolize the colonial trade.[36]

The principal objective of Gallatin's mission was to secure indemnification for the injuries inflicted on American commerce by Napoleon. Since American navigation in 1816 was finding the discriminations no very serious obstacle, he concluded that it would be wisest to drop the subjects of discriminating duties and the colonial trade until he had obtained a decision on the question of indemnity. In this way, he could prevent any attempt by the French government to balance commercial concessions against claims for damages.[37] He made

[36] Monroe to Gallatin, April 15, May 21, 1816, *Instructions*, VIII.

[37] Gallatin to Monroe, Sept. 12, 1816, July 12, 1817, Gallatin, *Writings*, II, 8, 40. Gallatin first introduced the subject of the removal of the discriminating duties in July, 1817. Richelieu, the foreign minister, was friendly, but felt that the organized French commercial interest was too much opposed to the proposition. He said that France did not as yet have a commercial treaty with any nation and that it might be inconvenient to treat with the U. S. alone,

representations against the quarantine regulations and the charges of the ship brokers, however. The quarantine restrictions were usually removed on the minister's representations, but not before considerable loss and inconvenience had been suffered by individuals.[38] The charges of the ship brokers, were, in effect, an additional discriminating duty, since they were larger on foreign than on French vessels. In October 1818, Gallatin obtained an order that American consuls might act as interpreters or brokers for American captains. A succeeding minister of the interior reversed the decision, however, and the brokers' fees remained, in the estimation of the American government, an abuse.[39]

The French government was itself interested in other phases of commercial relations. In January 1817, Hyde de Neuville, the minister at Washington, complained of the treatment of French wines in the tariff of 1816. He showed that the French light wines paid about eighty per cent on first cost, which was the same as was collected on the more spirituous Madeira. He repeated the complaint in April 1818 and again early in 1819. His arguments received the support of the Administration, and an Act of Congress of March 3, 1819, reduced the rates on the cheapest wines, which included most of the French wines, to fifteen cents per gallon.[40] In December 1817, Neuville demanded favored treatment for French vessels in the ports of Louisiana, contending that under the eighth article of the treaty of 1803, which stipulated perpetual most-favored-nation treatment for French vessels in Louisiana ports, those vessels were entitled to be excused

---

and that mutual legislation might be preferable to a treaty. Gallatin to Monroe, July 11, 1817, Gallatin, *Writings*, II, 38-39. Gallatin to Marquis of Dessolle, Oct. 25, 1819, *ASP, FR*, V, 33-34.

[38] Gallatin to Dessolle, May 17, 1819, Gallatin to the Secretary of State, May 22, 1819, *ASP, FR*, V, 31-32.

[39] Gallatin to the Secretary of State, May 21, 1819, *ASP, FR*, V, 24-25, and additional correspondence, *ibid.*, 25-30.

[40] Neuville to Secretary of State, Jan. 3, 1817, April 17, 1818, Nov. 21, 1818, Feb. 6, 1819, Notes from French Leg., IV, VI; *Statutes at Large of the U. S.*, III, 515; Neuville to Richelieu, Feb. 1, 1817, March 17, 1819, AAE, CP, EU, LXXIII, 76.

from the extra tonnage and merchandise duties, since British vessels were now excused from them in accordance with the convention of 1815. The minister also proposed a treaty which would make it easier for French shipmasters to apprehend deserting seamen in the United States.[41]

With serious dissatisfaction on both sides with the existing situation, there was ample reason for an attempt at a conventional arrangement. Gallatin was designated to carry on the negotiation in France, Monroe's entire cabinet being of the opinion that none could excel him as negotiator of commercial treaties.[42] He proposed to the French government in October 1819 the adoption of the American reciprocity policy, asserting that the United States would be obliged to retaliate if relief were not given from unjust discrimination. The Marquis of Dessolle, the minister for foreign affairs, admitted that the American reciprocity system was quite just, but declared that the organized merchants of France would prevent any great alterations in the existing policy, since they were convinced that equality of treatment would give the United States a decided superiority. He agreed, however, that the rates were too high, and proposed a reduction of one-third. Gallatin responded that the reduction would be entirely insufficient.[43]

Dessolle's attitude convinced the American envoy that no satisfactory counter-proposition would be offered, and he immediately outlined to Adams a proper mode of reprisal. He regretted that it was impracticable at the time to try to secure an amendment to the Constitution permitting the levy of a duty on goods exported from the United States in foreign ships. If such a duty were legal, it would be possible to penalize the competing French vessel the exact amount of the penalty inflicted on the American ship in France. The retaliation would be so complete and just that it would be

---

[41] Neuville to the Secretary of State, Dec. 15, 1817, June 16, 1818, *ASP, FR*, V, 152-153; Adams to Neuville, Dec. 23, 1817, *op. cit.*, V, 152-153; Adams, *Memoirs*, IV, 58-59; Neuville to Adams, Feb. 6, 1819, Notes from French Leg., VI; Adams to Neuville, March 31, 1819, Adams, *Writings*, VI, 539.

[42] Adams, *Memoirs*, IV, 505.

[43] Gallatin to the Marquis of Dessolle, Oct. 25, 1819, *ASP, FR*, V, 33-34; Gallatin to Adams, Dec. 9, 1819, *op. cit.*, V, 35.

difficult to attack it effectively. In the existing circumstances, the discrimination in favor of French vessels exceeded the freight earned on a cargo carried to France, and, consequently, the French marine was rapidly engrossing the trade between the two countries. Since a constitutional amendment allowing an export duty could not be obtained in time, he recommended a special tonnage duty on French vessels entering American ports equal to the average of the duties collected per ton on American produce imported into France in American vessels. He calculated that these duties were equivalent to $12.50 per register ton on a cargo of cotton, and $17 per ton on a cargo of tobacco. Vigorous retaliation, he felt, would force the French government to a serious negotiation. Gallatin's arguments were effectively supported by American merchants.[44]

In response to Gallatin's repeated recommendations of retaliation, Congress, apparently without opposition, passed an act, approved May 15, 1820, levying $18 per ton on French ships, beginning July 1, 1820.[45] This measure had an immediate and powerful effect on the negotiation, adverse at first, but probably favoring a successful outcome in the end. Gallatin added his criticism of the law to that of the French officials. He was strongly in favor of a high rate, but felt that $12 or $13 per ton would have been sufficient to show the determination of the United States without giving an excuse for a further advance in France. French officials were angered on three points: the unnecessary amount of the duty; the shortness of notice before the provisions were to become effective; and the publication of some of Gallatin's frank dispatches. While the government was now disposed to take

[44] Gallatin to Adams, Oct. 25, 1819, *ASP, FR,* V, 32-33; Memorial of the New York Chamber of Commerce, presented to the House of Representatives, Dec. 27, 1819, *ASP, C&N,* II, 403-405; Memorial of Twenty-four Ship Captains of New Orleans, presented to the House of Representatives Jan. 4, 1820, *ibid.,* 411-413. Gallatin repeated his arguments for a constitutional amendment empowering Congress to levy an export duty in his dispatch of Sept. 22, 1820, Gallatin, *Writings,* II, 167-173; cf. discussion of the constitutional prohibition of export duties, *ante,* pp. 100, 150-151.

[45] Gallatin to Secretary of State, Jan. 15, 1820, *ASP, FR,* V, 35; Gallatin to Adams, April 27, 1820, Gallatin, *Works,* II, 140; *Statutes at Large of the U. S.,* III, 605; *Annals,* XXXVI, 2245-2246.

the matter somewhat more seriously, it insisted that another retaliation would be necessary in order to satisfy French pride. It therefore enacted a law levying an additional tonnage duty of 90 francs per ton on American vessels, and provided for a ten per cent premium on cotton when imported from any part of America except the United States. The latter was understood to be an attempt to route United States cotton via the West Indies, thus evading American regulations. It was intimated also that sectionalism in the United States was being depended upon to help win the battle for France, since it was known that the southern planters were prone to attack anything likely to interfere with the markets for cotton and tobacco. Readiness was expressed by both Neuville and Pasquier, the latter now foreign minister, to negotiate on the basis of reciprocity—a reciprocity which would leave half the carriage between France and the United States in French bottoms.[46]

Since the dispute was endangering cordial relations between the two countries, Monroe and his cabinet gave careful consideration to the policy to be followed, and to the question of whether or not it was desirable to make any compromise with the French "reciprocity" principle that taxes should be applied until each country should possess half the trade. Gallatin, always conciliatory, had expressed the opinion that the principle might be accepted, provided the duties were made low enough, stating that he thought American vessels could pay as much as $2.30 per ton and still compete. Crawford was sympathetic toward that point of view, as was the President himself, at first. Adams led the fight for the preservation of the original reciprocity plan.

But, I observed, I did not see how we could possibly assent to the principle (he wrote in his diary). We had offered to all the world entire reciprocity. Great Britain and several other nations had ac-

[46] Adams, *Memoirs*, May 17, 1820, V, 123-124; Gallatin to Adams, July 5, July 11, July 31, Aug. 2, 1820, Gallatin, *Writings*, II, 148-150, 150-151, 153-164, 164-165; Adams to Gallatin, Sept. 13, 1820, Adams, *Writings*, VII, 66. The new French tonnage law of July 26, 1820, is in *Le Moniteur Universel*, July 29, 1820.

cepted the proposal. France now called upon us to agree to be clogged, in order to enable her people to hold competition with us. If we should assent, our own people would first be dissatisfied, and next, all the nations with which we have stood on terms of reciprocity. We should have clamor and discontent from all quarters.

Adams won for the moment, and at a cabinet meeting on November 1, 1820, it was unanimously decided that the principle proposed by France could not be accepted.[47]

The negotiation in France was terminated in the fall of 1820, when the foreign minister announced that he held the consideration of the eighth article of the Louisiana treaty inseparable from a discussion of discriminating duties. Gallatin had no instructions on this point. In fact, he had suggested to Adams as early as August 2, that the negotiation might well be transferred to the United States. Adams, of course, was unwilling to admit the Louisiana question into discussion. He had dealt with that subject fully when it had been proposed by Neuville in 1817. He held that the conditional clause was implied, even when not specifically expressed, in every statement of the most-favored-nation principle. Great Britain had purchased the right for her vessels to enter Louisiana without paying discriminating duties, by admitting American vessels into British ports without discrimination. France had no right to similar treatment without giving the equivalent. Moreover, the United States government was forbidden by the Constitution to make a special arrangement for Louisiana, since commercial regulations must be uniform throughout the union.[48]

The failure to reach a settlement in Paris induced the French government to transfer the negotiation to the United States. Neuville, who had returned to France and been designated ambassador to Brazil, was ordered back to Wash-

[47] Gallatin to Adams, Sept. 19, 1820, Dispatches, France, XX; Gallatin to Adams, Sept. 22, 1820, Gallatin, *Writings*, II, 167-173; Crawford to Gallatin, Gallatin, *Writings*, II, 143-146; Adams, *Memoirs*, V, 177-179, 195-287.

[48] Gallatin to Adams, Sept. 19, 1820, Dispatches, France, XX; Adams to Neuville, Dec. 23, 1817, *ASP, FR*, V, 152-153; Adams, *Memoirs*, IV, 58-59; Adams to Gallatin, Oct. 4, 1820, Adams, *Writings*, VII, 75-81.

ington for the purpose of concluding the commercial treaty.[49] As a conciliatory measure, Monroe recommended to Congress, in November 1820, that the new tonnage duties be refunded on those French vessels which had not had sufficient notice of the passage of the law, and the recommendation was carried into effect by an act of March 3, 1821.[50] The negotiation, which was formally opened at Washington, February 19, 1821, falls into two periods. The first extended through the spring and summer of 1821, and ended in disagreement in August of the same year. The second stage began early in the following year and terminated with the signature of a commercial treaty in June 1822.

Neuville opened the discussion by proposing the acceptance of the French interpretation of the eighth article of the Louisiana Purchase convention, which would give French vessels in Louisiana ports the same privileges as the British held under the treaty of 1815. The subject remained to vex the negotiation throughout its course.[51] Adams vigorously repeated and amplified the arguments he had used previously, claiming that Neuville's interpretation would make it impossible for the United States to have commercial treaties with other nations, and asserted that the United States could not grant as a gratuitous favor to France that which had been conceded to other nations for a valuable consideration.[52]

The French envoy then proposed a general commercial treaty including the following subjects: a reduction of the American duties on French wines; a reduction of the duty

[49] Gallatin to Adams, Oct. 19, 1820, Gallatin, *Writings*, II, 173.

[50] Richardson, *Messages and Papers*, II, 645-646; *Statutes at Large of the U. S.*, III, 642. The French government passed a similar law. Neuville to Adams, July 21, 1821, Notes from French Leg., VIII.

[51] Neuville to Adams, Feb. 23, May 15, June 30, Aug. 15, 1821, *ASP, FR*, V, 162-163, 171-177, 186-192, 193-194. The draft of Pasquier's instructions to Neuville, dated Oct. 18, 1820 are in AAE, CP, EU, LXXVII, 243-255. A lengthy analysis of the French claim in regard to the Louisiana treaty by the Comte d'Hauterive is *ibid.*, 238.

[52] Adams to Neuville, March 29, 1821, *ASP, FR*, V, 163-165. The refutation of Neuville's arguments was made again at great length in Adams to Neuville, June 15, 1821, *ibid.*, 180-184.

on French silks, or an increase on those from India and China; a reduction of the regular American discriminating duties; a reduction of the French discriminating duties on cotton, potash, rice, and tobacco from the United States; a consular convention on the basis of the previous one of 1788; and a settlement of the special ($18 and 90 franc) tonnage duties according to the wishes of the United States.[53] In response, Adams agreed to a reduction on French wines to ten cents a gallon in casks and twenty cents in bottles; an increase of duties on silks from beyond the Cape of Good Hope to thirty per cent ad valorem; and a consular convention on the basis of that of 1788,[54] if certain necessary changes could be agreed upon, otherwise an article providing for the mutual restoration of deserting seamen. In return for these concessions, however, he demanded abolition of the French government's monopoly of the purchase, manufacture, and sale of tobacco, and the removal of all discriminating duties on tonnage and merchandise, as in the British treaty of 1815.[55]

The propositions of the Secretary of State were so unreasonable from the French point of view that Neuville dropped the idea of a general commercial treaty and thenceforth the discussion was centered on the discriminating duties. Numerous projects and counterprojects were exchanged, but none of Neuville's offers went beyond a reduction of fifty per cent in the French discriminating duties on merchandise. This concession was made contingent upon a prior settlement in favor of France of the Louisiana controversy, and a prior agreement to make reparation for the seizure, in Spanish

[53] Neuville to Adams, undated memorandum, *ASP, FR,* V, 166.

[54] The consular convention concluded by Jefferson in Paris in 1788, after the rejection by Congress of an earlier one negotiated by Franklin, was the first treaty with a foreign nation to be ratified by the government under the Constitution. It was abrogated in 1798, together with the other French treaties. It was held objectionable by the American government because it was believed to grant too extensive privileges to French consuls, especially in allowing them to exercise jurisdiction in lawsuits involving French nationals residing in the United States. Bemis, *American Secretaries of State,* I, 252-259; Miller, *Treaties,* II, 228-244.

[55] Adams to Neuville, April 18, 1821, *op. cit.,* V, 167.

jurisdiction, of the French ship *Apollon*, by American customs officers.[56] The *Apollon* had anchored on the Florida side of the St. Marys River, apparently with the intent to evade the high tonnage duties on French vessels by carrying on trade in Georgia without making entry at an American port. The seizure, interpreted by Neuville as an insult to the French flag, became a very disturbing factor in the negotiation. To this case was added in a short time that of another French vessel, the *Jeune Eugénie*, seized on the African coast by Commodore Stockton, on the ground of being engaged in the slave trade.[57]

Adams continued to oppose a "reciprocity of advantages" calculated to so handicap American navigation that the French could keep pace with it. His furthest step to meet Neuville's demands was an offer to agree to a mutual discriminating duty of one and one-half per cent on the value of the cargo or a duty of $1.50 per ton on merchandise. He preferred the ad valorem duty, since American exports to France were more nearly equal to imports from France in value than they were in weight or bulk. He gave little attention to the demand for reparation for the seizure of the French vessels or to the matter of the interpretation of the Louisiana treaty. Obviously a deadlock had been reached, and the negotiation was suspended while Neuville awaited new instructions.[58]

Adams had shown an extremely unconciliatory spirit throughout the negotiation. In cabinet meetings he opposed concession on every point proposed by Neuville. It was only through the influence of the other members of the cabinet that he agreed to discuss reduction of duties on French articles, and a new consular convention on the basis of the old. At

[56] Neuville to Adams, April 21, 28, July 3, Aug. 15, 1821, *ASP, FR*, V, 167, 168-169, 186-192, 193-194; Adams to Neuville, April 26, May 11, June 27, Aug. 13, 1821, *ibid.*, 168, 169-170, 184-186, 192-193.

[57] Roth to Pasquier, Oct. 26, Dec. 30, 1820, Jan. 28, 1821, AAE, CP, EU, LXXVII, 259-266, 290-291, LXXVIII, 8-10; Neuville to Pasquier, April 14, May 31, Aug. 22, 1821, *ibid.*, 78-82, 129-133, 151-154.

[58] Adams to Neuville, May 11, June 27, Aug. 13, Aug. 20, 1821, *ASP, FR*, V, 169-170, 184-186, 192-193, 194. Neuville to Pasquier, April 22, Aug. 24, 1821, AAE, CP, EU, LXXVIII, 83-87, 155-162. Adams' answer on the subject of the *Apollon* is in *Writings*, VII, 137-160.

first his colleagues supported him in his refusal to depart from the strict reciprocity plan, although Crawford was critical. Then Gallatin reported his opinion that the French government now desired only an article that would give a semblance of acceptance of the "reciprocity of advantages" principle—a mere face-saving formula. Monroe, in spite of Adams' protests, then ordered him to experiment with an offer in accordance with Neuville's plan, with the object in view of determining how high a handicap for American navigation would be demanded.[59] This accounts for Adams' proposal of one and a half per cent ad valorem or one dollar and fifty cents per ton additional duty.

With the suspension of the negotiation in August, both countries were free to reëxamine the situation. It appeared that, as a result of their war of discriminating duties, over three-fourths of the carrying trade between France and the United States was now in the hands of Great Britain and other competitors.[60] Obviously neither was pleased with the result. In Paris, Gallatin labored to remove animosities and to influence the new instructions being prepared for Neuville. He continued to urge his government to compromise on the matter, asserting that if the French duties were reduced to one-fourth the existing rate, United States vessels could gain over half the carriage.[61]

When the negotiation was resumed early in 1822, the influence of Gallatin was evident in the new attitude of each party. New instructions authorized the French envoy to accept a rate of duty as low as twenty francs per ton and to postpone the Louisiana question to a later negotiation.[62] Neuville immediately agreed to drop all the extraneous questions which had hindered the work previously, and confine himself strictly to the commercial problem. He then

[59] Adams, *Memoirs*, V, 295, 342-345, 348-350, 353-354; Gallatin to Adams, March 29, 1821, Gallatin, *Writings*, II, 179-180.
[60] Gallatin to Adams, Jan. 30, 1822, Dispatches, France, XX.
[61] Gallatin to Adams, Sept. 26, 1821, *Writings*, II, 199-203; Oct. 23, 1821, *ibid.*, II, 206-208; Nov. 13, 1821, *ibid.*, 212-215.
[62] Drafts of the instructions dated Oct. 9 and Dec. 13, 1821 are in AAE, CP, EU, LXXIX, 190-195, 262-268.

offered to agree to a treaty which would provide for the reduction of the French discriminating duties to one-fourth
their existing amount, and for subsequent annual reductions
until all discrimination had disappeared. This proposition in
hand, the American cabinet had only to decide whether it
would agree to compromise or not. Adams continued to re-
affirm the desirability of adhering firmly to strict reciprocity.
Monroe, however, with Crawford strongly supporting him,
determined that a tax as high as four dollars per ton should
be accepted. This decision in reality decided the fate of the
negotiation. All that remained was for Adams and Neuville
to work out the technical details.[63] In the meantime, the last
obstacle to a treaty was removed by the federal courts, which
gave decisions satisfactory to France in the cases of the *Apollon* and the *Jeune Eugénie*.[64]

The treaty, concluded on June 24, 1822, dealt with only
two subjects: discriminating duties and return of deserting
seamen. It provided that an additional duty of twenty francs
per ton of merchandise in American ships might be collected
in France for two years, the amount thereafter to be reduced
by one-fourth annually until the duty disappeared or until
one or other party should denounce the treaty. Similarly,
the United States might levy a duty of not exceeding three
dollars and seventy-five cents per ton on merchandise from
France imported into American ports in French vessels. All
other charges on shipping, such as tonnage, lighthouse and
pilotage charges, were limited to ninety-four cents per ton
in the United States and five francs in France. In response
to Neuville's demand that something be done to stop
French sailors from deserting their ships to take advantage

[63] Adams to Neuville, Jan. 31, 1822, Notes to For. Leg., III; Neuville to
Adams, April 5, 1822, *ASP, FR*, V, 204-205; Adams, *Memoirs*, V, 487, 511,
529-533, 541-543; VI, 18, 22; Adams to Neuville, April 9, 1822, and subsequent exchanges, *ASP, FR*, V, 205-206, 207-212; Crawford to Gallatin,
May 12, 1822, Gallatin, *Writings*, II, 241-242; Neuville to Montmorency,
April 11, May 8, June 6, June 19, 1822, AAE, CP, EU, LXXIX, 120-123,
140-141, 144-145.
[64] Neuville to Montmorency, April 20, June 2, June 24, 1822, *ibid.*, 113-114,
188-189, 200.

of opportunities for more lucrative employment in America, its was stipulated that the consuls of the two countries should have authority to arrest such deserters, and to call upon the local civil officers for assistance in doing so. Two separate articles were appended. The first, providing for the refund of all the duties collected under the eighteen dollar and the ninety franc tonnage laws, was ratified by both parties. The second separate article, which stipulated that the extra duties authorized by the treaty should be payable only on the excess of imports over exports in the same vessel, was not ratified by the French government.[65]

With the commercial negotiation out of the way, Gallatin again took up in Paris the claims for Napoleon's spoliations. He was now confronted with the demand that the discussion of the construction of the eighth article of the Louisiana treaty should be combined with the claims negotiation. He defended the American point of view at least as ably as Adams had. He advised Adams that it would be better to allow the claims to wait rather than to entangle the two questions.[66] The American government offered to discuss the Louisiana matter before the claims negotiation, or to submit it to arbitration; but the French ministry continued to insist that claims could not be considered unless the subject of discriminating duties in the ports of Louisiana should be dealt with at the same time.[67] Consequently neither subject was settled during the period.

The treaty of 1822 proved to be a not very damaging deviation from the policy of strict reciprocity. American ship-

[65] Miller, *Treaties*, III, 77-90; Adams to Gallatin, Feb. 12, 1823, June 27, 1822, Instructions, IX; *Senate Executive Jour.*, III, 329-330; *Statutes at Large of the U. S.*, III, 747-748; Sheldon to Adams, June 28, 1823, Dispatches, France, XXII.

[66] Gallatin to Chateaubriand, Feb. 27, 1823, *ASP, FR*, V, 313-314; Gallatin to Adams, Feb. 27, 1823, Gallatin, *Writings*, II, 265-266.

[67] Adams to Menou, Aug. 12, 1823, Notes to For. Leg., III; Adams to Sheldon, Aug. 13, 1823, *ASP, FR*, V, 477; Adams to Brown, Dec. 23, 1823, Instructions, X; Chateaubriand to Brown, May 7, 1824, *ASP, FR*, V, 481; Brown to Adams, May 11, Dispatches, France, XXII; Adams to Brown, Aug. 14, 1824, Instructions, X, 205-206; Brown to Clay, Nov. 28, 1825, Dispatches, France, XXII; Brown to Clay, Sept. 8, 1827, Dec. 28, 1827, *ibid.*, XXIII.

ping soon gained and kept the upper hand. The two-year trial period expired in 1824, with France expressing a willingness to continue the experiment. The annual reductions were regularly made, until the extra duties were terminated in 1827, leaving only the ninety-four cent and five franc tonnage duties on the ships of the two nations in each other's ports. The United States government, apparently including Adams, was highly satisfied. The French government was not entirely pleased, however.[68] In 1827, the year of the removal of the final instalment of the extra duties, Mareuil, then minister at Washington, proposed a new negotiation, the purpose of which would be to increase the consumption of French wines, brandies, and silks by means of a reduction of customs duties on those articles. He suggested that, as compensation in addition to the continuance of the provisions of the treaty of 1822, France would be willing to reduce the duty on short staple cottons. Clay cordially expressed a readiness to enter such a negotiation. He was rather concerned, thinking Mareuil's proposal was a preliminary to the denunciation of the treaty. James Brown, who had succeeded Gallatin, gathered from interviews with the foreign minister that the treaty was in no immediate danger, although additional compensation would soon be demanded.[69] In 1828 the demands of the French government were partially met by legislation. The duties on certain French wines were reduced from fifteen to ten cents per gallon, and the rate on silks from the Orient was made ten per cent higher than that on silks from Europe.[70]

RECIPROCITY IN RELATIONS WITH PORTUGAL AND SPAIN

The erection of Brazil into a kingdom coördinate with Portugal in 1815 seemed to Monroe a proper occasion to

[68] Menou to Adams, March 31, 1824, Notes from French Leg., IX; Mareuil to Clay, Jan. 9, April 28, 1826, *ibid.*; Mareuil to Clay, Nov. 17, 1826, *ibid.*, X. For the opposition in France to the treaty, see W. H. Walker, *Franco-American Commercial Relations*, 50-52.

[69] Mareuil to Clay, May 16, 1827, Notes from French Leg., X; Clay to Mareuil, May 25, 1827, Notes to For. Leg., III; Brown to Clay, Sept. 27, 1827, Dispatches, France, XXIII.

[70] *Statutes at Large of the U. S., IV,* 309, 270-275.

attempt a commercial treaty, and Sumter, still minister at Rio de Janeiro, was instructed in June 1816 to suggest that the Portuguese minister at Washington be empowered to negotiate, since the dilatoriness of the government at Rio prevented negotiations there.[71] Early in 1819, Adams took up the subject in instructions to John Graham, who succeeded Sumter. He said that the State Department had insufficient information on Portuguese commerce for the preparation of adequate instructions. Sumter had been collecting information, and might have a report finished, which could be forwarded by Graham. It was known that other countries received advantages not extended to the United States, Adams stated. This government should discover the equivalent and purchase most-favored-nation treatment wherever possible. A decree of the Portuguese government at Rio, April 1818, he had learned, would put into effect after November 1, 1818, the principle of charging on the ships of each foreign state the same tonnage duty charged on Portuguese vessels in the ports of that state. This would be unobjectionable to the United States, but the same decree levied heavy discriminating duties on merchandise in foreign vessels. These were indirect tonnage duties and would have to be removed before Portugal could claim the advantages of the United States reciprocity act.[72]

Graham's overtures were not cordially received, since at the time the Rio government was very angry because of depredations on Brazilian commerce by privateers in the service of Artigas, the Uruguayan dictator, which had been fitted out in the United States.[73] Relations became somewhat strained over the matter of the privateers, and in 1822 the Portuguese government proposed a mixed tribunal to assess the damages done by them, and threatened reprisals on American commerce in the way of special concessions to competing countries. On the other hand, special favors were suggested if the American government should adopt a more

[71] Monroe to Thomas Sumter, June 10, 1816, Instructions, VIII, 81-82.
[72] Adams to John Graham, April 24, 1819, Instructions, VIII, 319-321.
[73] Graham to Monroe, Aug. 7, 1819, Dispatches, Portugal, III.

friendly attitude. This occasioned a tart letter from Adams, denying responsibility for the piracies. The atmosphere was not conducive to successful commercial negotiations.[74]

Representatives of the agricultural interest were much troubled at a Portuguese duty of two dollars per barrel on flour, which had been removed prior to the war, and reënacted afterward, it was believed in retaliation for the American duties on Madeira and Fayal wines. This was an important reason why a portion of Congress, at any rate, supported the dispatch in 1822 of General Dearborn to Lisbon,[75] to which city the court had returned from Brazil the previous year. Adams in his instructions gave little emphasis to the flour duties. The proposal of Portugal to give the United States special commercial advantages not given to other nations would not be acceptable even if unconnected with the matter of indemnification for alleged piracies. Perfect reciprocity was the American policy; the treaty of 1815 with Great Britain contained the only principle upon which the United States would be inclined to treat with Portugal. As to the complaints concerning the American duties on Portuguese wines, Adams observed that they were moderate in relation to price and duties charged on the same articles by the British.[76] This is a good illustration of the concentration on navigation and disregard of restrictions on imports during this period.

Dearborn proposed a commercial treaty to the Portuguese government in October 1822, and found it not indisposed to a liberal arrangement. However, delay followed delay because of the problem of settling relations with Brazil, and of constitutional and dynastic difficulties at home.[77] It was not

[74] Joseph Amado Grehon to Adams, April 1, May 3, 1822, Notes from Portuguese Leg., I; Adams to Amado Grehon, April 30, 1822, Adams, *Works*, VII, 247-250.

[75] Speech of Samuel Smith in House of Representatives, April 5, 1822, *Annals*, XXXIX, 1475-1476; Speech of Senator Lloyd of Mass., April 13, 1824, *Annals*, XLI, 515-518.

[76] Adams to Dearborn, June 25, 1822, Instructions, IX, 130-131.

[77] Dearborn to Adams, Oct. 10, 1822, Dec. 13, 1822, Dispatches, Portugal, VI.

until January 1823 that the Count da Sapa was designated to begin the negotiation.[78] Some progress was made toward a treaty basis, but Dearborn stated, "I have an opportunity for the fullest exercise of my stock of patience."[79] He soon became convinced that the delays were due to the British treaty of 1810, from which the Portuguese government was trying to secure release. There was at the time considerable popular opposition to British interference in Portuguese affairs. The Cortes had recently adopted a report in favor of suspending the article of the British treaty limiting import duties on British produce to fifteen per cent.[80]

In the spring of 1823, a reactionary revolution forced out the liberal monarch, John VI. Although the Great Powers intervened to secure his restoration, there was no longer any great possibility of a successful negotiation.[81] At a conference November 14, 1823, Palmella, the new foreign minister, admitted that the British treaty would prevent any project satisfactory to the United States. However, a navigation convention similar to the British treaty with the United States might still be possible.[82] But this project made no headway, and on January 1, 1824, Dearborn wrote: "I am fully convinced that there remains no probability of effecting any satisfactory arrangement with this government at present, and consequently that my remaining here can be of very little if any use."[83]

Dearborn's successor, T. L. L. Brent, also began a negotiation for a commercial treaty, but eventually encountered the same obstacle, namely, the fact that Portuguese relations with Great Britain made it impossible to conclude a satisfactory treaty with the United States. In this case, the claim was that the British treaty had expired and nothing

[78] Dearborn to Adams, Jan. 30, 1823, *ibid.*
[79] Dearborn to Adams, Feb. 20, 1823, *ibid.*
[80] Dearborn to Adams, March 3, 1823, Dispatches, Portugal, VI.
[81] Dearborn to Adams, July 15, 1822, June 4, Oct. 25, Nov. 7, 1823, Dispatches, Portugal, VI.
[82] Dearborn to Adams, Nov. 27, 1823, Dispatches, Portugal, VI.
[83] Dearborn to Adams, Dispatches, Portugal, VI.

could be done for the United States until it was decided what the revised British treaty should contain.[84] In March 1827 Brent protested to the minister of foreign affairs against the continued discrimination in favor of Great Britain to the disadvantage of the United States, and intimated that in return for most-favored-nation treatment his government might be able to reduce the duties on Portuguese wines.[85] Both parties believed a treaty would be advantageous, but the determination necessary to carry it to completion did not exist in the Portuguese government at this time.

Forsyth, on assuming the office of minister to Spain in 1819, was instructed by Adams to endeavor to secure a treaty on the basis of that with Great Britain. The principal purpose was to secure the removal of a special duty of twenty *reales de vellón,* or approximately one dollar per ton on American vessels, the general levy on foreign vessels being one *real* per ton. The collection of this tax dated from October 20, 1817.[86] Forsyth presented a memorandum to the Spanish court, in which he pointed out three justifiable complaints of the treatment administered to American ships. Ships of most other nations were allowed eight days in which to amend their manifests after arrival, those of the United States only twenty-four hours. One dollar (20 reals) per ton tonnage duty was levied on United States vessels only, and was even collected from ships touching but not unloading at a Spanish port. All American vessels arriving in Spain were obliged to submit to a vexatious quarantine whenever a serious epidemic was reported in any of the coast cities of the United States.[87]

[84] Brent to Clay, Jan. 9, May 4, 1826, Jan. 10, March 16, April 24, 1827, Dispatches, Portugal, VI, VII.

[85] Brent to Clay, March 16, 1827, Dispatches, Portugal, VII.

[86] Adams to Forsyth, March 8, 1819, Instructions, VIII, 306; Geo. W. Erving to Adams, Nov. 11, 1817, April 3, 1818, Dispatches, Spain, XIV, XV. The royal order, dated Oct. 20, 1817, levying the tax is in AHN, Estado, legajo 5560, expediente 25. The duty had been levied in Cuba several months previously. It was justified as being in retaliation for the United States tonnage duties. The difference was that the United States duties were general, whereas the Spanish levy applied to United States vessels only. Martin de Garay to Pizarro, July 5, 1817, *ibid.*

[87] Forsyth to Adams, July 13, 1820, Dispatches, Spain, XVIII.

By new regulations adopted in 1820, American cotton was prohibited. Corn laws prevented the sale of American grain and flour until the price of the domestic articles became exorbitant.[88]

From 1821 to 1822, during the constitutional régime, it appeared that the Spanish government was preparing to pursue a policy of real liberality in commerce. The special tonnage duty was extended to all foreign vessels, those of the United States being thus relieved from discrimination in that respect; and the duties on fish and staves were reduced. Adams felt that the only obstacle to applying the reciprocity act to Spanish vessels was the fact that a decree was still in force levying thirty-three and one-third per cent more on goods in American than in Spanish ships.[89]

The restoration of the absolute monarchy in 1823 soon put a stop to this liberal march, however. In 1824, Hugh Nelson was complaining that the tonnage duty was again twenty times as high on American as on other vessels, that Americans alone were refused an eight-day period in which to amend their manifests, and that American staves were discriminated against in favor of those of Hamburg. The refusal to receive more American produce restricted the market in the United States for Spanish wines, he contended.[90] The Spanish reply was a definite refusal to alter the existing system.[91] Clay instructed A. H. Everett, on his replacing Nelson in 1825, to begin a negotiation looking toward the settlement of the matters about which Nelson had complained; but although the minister for foreign affairs promised to nego-

[88] Forsyth to Adams, Nov. 12, 1820, *ibid*.

[89] Adams to Forsyth, June 20, 1821, Instructions, IX, 95-97. Forsyth to Adams, Nov. 22, 1820, Dispatches, Spain, XVIII. Forsyth to Adams, March 21, 1822, Dispatches, Spain, XX. The deliberations of the *Consejo de Estado* on Forsyth's propositions are in AHN, Estado, legajo 118, expediente 37. Although the Council declared against a reciprocity treaty in the existing state of Spain's industry, it decided, in a *consulta* of July 20, 1822, in favor of concessions on every point except that of extending the period in which manifests might be amended. The twenty-four hour limit must be retained, it was held, in order to prevent smuggling. *Ibid.*, pp. 75-101.

[90] Hugh Nelson to Adams, Dec. 13, 1824, Dispatches, Spain, XXIV.

[91] Hugh Nelson to Adams, April 6, 1825, Dispatches, Spain, XXIV.

tiate, he eventually informed Everett (1827) that his government was determined to make no change. The prohibitions on cotton, sugar, and rice were, however, removed in 1826.[92]

FURTHER LIBERALIZATION OF RECIPROCITY POLICY

The second extension of the reciprocity principle developed from discussions between 1818 and 1827 with the governments of the Scandinavian states, particularly Sweden, although the first authoritative expression of it was made in the treaty with Central America in 1825. It consisted in the agreement to abandon all discriminating duties on merchandise, regardless of origin, when imported in the vessels of any country whose government would grant similar treatment to American vessels. The treaty of 1816 between the United States and Sweden removed the discriminating tonnage and merchandise duties on each other's ships when laden with their country's own produce. Each nation had, after the passage of the American act of 1817, a navigation law which forbade the importation in the vessels of the other of the produce of a third country. At the instance of the Swedish government, an attempt was made in the treaty of 1816 to liberalize somewhat its navigation law by providing that, with the addition of an extra duty of only ten per cent, United States ships might import West India goods into Sweden and Norway, and Swedish and Norwegian ships might import Baltic goods into the United States. The Senate, however, refused to accept these articles. The Swedish government then offered to drop the proviso for the ten per cent extra duty, but the United States took no action.[93]

Swedish-American commerce flourished in the years immediately following the treaty of 1816. Christopher Hughes,

[92] Clay to A. H. Everett, April 27, 1825, Instructions, X, 300-302; Everett to the Duke del Infantado, Jan. 30, 1826, Dispatches, Spain, XXV; Everett to Clay, March 25, April 5, 1826, Dispatches, Spain, XXV; Everett to Clay, Feb. 15, Feb. 27, July 28, 1827, *ibid.*, XXVII.

[93] Miller, *Treaties*, II, 601-616; Adams to Jonathan Russell, June 22, 1818, Adams, *Writings*, VI, 351-352; Adams to G. W. Campbell, June 28, 1818, *ibid.*, 359; Christopher Hughes to Adams, May 18, 1820, Dispatches, Sweden, III; Stackelberg to Adams, Aug. 9, 1820, Notes from Swedish Leg., II.

American chargé at Stockholm, reported that in 1822 Sweden exported to the United States in sixty-one American and nine Swedish vessels about 18,000 tons of iron or almost three-fifths the total iron exports of the country.[94] To further encourage its trade with the United States, the Swedish government in 1821 opened the ports of Norway (not Sweden) to United States vessels on the same terms as to those of Sweden and Norway, i.e., the discrimination based upon the origin of the cargo was removed entirely. The purpose was to provide in Norway an entrepôt for United States and West India goods, where ships could unload, and while waiting a market in northern Europe, proceed to Sweden for a cargo of iron. The reciprocal favor was requested of the United States. In August 1821, Monroe issued a proclamation extending the Reciprocity Act of 1815 to the shipping of Norway, the only concession which legislation permitted. This did not place Norwegian vessels on any better footing than they enjoyed under the treaty of 1816, except that they were relieved from the provisions of the Navigation Act of March 1, 1817, thus being permitted to import goods of non-native origin on payment of the usual extra duties.[95] The request for the full privileges of natives in American ports was referred to Congress by Monroe in 1822, but no action was taken. Adams explained to the Swedish minister that the removal of the discrimination based on the origin of goods was a step which the United States could not take without injury to its own interests unless it were adopted by the other important maritime nations.[96] The Swedish government continued its liberal measures, and in 1824 provided for the admission

---

[94] Hughes to Adams, Dec. 8, 1820, Apil 14, 1823, Dispatches, Sweden, III, IV.

[95] Hughes to Adams, Jan. 30, 1821, Dispatches, Sweden, III; Adams to Hughes, May 17, 1821, Instructions, IX; Adams to Stackelberg, July 23, 1821, Notes to For. Leg., III; Stackelberg to Adams, Aug. 16, 1821, Notes from Swedish Leg., II; Richardson, II, 96-97; *ASP, FR*, IV, 868-869; Adams to Stackelberg, Aug. 21, 1821, Notes to For. Leg., III; James Anderson to Severin Lorich, Sept. 24, 1822, Notes from Swedish Leg., II.

[96] Adams, *Memoirs*, V, 489; *ASP, FR*, IV, 868; Adams to Stackelberg, Jan. 23, 1824, Notes to For. Leg., III.

of American vessels carrying West India produce into Swedish ports on the same terms as Swedish vessels, probably with the object of encouraging the direct exchange of American produce for iron. The United States was, of course, unable to reciprocate this concession immediately.[97]

In 1825, however, Clay and Adams came to the conclusion that it would be best to take the final step in the liberalization of maritime trade. Adams, in his first annual message, December 1825, recommended yielding the discriminating duties on vessels carrying produce other than that of their own countries, provided American vessels were granted similar concessions. A bill was introduced and passed in the Senate, but was allowed to die in the House.[98] Clay, not waiting for legislation, proceeded immediately to incorporate the new principle in his commercial diplomacy. The first treaty containing it was that with the Confederation of Central America, concluded December 5, 1825, although a treaty with Denmark admitting the point with slight limitations was proceeding simultaneously.[99]

The Russell treaty with Sweden expired in 1826, and in the following year a new negotiation was begun at Stockholm by J. J. Appleton, American chargé. Clay instructed him to obtain complete mutual national treatment of vessels if possible, as provided in the treaty with Central America. If necessary, he might allow Sweden to retain the monopoly of the trade between home ports and the West India colony of St. Bartholomew, provided the United States might trade between the island and any other country. If this were not agreed to, then he was simply to try to secure the renewal of the treaty of 1816.[100] Appleton's treaty was concluded July

---

[97] Stackelberg to Adams, June 28, 1824, Notes from Swedish Leg., III; Adams to Stackelberg, July 13, 1824, Notes to For. Leg., III; Clay to Severin Lorich, May 10, 1825, Notes to For. Leg., III.

[98] Richardson, *Messages and Papers*, II, 301; *Register of Debates*, II, 69-76; Speech of Senator Woodbury, Feb. 6, 1828, *ibid.*, IV, 237-243.

[99] Miller, *Treaties*, III, 209-238.

[100] Clay to Severin Lorich, Sept. 20, 1825, Notes to For. Leg., III; Clay to Stackelberg, Oct. 31, 1826, *ibid.*; *ASP, FR*, VI, 367-368, *Statutes at Large of the U. S.*, IV, 206; Clay to J. J. Appleton, Jan. 12, 1827, Instructions, XI, 231-237.

4, 1827. It provided for the removal by the two governments of all discrimination against each other's shipping, except for certain trade, unimportant for the United States, between the Kingdom of Norway and Sweden, its colony of Finland, and the Russian Empire. Sweden agreed to admit American vessels to her colony of St. Bartholomew on equal terms with native, even to the carriage between the island and the mother country.[101]

The government of Denmark attempted in 1818 to secure the benefit of the reciprocity act of 1815, but proved unable to establish the absence of discrimination against American vessels in Danish ports.[102] Failing in this effort, that government made overtures for a treaty, one purpose of which would be to extend the principle of national treatment of each country's vessels to cover all goods regardless of origin. Adams was, however, unwilling to agree to the removal of the limitation, and, in order to dispose of the proposition, offered to accept it as the equivalent for the reduction of the Danish Sound Dues on American vessels. The Danish minister continued willing to negotiate, but Adams remained aloof.[103]

The proposal to negotiate was renewed early in 1825, but encountered delays due to the death of the Danish foreign minister, and to the change of administration in the United States.[104] As late as November 1825, Clay expressed opposition to the proposal to admit, on the same terms as American vessels, Danish vessels with non-Danish produce.[105] The treaty was not concluded until April 26, 1826. In the meantime, the treaty with Central America had been ratified by the Senate, and there was no longer any reason for withholding the same terms from Denmark. The treaty provided that each nation should receive the shipping of the other on the

[101] Appleton to Clay, July 11, 1827, Dispatches, Sweden, V; Miller, *Treaties*, III, 283-308.

[102] Adams to Pedersen, March 6, 1818, Notes to For. Leg., II, 281.

[103] Adams, *Memoirs*, IV, 196-197, 204.

[104] Adams, *Memoirs*, IV, 514; Clay to Pedersen, March 25, 1825, Notes to For. Leg., III.

[105] Clay to Pedersen, Nov. 7, 1825, Notes to For. Leg., III.

same terms as its own, without regard to the origin of the cargo, with certain enumerated exceptions. These exceptions permitted Denmark to retain the monopoly of the trade with Greenland, Iceland, and the Faroe Islands, and that between the Danish West Indies and the home ports, although Americans were allowed to carry from the West Indies to all other foreign countries. Each country reserved the right to regulate its trade with the Far East without regard to the treaty; i.e., the United States did not yield its right to discriminate against Danish ships in the China trade.[106]

RELATIONS WITH GERMANY, RUSSIA, AND THE ITALIAN STATES

Through Frederick Greuhm, its minister at Washington, the Prussian government requested in 1817 the application of the act of 1815 to Prussian vessels. The American government delayed complying, and a year later the request was renewed. In April 1818, Congress extended the reciprocity policy in the case of The Netherlands to include the produce of the interior adjacent territories, usually shipped from Dutch ports. Greuhm asked the same privilege for the shipping not only of Prussia, but also for that of the Hanse towns of Hamburg and Bremen, the ports from which Prussian produce was usually exported.[107] Hamburg and Bremen had applied for reciprocity privileges in 1815, and had encountered the delay experienced at first by all the small maritime states. They were granted the privileges of the act of 1815 in July and August, 1818, but this gave little satisfaction, since it relieved their vessels from discrimination only when carrying native produce.[108] Monroe recommended

---

[106] Miller, *Treaties*, III, 239-248.

[107] Greuhm to Adams, Nov. 21, 1817, enclosing Hardenburg to Greuhm, June 30, 1817, Notes from Prussian Leg., I; Greuhm to Adams, Nov. 14, 1818, *ibid.*

[108] Burgomasters and Senate of Hamburg to the President, Nov. 13, 1815, *ASP, C&N*, II, 197; Richardson, II, 37-38; *ASP, C&N*, II, 197-198. Lübeck came under the arrangement, Oct. 30, 1819. Richardson, II, 73; Consul General Buck to the Secretary of State, Jan. 23, 1819, and an undated letter of the Burgomasters of Bremen to the President, *ASP, C&N*, II, 198-199.

favorable action on the requests of Prussia, Hamburg, and Bremen in a message to Congress February 8, 1819. In the Senate the proposition encountered the opposition of Samuel Smith and others, on the ground that Prussia levied a heavy transit duty on American tobacco from the Netherlands, which had an adverse effect upon the price of that article in the Dutch market. However, the bill containing the concession was passed by a large majority, and was approved March 3, 1819.[109]

The Prussian government, like the governments of the Scandinavian countries, was very much interested in securing the removal of the remaining discrimination in the ports of the United States. Hoping that the bill providing for that removal, then under consideration in Congress, would pass, the King repealed the remaining Prussian discrimination in 1826. In 1828, Clay and Niederstetter, the latter then Prussian minister at Washington, entered upon the negotiation of a new treaty of commerce, the previous convention of 1799 having expired in 1810. The treaty which, like that with Central America, contained the complete reciprocity principle without exception, was concluded May 1, 1828. On the recommendation of the President, Congress made the reciprocity article retroactive to the date of the Prussian equalization law of 1826.[110] By the same act, the President was authorized to remove by proclamation the discriminating duties on all goods regardless of origin when imported in the vessels of any nation which did not discriminate against American vessels under the same conditions. Thus, after long hesitation, the principle of complete free trade for the carrier was offered generally to foreign nations by Congress. In 1827, the three Hanseatic republics, Hamburg, Lübeck, and Bremen, dispatched a special minister, Vincent Rumpf, to

---

[109] Richardson, II, 52-53; *Annals*, XXXIV, 1425; *Statutes at Large of the U. S.*, III, 510.

[110] Miller, *Treaties*, III, 427-455; Richardson, II, 403; *Statutes at Large of the U. S.*, IV, 308-309; Speech of Senator Woodbury, Feb. 6, 1828, *Register of Debates*, IV, 237-243; see also Niederstetter's dispatches of April 26 and May 2, 1828, Prussia, Auswärtiges Amt, Abt. II, Rep. 6, Handel, Nord Amerika, III, Pt. II.

Washington for the negotiation of a commercial treaty.[111] This treaty, very similar to the Prussian, was completed and signed December 20, 1827.[112]

Although autocratic Russia and democratic America were the best of friends during this period, no serious attempt at a commercial treaty was made. The United States proposed a negotiation on two different occasions, once through the peace commissioners at Petrograd in 1813, and once through the minister to Russia, William Pinkney, in June 1817. Both offers were courteously declined.[113] Pinkney reported that a commercial treaty was unnecessary since no distinction was made in Russian ports between foreign and Russian vessels. It was the confirmed Russian policy to favor small navy powers, and consequently it was very unlikely that the Russian navigation system would be changed in the future to the disadvantage of the United States. No reduction of customs duties which would be likely to be conceded in a treaty could be expected to result in increased purchases of American produce.[114]

Adams adopted the attitude recommended by Pinkney, and declared himself satisfied with Russian policy.[115] To Monroe who, at a time of strained relations between Russia and Great Britain during the Greek Revolution in 1821, desired a strong attempt at a commercial treaty, Adams explained that

. . . our true policy was to be always willing and ready to treat of commerce with Russia, and rather desiring it; because that desire

---

[111] James Brown to Clay, May 12, 1827, Dispatches, France, XXIII; Gallatin to Clay, May 3, 1827, Dispatches, Great Britain, XXXIV; Rumpf to Clay, asking interview for Nov. 5, 1827, U. S. Dept. of State, Hanseatic Notes, I; Moritz Lindeman, "Zur Geschichte der älteren Handelsbeziehungen Bremens mit den Vereinigten Staaten von Nord Amerika" in Bremisches Jahrbuch, X (1878) 137-145; Ernst Baasch, "Beiträge zur Geschichte der Handelsbeziehungen zwischen Hamburg und Amerika," in Hamburgische Festschrift zur Erinnerung an die Entdeckung Amerikas, I, No. 3, 105-117.

[112] Miller, Treaties, III, 387-404.

[113] Adams, Memoirs, II, 498-499; Pinkney to the Secretary of State, June 10, 1817, Dispatches, Russia, VI; Monroe to Pinkney, May 10, 1816, Instructions, VIII.

[114] Pinkney to Adams, Sept. 25, 1817, Dispatches, Russia, VI.

[115] Adams to G. W. Campbell, June 28, 1818, Adams, Works, VI, 368-369; Adams to Middleton, July 5, 1820, Instructions, IX.

would always be received as a mark of esteem and respect; but we can really obtain nothing from Russia of any importance in a commercial treaty. She had no discriminating duties, no colonial monopolies to remove. All the trade between us is carried on in our vessels. She imports from us sugar, coffee, and raw cotton without heavy duties; and all we could possibly obtain would be a trifling reduction of them. For everything thus obtained an equivalent would be exacted. . . .'[116]

However, he included navigation and commerce in the full power sent to Henry Middleton for the negotiation on the Northwest Boundary in 1823.[117]

The Russian minister to the United States declared in 1815 that Russia had complied with the terms of the reciprocity act, and asked its application with regard to Russian vessels. The subject was not pressed at that time, however.[118] The request was repeated in 1823. In the act of 1824, Russia was included among those countries whose vessels might import without discrimination their own produce and the produce of any other countries usually shipped from their ports.[119] It was discovered later that the Russian government actually discriminated against foreign vessels in requiring them to pay a small tonnage duty at each entry, whereas Russians paid only once a year. The point was of no great importance, since American ships ordinarily made only one entry in a Russian port each year. However, Clay declared that he expected the Imperial government to remove the inequality at an early date.[120]

The Austrian Empire also showed an interest in commercial relations with the United States. An intimation of a desire to learn how trade might be promoted came in an indirect way from Metternich in 1815.[121] In 1825, Baron Lederer, the Austrian consul general, inquired of Clay as to the pos-

---

[116] Adams, *Memoirs*, V, 429-431.

[117] Adams to Middleton, July 29, 1823, Instructions, X.

[118] Daschkoff to Monroe, May 6, 1815, Notes from the Russian Leg., I.

[119] Baron de Tuyll to Adams, Dec. 9, 1823, Jan. 27, 1824, Notes from the Russian Leg., I; *Statutes at Large of the U. S.*, IV, 2-3.

[120] Baron de Tuyll to Adams, Feb. 16, 1825, Notes from the Russian Leg., I; Clay to Baron de Tuyll, April 5, 1825, Notes to For. Leg., III.

[121] Monroe to Adams, Dec. 12, 1815, Instructions, VIII.

sibility of securing the removal of the duties on Austrian vessels. He was advised to secure full powers for a treaty, which he did. However, Adams' administration terminated before the negotiation was completed.[122] Hanover made application for the advantages of the act of 1824 through the British minister in Washington in 1827, and the President issued the necessary proclamation July 1, 1828.[123] The same advantages were extended to the Papal States by a proclamation of June 7, 1827.[124]

CONTROVERSIES WITH REGARD TO TRADE WITH
EUROPEAN COLONIES

The attempt of the United States to enforce its policy in the trade with the British West Indies has received far more attention in historical writing than any other aspect of the fight for commercial reciprocity. Consequently, the episode has seemed to occupy a more important position than the economic value of the trade or the real significance of the diplomatic controversy justifies. During the period from 1815 to 1829, the trade with the British West Indies constituted only a small fraction of the country's foreign trade, and even of the total trade with the British Empire. It was no longer of outstanding significance in the total of American commerce with the West Indies, being exceeded by far by the trade with the island of Cuba alone.[125] The great attention given the subject has been due to a considerable extent to the fact

[122] Clay to Lederer, Dec. 20, 1825, Notes to For. Leg., III; Adams, *Memoirs*, VIII, 73; Clay to Lederer, Nov. 22, 1828, Notes to For. Leg., IV; Adams' 4th Annual Message, Dec. 2, 1828, Richardson, II, 409.

[123] Clay to Vaughan, Jan. 7, 1828, Notes to For. Leg., III; Richardson, II, 404-405.

[124] Richardson, III, 376-377; Adams, *Memoirs*, VII, 291.

[125] The annual value of the trade between the United States and the British West Indies during the years from 1815 to 1829 did not vary greatly from its annual value during the early years of the republic. However, the total exports from the United States had increased from about $20,000,000 in 1792 to nearly $100,000,000 in 1825. Great Britain's share of the total commerce between the United States and the West Indies amounted in 1816-1817 to less than one-fourth. These conclusions are drawn from a study of Pitkin, *Statistical View*, 167-168, 177, 212-213, 219, 222, 225, 242, 219, 234, 236; Seybert, *Statistical Annals*, 140-141.

that here occurred one of those cases of a specific foreign policy becoming an issue in a heated political battle. Until the opportunity occurred for the opposition to the Adams administration to make political capital out of the subject, the West India controversy aroused surprisingly little popular interest.[126]

The efforts made during the administrations of Monroe and Adams to control the West India trade are of real significance, however, in that the series of regulations and negotiations illustrate the conditions and methods of American reciprocity policy, and the handicaps and advantages of the United States in carrying on commercial warfare. With the exception of the fight to force the abandonment of the French discriminating duties on American shipping, and a minor battle with Nova Scotia and New Brunswick over the carriage of plaster of Paris, the attempt to wrest the West India carrying trade from the British is the only early example of a commercial war carried through to a conclusion by the United States. Altogether, five major pieces of legislation, two important presidential proclamations, and five diplomatic negotiations were directed toward a settlement of this question. The national power derived by the United States from its foreign trade is clearly brought out in the struggle, while the difficulties in carrying to a successful conclusion a determined foreign policy, inherent in the prevailing sectionalism and faction then existent in American politics, and in rigid constitutional provisions, are also shown.

Neither the United States nor Great Britain attempted a policy of conciliation or of meeting the just demands of the opposing party. The United States insisted upon "complete reciprocity" or free competition for its shipping. The adoption of this scheme meant that the United States, because of its favorable geographical location, would drive British shipping almost entirely from the intercourse. The West India

---

[126] Benns, *American Struggle*, 45, 52, 59, 71, 76-77, 89, 99, 111; Adams, *Memoirs*, IV, 495, 504; Addington to George Canning, Sept. 28, 1823, PRO, FO, 5, vol. 177.

policy of John Quincy Adams was undoubtedly partially motivated by his desire to see the European colonial system broken down in America, and to promote the leadership of the United States in the New World. The British government, on the other hand, held that permission to participate in the colonial trade was a boon which the mother country could grant or withhold as her own interests might dictate. The various proposals made by that government in order to preserve the West India planters from ruin covered a plan to direct the trade along routes which were beyond the reach of the regulations of the United States. Adams was not far wrong when he characterized the British Act of 1822, the best proposition offered the United States, as being based on stratagem.[127]

The West India policy of the United States was directed solely to securing the advantage of navigation. The expansion of markets for American produce was not an object.[128] Until the reverse of 1827, American policy was clearly and firmly stated: Let the British regulate the importations into the West Indies as they please. Let them limit the trade to

[127] Stratford Canning to George Canning, Feb. 8, 1823, PRO, FO, 5, vol. 175. For evidence of American awareness of the plan to force the trade through the North American colonies so that British vessels would have the carriage, and to make use of the circuitous voyage to the disadvantage of American shipping, see Stratford Canning to George Canning, June 6, 1823, PRO, FO, 5, vol. 176; Adams to Rush, May 7, 1819, *ASP, FR*, IV, 403; Gallatin to Clay, Oct. 27, 1826, Gallatin, *Writings*, II, 335-337.

That Adams knew what he was talking about in resisting the British proposals is proved by the event after the so-called "reciprocity" of 1831. Under this arrangement, which was an unconditional compliance with the British acts of 1825, the value of the exports made directly from the United States to the British West Indies, to which the reciprocity rule applied, amounted in 1833 to only a little over a million, while the exports to the North American colonies, most of which were destined to the West Indies, reached nearly four and one-half millions. Pitkin, *Statistical View*, 212-213.

[128] Here and there one finds a suggestion of the possibility of favoring the exchange of American and West India products. Adams once mentioned to Stratford Canning the possibility that Congress might decide to exclude British West Indian rum in retaliation for the exclusion of salted provisions produced in the United States. Adams, *Memoirs*, VI, 104; see also William King to Rufus King, King, *Correspondence*, VI, 117-118. According to Tazewell, *A Review of the Negotiations*, 38-39, the first American attack on the restrictions in the British West Indies was in the tariff of 1816, when the rates on rum and sugar were made practically prohibitive.

a few articles of import and export, or let them prohibit it altogether if they wish. The United States would have no right to complain. But if they decide to purchase any supplies from the United States, they must allow American vessels to compete freely for the carriage of them.[129] The confidence with which the principle was asserted and with which the measures of execution were taken was derived in a large degree from the conviction that the United States was in no degree dependent upon the British West Indies for supplies, while those islands were dependent upon their northern neighbor for necessities.[130]

In the negotiation of 1815, on the refusal of their opponents to discuss the colonial trade, the American commissioners insisted on the inclusion in the commercial treaty of an article reserving the right of each party to regulate that intercourse. Although the provision seemed to express an intention not to continue to allow British shipping a monopoly, it was not until after some experience of the effects of the treaty of 1815 that the demand for retaliation came emphatically to the front in Congress. The effect of the treaty was to destroy that reciprocity in the direct trade between the United States and Great Britain, the guarantee of which had been the purpose of the two governments. It was soon found that American vessels were being pushed out, not because they could not be operated more cheaply than British, but because the British had a triangular route from Great Britain to the United States, to the West Indies and back to Great Britain, from two legs of which American vessels were excluded by British regulations. They could well afford to undercut the Americans in the leg in which there was competition, since losses could be recovered in the other voyages.[131]

When pressed by Adams in 1815 and 1816, to negotiate

[129] Monroe to Adams, May 21, 1816, Instructions, VIII; Adams, *Memoirs*, III, 391-394.
[130] Benns, *American Struggle*, 51; R. King to Christopher Gore, April 12, 1818, King, *Correspondence*, VI, 139-140.
[131] Benns, *op. cit.*, 34-35.

a settlement of the controversy, Castlereagh first refused, then delayed, and finally, on the eve of the first step in the American retaliatory system, submitted an offer far short of anything the American government felt it could honorably accept, perhaps in the hope of further staving off adverse regulations. These proposals, handed to Adams early in 1817, provided for admitting American vessels of very limited tonnage with cargoes restricted to a few of the less important (from the American standpoint) articles to designated ports in the islands; for admitting American vessels under very favorable conditions to an entrepôt in Bermuda; and for an unlimited trade to Turk's Island for salt. The proposals were not seriously considered in the United States.[132]

Castlereagh's attitude throughout was one of extreme good feeling. He repeated again and again that his government would have no right to resent retaliation by the United States. In fact he advised Adams on one occasion that the triangular voyages which were taking from the United States all the advantages of the treaty of 1815 could be eliminated, either by prohibiting them or taxing them heavily.[133] He gave the impression of laboriously seeking some plan which would satisfy British interests and at the same time allay the resentment of the United States. He informed Bagot at Washington that it was his object "to narrow as much as possible jealous and controversial points between the two governments." He could view with considerable toleration the American retaliatory measures because they "would in many respects operate beneficially to increase our colonial trade in provisions and lumber."[134]

Early in 1817, Congress took a cautious step toward the objective of destroying Britain's monopoly of the West India carrying trade and her increasing share of the direct trade to

---

[132] Adams, *Memoirs*, III, 422-423, 489-492; Adams to Monroe, Sept. 18, Sept. 27, Oct. 5, 1816, March 20, 1817, Adams, *Writings*, VI, 87, 95, 103-104, 167-168; Adams to Castlereagh, Sept. 17, 1816, *ibid.*, 81-83; Gallatin to Adams, April 16, 1817, Gallatin, *Writings*, II, 29-30.

[133] Adams, *Memoirs*, III, 422-423; Adams to Monroe, March 20, 1817, Adams, *Writings*, VI, 167-168.

[134] Castlereagh to Bagot, March 22, 1817, PRO, FO, 5, vol. 120.

Great Britain. An additional tonnage duty of two dollars per ton was levied on foreign vessels arriving from ports ordinarily closed to American vessels.[135] This law had only slight effect on the British system, however, since it placed no impediment in the way of British vessels coming directly from Great Britain to the United States and then proceeding to the West Indies. The British government did not increase the concessions contained in the offer above referred to.[136] Consequently a navigation act with teeth in it was adopted April 18, 1818. This provided that after Sept. 30, 1818, the ports of the United States should be closed to British vessels coming from ports ordinarily closed to American vessels, and British vessels lading in American ports were to be required to give bond not to land their cargoes in any port closed to American vessels.[137] The act was adopted with only two dissenting votes in the Senate and sixteen in the House. There was no indication of sectionalism in the vote.[138]

The act of 1818 was quite effective in reducing the advantages held by British navigation. Between 1817 and 1819, British shipping in American ports dropped from 174,935 to 36,333 tons.[139] That an American monopoly based on carriage to non-British islands in the West Indies was not completely established, was due to the manipulation of customs

[135] *Statutes at Large of the U. S.*, III, 344, 369. This act preceded by only a short time the Navigation Act of 1817. Benns (*American Struggle*, 46-47) is in error in supposing that the Navigation Act of 1817 prohibited imports from the West Indies in all British vessels except those owned and registered in the West Indies. That such an effect was expected by certain persons at the time is shown in William King to Rufus King, Feb. 24, 1818, King, *Correspondence*, VI, 117-118. However, the Treasury Department ruled that a vessel owned in any part of the British Empire could import goods from any other part. Mayo, *Synopsis of the Commercial and Revenue System*, 45-46.

A provision for refusing drawbacks to foreign vessels destined to ports closed to American vessels was included in the general impost law. Rush to Adams, Jan. 5, 1818, Dispatches, Great Britain, XXII; *Statutes at Large of the U. S.*, III, 313-314.

[136] Rush to Adams, April 15, 1818, Dispatches, Great Britain, XXII.

[137] *Statutes at Large of the U. S.*, III, 432-433.

[138] Rufus King to Christopher Gore, April 12, 1818, King, *Correspondence*, VI, 139-140; Benns, *American Struggle*, 52.

[139] Benns, *op. cit.*, 64; see also Gallatin to Adams, Nov. 7, 1818, Dispatches, Great Britain, XVIII; Adams, *Memoirs*, IV, 181.

duties by the British government, the effect of which was to route much American produce to the West Indies via St. Johns and Halifax and via Bermuda, routes the greater part of which was monopolized by British shipping.[140] Bermuda was not affected by the American act because it was "ordinarily" open to American vessels; the New Brunswick and Nova Scotia route could be reached only by prohibiting British vessels in the short voyage between the United States and those provinces, the trade in United States vessels not being touched. The handicaps in the way of trade increased considerably the hardships of the West India planters.[141]

After the adoption of the navigation act of 1818, the United States again offered to negotiate. The general commercial treaty of 1815 was due to expire in 1818, and other important questions, particularly boundary and the Newfoundland fisheries problems, had reached the stage where an attempt at settlement seemed desirable. Richard Rush, the regular minister, was not considered of sufficient stature for the work, and Gallatin was transferred temporarily from Paris to assist him.[142] These envoys were very much surprised to find that the navigation law of 1818 had brought about a considerable alteration in the British attitude respecting the West India trade. The government agreed to accept an arrangement which, on the face of it, seemed to promise a reasonable degree of reciprocity. It offered to admit American vessels from the United States into the ports of the West India colonies on exactly the same terms as British vessels from the United States. The plan contained, however, a proposition to limit the number of articles which might be carried in the direct trade between the West Indies and the United States in either American or British ships. Gallatin and Rush suspected that it was intended to allow an indirect trade through Nova Scotia and New Brunswick in articles excluded from the direct trade, and also to draw a supply of United

---

[140] Rush to Adams, June 4, 1818, Dispatches, Great Britain, XXII.
[141] Benns, *American Struggle*, 64-66.
[142] Adams to Rush, May 21, 1818, Adams, *Writings*, VI, 327-332; Adams to Gallatin, May 22, 1818, *ibid.*, 332-336.

States produce through the northern colonies by means of the device of levying in the West Indies higher duties on American produce than on that of those colonies. In this way reciprocity would be granted on paper, but the produce of the United States would continue to go to the West Indies in British vessels. The American envoys proposed the inclusion of provisions to obviate these difficulties, but the British refused. They then referred the British proposals to Washington, where both the Administration and the Senate approved the attitude adopted by Rush and Gallatin.[143]

The United States next proceeded to strengthen its retaliatory system, concluding that that was the best means of inducing the British government to go the whole way toward reciprocity. An additional navigation act was adopted in 1820, which closed the ports of the United States to British vessels, not only from the ports usually closed to American shipping, but from all the British colonial ports in America. Going further, the act prohibited the import of goods, even in American vessels, from British colonial ports except when the goods were imported directly from the colony producing them.[144] By this means the circuitous trade in United States and West India goods in British ships to Bermuda, Nova Scotia, and New Brunswick was effectively stopped. American produce could still go to St. Johns and Halifax in American vessels, but it could not be there exchanged for British or West India produce. All goods from the United States sold in the British West Indies must now go in American vessels to the Dutch, Danish, Swedish, Spanish, or French islands and there be transshipped to British vessels for conveyance to their destination. This brought about such an increase in the prices which the West India planters had to pay for provisions that conditions in the islands became extremely serious during 1820-1821.[145] Simultaneously there

[143] Rush and Gallatin to Adams, Oct. 20, 1818, *ASP, FR*, IV, 381-382; Adams, *Memoirs*, IV, 315-316; Adams to Rush, May 7, 1819, Instructions, VIII, 337-338; Rush to Adams, Sept. 17, 1819, Dispatches, Great Britain, XXIV; Benns, *American Struggle*, 55-59.

[144] *Statutes at Large of the U. S.*, III, 602-604; Benns, *op. cit.*, 69-71.

[145] Ragatz, *Fall of the Planter Class*, 338-339, 342-361; Benns, *op. cit.*, 72-75.

arose a considerable clamor in the southern states against the policy of retaliation, on the ground that it was injuring the market for farm produce in order to help the northern navigating interest. For a time there was some doubt as to which of the domestic oppositions would force its government to yield first.[146]

The West India planters obliged the British government to take action first, however. The result was the West Indian and American Trade Act of July 24, 1822. In this legislation the British government receded from one of the positions which had prevented an agreement in 1819. The new law provided that the same list of articles might be imported from the United States directly into the West Indies as might be imported indirectly by way of the North American colonies. That which had seemed to amount almost to an open declaration of intention to favor a circuitous trade was thus abandoned. On the other hand, the policy of levying discriminating duties on American produce, with the avowed object of encouraging the industry of the North American colonies, was reaffirmed. The law contained a schedule of such duties, amounting to about ten per cent ad valorem on livestock, provisions, lumber, and lumber products, articles which constituted the principal exports of the United States to the West Indies.[147]

The American government decided to secure the advantages of this act by complying with its provisions. In fact Congress, on learning that a bill for regulating the West India trade was under consideration in Parliament, had authorized the President to proceed *pari passu* with the British government in reopening the trade.[148] A proclamation issued by Monroe on August 24, 1822, opened the ports to British vessels coming directly from and loaded with the produce of

---

[146] *Annals*, XXXVIII, 173, 224, 803, 1033, 1113; *ASP, C&N*, II, 521-522; S. Canning to Londonderry, Dec. 30, 1821, PRO, FO, 5, vol. 159; *Annals*, XXXVII, 1490-1498, 1505-1522; Gallatin to Monroe, Feb. 4, 1822, *Writings*, II, 232-233; Benns. *op. cit.*, 76-81.

[147] The act is in *ASP, FR*, V, 231-236; Benns, *American Struggle*, 83-85.

[148] *Statutes at Large of the U. S.*, III, 681-682.

the British West Indies, and also to those coming from the
North American colonies carrying the produce of those regions.[149] The proclamation did not remove the regular tonnage duty of one dollar per ton nor the ten per cent additional on the duties collected on merchandise. To Stratford
Canning's complaint and assertion that no similar duties were
collected in the British colonies, Adams answered that the
President did not have authority under the act for reopening
the trade to the British colonies, to remove those duties,
which were levied by a general law. He argued, however, that
these duties were no more than sufficient to countervail the
high export and import duties in colonial ports, and the
limitation of American shipping to enumerated ports in the
colonies, to enumerated articles of import and export, and
to the direct trade only between the United States and the
colonies—restrictions which had no counterpart in the regulations of the United States.[150] The British government continued to press the claim for removal of the discriminating
duties.[151]

The proclamation of the executive was superseded by an
act of Congress on March 1, 1823. This law continued the
system of the proclamation, providing in addition that the
discriminating duties should be removed whenever the
British would agree to admit American produce into colonial
ports on the same terms as goods "from elsewhere."[152] The
term "elsewhere" was intended to mean the other British
colonies as well as foreign nations. Just as Parliament had
established by legislation in 1822 a system which the American government had refused to accept in a conventional arrangement in 1819, so Congress replied with a system re-
asserting the demands which the American representatives

---

[149] Richardson, *Messages and Papers*, II, 184-185.

[150] Stratford Canning to Adams, Oct. 25, 1822, Notes from the British Leg.,
XII; Adams to Stratford Canning, Nov. 11, 1822, Adams, *Writings*, VII,
323-327.

[151] Stratford Canning to Lord Bathurst, Dec. 4, 1822, PRO, FO, 5, vol. 169;
Rush to Adams, Oct. 26, 1822, Dispatches, Great Britain, XXVIII; Stratford
Canning to George Canning, Feb. 8, 1823, PRO, FO, 5, vol. 175.

[152] *Statutes at Large of the U. S.*, III, 740-742.

had made in the last negotiation. In other words, the United States insisted that as long as Great Britain reserved the right to favor British shipping by manipulating customs duties so as to draw American supplies through the adjoining colonies, the United States would penalize British shipping in the direct trade with the colonies by continuing to collect the discriminating duties on tonnage and merchandise.[153]

Adams took a very high tone in his discussions with Stratford Canning regarding this legislation. He told him that the prohibitory laws and trade through the "neutral" islands in the West Indies was best for the interests of the United States.[154] When the British minister threatened that his government would levy similar retaliatory duties in the West Indies, the Secretary of State became almost truculent.

It was not to be expected (he said) that the colonial intercourse could remain with satisfaction to either party on its present footing. The Act of Congress relating to that trade had been passed with a full knowledge of its being at variance with the Act of Parliament on which it was bottomed, and at the open risk of its leading to a fresh exclusion of the United States vessels from the enumerated colonies. Great Britain was indeed at liberty to maintain the discriminating duties on her side, but in that case her principal object in opening the West Indies would be frustrated by the enhanced price of articles essential to the wants of the colonies.[155]

The attitude of the American government and people caused Stratford Canning to doubt the wisdom of making concessions to the United States. He reported that the decision of the British government in 1822 to open the islands had been received in the United States as a "national triumph," and accepted as proof of "the irresistible truth of the principles proclaimed by the American government," and of the superior capacity of American statesmen. He strongly recommended the adoption by Great Britain of a permanent system, and suggested that the national credit would suffer

[153] See Rufus King to G. King, Jan. 7, 1823, King, *Correspondence*, VI, 493; Adams to Rush, June 23, 1823, Instructions, IX.
[154] Stratford Canning to George Canning, Feb. 8, 1823, PRO, FO, 5, vol. 175.
[155] Stratford Canning to George Canning June 6, 1823, PRO, FO, 5, vol. 176.

less from admitting Americans to all commercial privileges than from the continued pursuit of "a policy which aims at exclusion and ends in concession."[156]

On July 17, 1823, an order in council was issued which levied in the colonial ports discriminating duties equal to those still collected by the United States on British vessels from the colonies.[157] In the fall of 1823 a renewed effort was made to settle the dispute by negotiation in London. Rush represented the United States, and Stratford Canning and Huskisson, Great Britain. Rush demanded the abandonment of the preferential duties in favor of the North American colonies. The British plenipotentiaries emphatically rejected the claim as being derogatory to the character of their country as an independent commercial power. The result was a deadlock, and both parties agreed to suspend the negotiation for the time being.[158]

As a result of the law of 1823, a substantial monopoly of the carrying trade to the British islands was secured by the shipping of the United States. The British government was entirely dissatisfied, not only because British navigation was practically excluded, but also because the arrangement did not solve the problem of cheap supplies for the planters. The American and British discriminating duties were a heavy tax, and American merchants frequently demanded payment for their provisions, lumber, and livestock in specie or bills on London in preference to the productions of the islands. The ministry also felt that the United States government had been entirely too arrogant in making its demands.[159]

The Monroe Doctrine and various American acts indicating aspirations to leadership in the New World aroused Can-

[156] *Ibid.;* see also Stratford Canning's dispatch of May 8, 1822, PRO, FO, 5, vol. 168.
[157] Benns, *American Struggle*, 99; George Canning to Stratford Canning, July 11, 1823, PRO, FO, 5, vol. 174; Addington to George Canning, Sept. 28, 1823, PRO, FO, 5, vol. 177.
[158] Rush to Adams, Aug. 12, 1824, Dispatches, Great Britain, XXXI; George Canning to Addington, Sept. 7, 1824, PRO, FO, 5, vol. 184; Benns, *op. cit.*, 101-103.
[159] Benns, *op. cit.*, 103-105.

ning to compete for that leadership and to do whatever possible to check American rivalry. As a step in this direction, it was determined to try to counter the unreasonable demands of the United States by attempting to supply the needs of the sugar islands from the newly liberated Spanish colonies, from Europe, and from the North American colonies.[160] To carry into effect the new "permanent" policy, Parliament adopted three new acts for the regulation of the colonial trade, these acts to take effect on January 5, 1826. One provided for the admission of the produce of all countries of America, Europe, Africa, and Western Asia into the West Indies, and stated the duties to be collected. Incidentally, a duty was levied on several articles which had formerly been admitted free from the United States. The other two acts related to navigation, one providing for the limitation of the trade between the colonies and Great Britain to British ships; the other offering to open the foreign trade of the colonies to all countries which, having colonies, would extend similar privileges in those colonies to British ships, or, having no colonies, would extend general most-favored-nation privileges to British vessels.[161]

The way in which the United States was to be affected by the new legislation was not very clearly set forth by the British government. The acts were never officially communicated, nor was any suggestion ever made that action by the United States was expected. American opinion questioned the "liberality" of the new system, and government officials, both American and British, were doubtful of the meaning of the laws. The attitude adopted by the Administration was that Great Britain certainly did not intend to upset the arrangement of 1822, and would except the United States from the application of the acts, especially since the suspended negotiation of 1824

[160] Benns, *ibid.*, 106-107; Temperley, "The Later American Policy of George Canning," in *AHR*, XI, 779-797; Perkins, *The Monroe Doctrine, 1823-1826*, 247-253; Rippy, *Rivalry of the U.S. and Great Britain*, 112-124.

[161] The acts are in *ASP, FR*, VI, 306-323. See Benns, *American Struggle*, 107-109.

was expected soon to be resumed.[162] In fact, the acts were not applied to the United States on the date which had been set for the closing of the ports to the shipping of all nations which had not complied with the terms. The subject was brought to the attention of both houses of Congress in the spring of 1826, but on the intimation by the Administration that a settlement by negotiation was preferred, no legislative action was taken. The Senate committee on commerce reported that the British acts did not offer fair reciprocity.[163] In failing to act before the adjournment of Congress in 1826, it appears that the United States lost the last opportunity of an amicable settlement, for Canning expressed, as late as March 8, a readiness to settle on the basis of mutual repeal of the extra tonnage and merchandise duties.[164]

The American government was extraordinarily slow in renewing the suspended negotiation. Rufus King, who succeeded Rush at London, never received instructions. In commenting on the fact, he expressed the feeling that it was just as well that he had not been instructed, since there was no indication that the British government was prepared to make concessions.[165] No effort to undertake a settlement was made until Gallatin was sent to replace King in June 1826. The opinion was held in Great Britain that the delay was intentional, with the object of further testing out the British regulations.

Gallatin was instructed to abandon the contention that there must be no discrimination in favor of goods imported into the West Indies from the North American colonies. He was to claim instead the right for the vessels of the United States to carry from the British islands to any non-British port.[166]

---

[162] Benns, *op. cit.*, 109-114; Clay to Cambreleng, Dec. 25, 1825, *Br. and For. State Papers*, XIV, 493-494; Sir James Kempt to Vaughan, Dec. 6, 1825, PRO, FO, 5, vol. 210; Vaughan to George Canning, Jan. 20, 1826, *ibid.*, vol. 209.

[163] Benns, *op. cit.*, 115-117; *Register of Debates*, II, 576-590; Adams, *Memoirs*, VII, 114-116; Vaughan to Canning, March 1, 1826, PRO, FO, 5, vol. 211.

[164] George Canning to Vaughan, March 8, 1826, PRO, FO, 5, vol. 209.

[165] King to Clay, Feb. 5, March 3, 1826, Dispatches, Great Britain, XXXII.

[166] Clay to Gallatin, June 19, 1826, *ASP, FR*, VI, 248-249.

The reason for the abandonment of the ground previously taken with regard to the preferential duties is not clear. The intention of the British to force the trade through the North American ports was never more evident than in the acts of 1825. Possibly the fact that American shipping had so completely monopolized the trade under the arrangement of 1822 convinced Clay that the danger had been overemphasized. The retreat seems to have been due to Clay and not Adams. The latter never cared a great deal whether a settlement were ever made, thinking the American retaliatory laws and indirect trade by way of the foreign West Indies better than the deceitful concessions of the British. It seems more probable, however, that the advanced position was abandoned because Congress could no longer be depended upon to carry on the fight, since party and sectional advantage was now the primary objective of the members of that body. The demand for national treatment for American vessels was a difficult one to defend against politicians who knew little about the mechanics of commerce.

Gallatin found on reaching England that even the amended demands now stood no chance of being accepted by Great Britain. He was immediately confronted with the fact that an order in council had been issued closing the West Indian ports to American vessels.[167] Canning then resolutely refused to negotiate on the subject of the West India colonial trade "so long as the pretension recorded in the Act of 1823, and there applied to British colonies alone, remains part of the law of the United States," declaring that his government could not hold itself bound to remove its interdict "whenever it may happen to suit the convenience of the foreign government to reconsider the measures by which the application of that interdict was occasioned."[168] It seems probable that Canning

[167] The order, dated July 27, 1826, is in *ASP, FR*, VI, 333-335. See also, Benns, *op. cit.*, 117-119.

[168] Canning to Gallatin, Sept. 11, 1826, *ASP, FR*, VI, 253. Gallatin saw the opportunity to counteract the refusal of the British to negotiate on the West Indies by refusing to renew the Convention of 1815, which was an object with the British. He asked instructions, but Clay ordered him to keep the two questions separate. Gallatin to Clay, Sept. 20, 1826, Gallatin, *Writings*, II, 327-328; Clay to Gallatin, Oct. 31, 1826, Instructions, XI.

was delighted at the opportunity to humiliate the government which had had the temerity to announce a program of leadership in the new world. Furthermore, Huskisson, who, as President of the Board of Trade, had fathered the legislation of 1825, was finding the shipping interest very critical of his tampering with the navigation laws, and hoped to regain its support by adopting a hostile attitude toward Britain's chief maritime rival.[169]

The Administration, devoid of support at home, made every possible effort, short of abject apology, to induce the British government to reconsider its attitude. In April 1827, Clay authorized Gallatin to agree to settle the matter by mutual legislation instead of a convention, offering to yield the circuitous trade from the United Kingdom to the West Indies by way of the United States.[170] Gallatin did not cease his efforts until October 1827. His last offer was an unqualified compliance with the British acts of 1825, provided the British would agree in advance to extend the advantages of those acts in return for a favorable act of Congress. Huskisson and Dudley declared that their government could not commit itself in advance as to whether it would open the ports; all would depend on circumstances and conditions at the time.[171]

[169] For Gallatin's view that the British policy was dictated by Huskisson who wished to curry favor with the shipping interest, see Gallatin to Clay, Dec. 21, 29, 1826, Feb. 22, April 21, April 28, Aug. 14, 1827; Gallatin, *Writings*, II, 348-349, 360-361, 372, 382, Dispatches, Great Britain, XXXIII. In two speeches in defense of his shipping policy, made in Parliament May 12, 1826 and May 27, 1827, Huskisson stressed the danger to British interests of the commercial and naval development of the United States. Huskisson, *Speeches*, III, 48-49, 109-115.

[170] Clay to Gallatin, April 11, 1827, *ASP, FR*, VI, 970-975; Gallatin to Lord Dudley, June 4, 1827, *ibid.*, 975-976.

[171] Gallatin to the Secretary of State, Sept. 14, 1827, *ASP, FR*, VI, 978-979.

Following the interview with Gallatin at which he had refused to commit himself as to what action would be taken in case the United States should comply with the acts of 1825, Dudley sent an instruction to Vaughan at Washington, which is very revealing of the British attitude: "The case betwixt the two countries is shortly this. An advantage, which it is our unquestioned right to give or to withhold, was offered to America under certain conditions. Those conditions she did not choose to accept,—probably in the hope that we should at last find ourselves obliged to give the advantage without receiving the equivalent. Whether or not she entertained this expectation, the event did not correspond with it. We persevered, and with less inconvenience than we had apprehended.

A year later Barbour, who succeeded Gallatin, seized an opportunity to sound Lord Aberdeen, then foreign minister, as to what the attitude of his government would be in case Congress should make a legislative compliance with the British arrangement of 1825, but that minister avoided committing himself.[172]

In the meantime Adams, as soon as he had learned of the final refusal of Canning to negotiate, and of the Order in Council of July 27, brought the matter of American policy before the cabinet.[173] It was determined to refer the whole subject to Congress without recommendation. Privately, Adams advised a program of complete non-intercourse with the British colonies.[174] Adams' wishes were, however, no longer a guide for the Senate and House of Representatives. Both houses decided that it was proper to comply with British demands, and each house passed a bill to that effect. They disagreed, however, on the details of the desired legislation, with the result that no law was enacted.[175] In the absence of Congressional action, nothing remained but for Adams to issue a proclamation putting into force again the American restrictive acts of 1818 and 1820.[176] These remained in force throughout the remainder of the period under review. As previously, they had the effect of giving to American shipping a practical mo-

---

"Disappointed in the result, America now proposes . . . to accept those conditions she so long refused to comply with. We do not treat this conduct as affronting; we do not even complain of it. Her right to decline is as clear as ours to offer. But we do not think it consistent with the dignity or the interest of this country for it to appear to all the world that an offer which . . . had been made in a spirit of fairness and conciliation, may be rejected for the chance of an uncompensated concession on our part; and then if the experiment fail, may be re-proposed with a certainty that if nothing has been gained, nothing at least has been lost by the delay." Lord Dudley to Vaughan, Oct. 6, 1827, PRO, FO, 5, vol. 222.

[172] J. Barbour to Clay, Oct. 2, 1828, Dispatches, Great Britain, XXXVI.

[173] Adams, *Memoirs*, VII, 166, 174-175.

[174] Clay to Gallatin, Dec. 28, 1826, Instructions, XI, 223-225; Richardson, II, 355; Adams, *Memoirs*, VII, 164, 213-214.

[175] Adams to Gallatin, March 20, 1827, Gallatin, *Writings*, II, 364-368; *Register*, III, 501-504.

[176] The proclamation is dated March 17, 1827, Richardson, II, 375-376; Adams, *Memoirs*, VII, 231, 234, 236-239; Benns, *American Struggle*, 144.

nopoly of the carriage of supplies for the British islands, the route being via the Spanish, Dutch, Swedish, and Danish islands. No serious damage was done either to American shipping or agriculture, but the humiliating defeat which Adams had suffered was seized upon by the opposition as one of the big issues in the campaign of 1828.[177]

The policy of the United States toward the trade with the British North American colonies was not during this period primarily concerned with reciprocity in customs regulations. The commerce in itself was not of outstanding importance. It became a matter of significance from the American point of view, only in connection with the subject of the Indian trade, the navigation of the St. Lawrence, and the West India trade controversy. The close connection between the North American and the West India colonial trade has already been noted.

In the commercial negotiation of 1815, the American commissioners proposed an article providing for the free navigation of the lakes and rivers through which the northern boundary passed, reciprocal national treatment for vessels, mutual free admission of furs, and admission of all other articles at the same rate of duty as when imported into the Atlantic ports. They announced specifically that the British merchants would not be allowed to trade with the Indians on the American side. Political and not commercial considerations were back of this determination. The British negotiators offered little resistance to exclusion from the Indian trade. They refused, however, to admit American vessels into the St. Lawrence and its tributaries where the waters were entirely within British territory. Freedom of navigation on the British side of the Great Lakes without access to the St. Lawrence would have been of little value to the United States since American vessels would have been unable to reach the principal Canadian ports. Consequently the article was

[177] See Foot's speech in Senate, Feb. 6, 1828, *Register*, IV, 244; Adams to Gallatin, Dec. 12, 1827, Gallatin, *Writings*, II, 398-399; Benns, *op. cit.*, 156-157; Barbour to Clay, Oct. 2, 1828, Dispatches, Great Britain, XXXVI.

dropped.[178] In March 1817, Castlereagh again offered the article which the Americans had rejected in 1815. The subject was also considered in the negotiations of 1823-1824 and 1826-1827. Throughout the period the American government continued to maintain that it could accept no commercial arrangement with regard to the North American colonies unless it should contain a provision for the navigation of the St. Lawrence at least to Montreal and Quebec.[179]

During the first few years after the war, the customs regulations on the British side did not offer ground for serious complaint to American producers. The importation into the colonies of the type of goods consumed in the West Indies was encouraged; East Indian and European goods were imported into Canada via the United States; and furs came into the United States from Canada. Later regulations were not quite so favorable, and an interest in tariff reciprocity began to develop on the American side of the border. As long as the British policy of routing United States produce to the West Indies by way of the North American colonies continued, however, the American government had a good reason for not favoring to any great extent the exchange of goods across the northern boundary.[180]

A very irritating episode in the commercial relations with the neighboring British colonies was the attempt of the pro-

[178] Clay and Gallatin to the Secretary of State, May 18, 1815, American Plenipotentiaries to the Secretary of State, July 3, 1815, and enclosures, *ASP, FR*, IV, 9-10, 12-13, 15-16, 17-18; Moore, *Canada and the United States*, 95-98.

[179] Adams to the Secretary of State, March 20, 1817, *ASP, FR*, V, 367-368; Adams to Rush, June 23, 1823, *op. cit.*, V, 518-519; Rush to Adams, Aug. 12, 1824, *ibid.*, 539-543; Gallatin to Clay, Sept. 13, 1826, Gallatin, *Writings*, II, 322-325; Gallatin to Clay, Sept. 21, Dec. 5, 1827, *ibid.*, 388-389, 395-396.

[180] Moore, *op. cit.*, 99-123; Adams to Castlereagh, Sept. 17, 1816, Adams, *Works*, VI, 81-83; Report by James Monroe on "Obstructions to American commerce in the provincial and colonial possessions of Great Britain," in *ASP, C&N*, II, 30-31; Gallatin to Adams, April 16, 1817, Gallatin, *Writings*, II, 29-30; "Report of Mr. Russell from the Committee on Foreign Affairs, communicated to the House of Representatives, Jan. 21, 1823," in *ASP, FR*, V, 224-225; Gallatin to Clay, June 29, 1826, Sept. 21, 1827, Dec. 5, 1827, Gallatin, *Writings*, II, 313-317, 388-389, 395-396; "Memorial of delegates from twenty towns in St. Lawrence County, N.Y.," Jan. 24, 1827, *ASP, FR*, VI, 382; Adams, *Memoirs*, VII, 488.

vincial governments of Nova Scotia and New Brunswick to maintain a monopoly for British shipping in their trade with the United States. Their principal article of export was plaster of Paris, on which a heavy export duty was laid. In 1817, in order to prevent smuggling and the landing of the plaster in the neighboring Maine ports from which American shipping would have the better of the competition in the carriage, both provinces passed laws limiting the ports from which the article could be shipped, and establishing a heavy penalty for landing cargoes at any United States port east of Boston. These laws aroused the government at Washington to retaliation. A law was rushed through Congress prohibiting the importation in foreign vessels of plaster of Paris from ports closed to American vessels. The closing of the principal market for the chief article of export had the desired effect, and Nova Scotia and New Brunswick soon repealed the objectionable laws.[181] Adams was jubilant, feeling perhaps that this easy success was harbinger of victory in the more important battle over the West India trade then beginning. He characterized the proclamation which he drafted for restoring the trade as "one of the most significant acts, though upon a very insignificant subject, that the Government of the United States will have issued since the Declaration of Independence."[182]

The commerce with the British colonies in America was the only colonial trade which required retaliative action on the part of the United States government during the terms of Monroe and Adams. While none of the European governments were prepared, in the years immediately following the adoption of the American reciprocity act, expressly to surrender the regulations of the old colonial system, in actual practice they relaxed or abandoned them. The Spanish colonies of Cuba and Porto Rico were open to American shipping with no greater restrictions than very high import duties

[181] *ASP, C&N*, II, 31-32; *Statutes at Large of the U. S.*, III, 361-362; "Proclamation of the Lieutenant Governor of New Brunswick, April 10, 1818" in Bagot to Adams, June 15, 1818, Notes from British Leg., XI; Richardson, *Messages and Papers*, II, 34-37.
[182] Adams, *Memoirs*, IV, 81.

on certain articles.[183] Colonial trade played a rather important rôle in the negotiation with the Netherlands in 1817, the Dutch government refusing determinedly to consent to any treaty stipulations with regard to it. However, St. Eustatius and Curaçao were opened to American vessels. The general policy was to close Surinam (Dutch Guiana) to all foreign commerce; but some trade, subject to strict regulation and high duties, was carried on with the United States.[184]

Although it had been liberalized considerably by the regulations of the governors the ordinance of 1784 was still the basic commercial law of the French West Indies. A royal decree of 1826 offered freedom from all restrictions in Guadeloupe and Martinique on a reciprocal basis. The Adams administration did not think it worth while to suggest compliance, since no new privilege would have been obtained. In 1828 the opposition in Congress sharply called attention to the omission, alleging that the French West India trade was on the point of being "lost" as the British had been. An act of May 9, 1828, met the terms of the French decree and provided for relief from discrimination for French vessels arriving from either of the two islands and laden with their produce.[185]

By the Swedish treaty of 1816, the vessels of the United States were guaranteed the treatment of native vessels in St. Bartholomew on the direct voyage from the United States with American produce. The reciprocal favor was granted in the United States, however, only to Swedish and Norwegian vessels owned and naturalized in the island. The treaty of 1827 removed all restrictions on shipping.[186] American shipping was received very favorably in the Danish West Indies throughout the period. By the treaty of 1826 all discriminations were abolished by the two nations, except that the

[183] *ASP, C&N*, II, 638; *ASP, FR*, V, 5.
[184] *ASP, C&N*, II, 354; *FR*, V, 5; Westermann, *The Netherlands and the United States*, 217-223.
[185] *ASP, FR*, V, 5; VI, 825-829; *Statutes at Large of the U. S.*, IV, 269; *Register of Debates*, IV, 553-570.
[186] Miller, *Treaties*, II, 601-616, III, 283-308; *ASP, FR*, V, 5; *ASP, C&N*, II, 636, 638; see above, p. 217.

Danes retained a monopoly of the trade between their islands and the homeland.[187]

Of the East India colonies of European powers, only those of Great Britain and the Netherlands were of importance to American commerce. Those of the Netherlands were included in the negotiation of 1817, but were not again discussed after that failure. The trade consisted principally in the exchange of specie for spices. American vessels were admitted, though heavy export duties were charged.[188] The trade to India was an important subject in the Anglo-American negotiation of 1815. By the Jay Treaty, United States vessels from any port whatever had had the right to enter the principal Indian ports and to export Indian produce directly to the United States. The unratified Monroe-Pinkney treaty of 1808 had contained a similar clause, but limited the trade to American vessels arriving directly from the United States. The American commissioners in 1815 at first asked to be admitted to the indirect trade both to and from Indian ports. This the British negotiators refused, and insisted that their best offer was the provision of the Jay Treaty. The Americans were anxious to have their privileges extended to include the voyage from India to China, but this was also refused. Adams was largely responsible for the inclusion of a stipulation with regard to India. Both Clay and Gallatin questioned the value of the intercourse because it drained specie from the United States.[189]

COMMERCIAL POLICY IN RELATIONS WITH
LATIN AMERICA

A very important phase of the work for commercial reciprocity appears in the relations between the United States and the new nations of Latin America. In fact, the Latin American policy of the Monroe and Adams administrations had its

---

[187] *ASP, FR*, V, 5; *ASP, C&N*, II, 358, 638; see above p. 218.

[188] *ASP, C&N*, II, 33, 354; see above, pp. 188-190.

[189] Clay and Gallatin to the Secretary of State, May 18, 1815, American Plenipotentiaries to the Secretary of State, July 3, 1815, and enclosures, *ASP, FR*, IV, 9-10, 12-13, 15-18; Adams, *Memoirs*, III, 210-212, 219, 226-228, IV, 181; Adams to Jonathan Russell, Oct. 10, 1815, Adams, *Writings*, V, 413-416; Gallatin to Monroe, Nov. 25, 1815, Gallatin, *Writings*, I, 662-665; *ASP, C&N*, II, 33; Adams to Secretary of State, July 30, 1816, Adams, *Writings*, VI, 55-57.

origins, to a considerable extent, in the same considerations which dictated the reciprocity program. Monroe, and especially Adams, declared open war on the European "system." The aspect of that system with which Americans were most familiar, and with resistance to which the government had been occupied ever since its establishment, was the "excluding and exclusive" commercial system. The policy toward the British West India trade and the Monroe Doctrine are outstanding examples of this hostility to the old colonial order. Expressions indicating emphasis on the commercial aspect of Latin American independence, in the period before the Monroe Doctrine, are numerous. In the Cabinet Memorandum of Oct. 22, 1808, Jefferson and his aids expressed "the strongest repugnance to see you [the Spanish-American patriots] under subordination to either France or England, either politically or commercially."[190] Clay, of course, in his early attempts in Congress to force recognition of the revolutionary governments, stressed the commercial advantages which would flow to the United States.[191] Adams had little expectation of immediate commercial advantages, at least in the Spanish areas, and believed that the liberated colonies were likely to be competitors of the United States, except in shipping. Nevertheless he was extremely active in forwarding the adoption of the American reciprocity policy by the new governments. In a conference with Stratford Canning on the British colonial trade in 1822, he boasted that the liberation of the Spanish colonies would mean the end of exclusive commercial policies everywhere.[192]

The United States government made no unusual efforts to favor the commercial enterprize of its citizens in Latin America beyond the program of securing free competition. Monroe stated in 1817 the policy to which he and his successor strictly adhered:

[190] Adams, *History of the U. S.*, IV, 341.

[191] H. L. Hoskins, "Hispanic American Policy of Henry Clay, 1816-1828," *HAHR*, VII (1927) 464-465.

[192] Adams, *Memoirs*, Nov. 25, 1822, VI, 104; Adams to R. C. Anderson, May 27, 1823, Manning, *Diplomatic Correspondence*, I, 199-206; J. F. Rippy, *Rivalry of the United States and Great Britain*, 115-118.

Should the colonies establish their independence, it is proper now to state that this Government neither seeks nor would accept from them any advantage in commerce or otherwise which will not be equally open to all other nations.[193]

A very determined stand, however, was taken against the granting of special privileges to any other nation.[194] Because of the self-denying declarations of Great Britain and France in 1823, the principal thing which the United States had to resist was the tendency of some of the new states to exchange special commercial favors among themselves, to the disadvantage of the United States and Europe.[195] After the new governments were recognized, there was no great haste to enter into commercial treaties with them. European nations had concluded treaties with some of the new republics before the United States entered negotiations. In most cases, there was little trade to protect. Moreover, the new states were prone to disorders, arbitrary changes of policy, and unstable

[193] First Annual Message, Dec. 2, 1817, Richardson, II, 582. Certain students of the relations of the United States and Latin America, misinterpreting the most-favored-nation formula, have concluded that the United States sought favors beyond those of other nations. See H. L. Hoskins, "Hispanic American Policy of Henry Clay, 1816-1828," *HAHR*, VII (1927) 473; H. C. Evans, *Chile and its Relations with the United States*, 29.

[194] The special investigative commission composed of Caesar Rodney, John Graham, and Theodoric Bland, which visited South America in 1817, was instructed to report on the commercial conditions in each country and to specify whether or not all nations paid the same import and export duties. Manning, *Diplomatic Correspondence*, I, 44. For examples of the activities of American agents in guarding against the conferring of special privileges on other nations, see C. S. Todd to Adams, March 6, and July 29, 1823, *ibid.*, II, 1244-1245, 1265; J. M. Forbes to Manuel José García, Dec. 6, 1824, *ibid.*, 642-643; Samuel Larned to Clay, Nov. 1, 1827, *ibid.*, II, 1122-1123.

[195] Adams' message to the Senate, Dec. 26, 1825, Richardson, II, 318. The idea of reserving the right of granting exclusive privileges to Spain in return for a recognition of independence was held in certain quarters. *Ibid.*; Memorandum of the Polignac-Canning Conference, Oct. 9-12, 1823, Manning, III, 1498. Another proposal was to grant them to the first nation extending recognition. Adams to D. C. De Forest, Dec. 31, 1818; Adams to Monroe, Jan. 28, 1819, *ibid.*, 83-84. In 1823, Adams declared that the principal American objection to the plan to provide European monarchs for the former Spanish colonies arose from the fact "that they are always connected with systems of subserviency to European interests: to projects of political and commercial preferences to that European nation from whose stock of Royalty the precious scion is to be engrafted." Adams to C. A. Rodney, May 17, 1823, Manning, *op. cit.*, I, 190-191.

regulations. These conditions in some cases delayed or prevented treaties.

The first treaty between the United States and a Latin American republic was concluded with Colombia in 1824. The negotiation came near the end of the experimental period of the reciprocity law, which, by the act of 1818, was to expire in 1824. For this reason, Richard C. Anderson, who conducted the negotiation in Colombia, was not instructed to include in the treaty the specific reciprocity provisions with regard to shipping. He was simply required to secure a guarantee of most-favored-nation treatment for American trade.[196] No question of importance regarding the regulation of commerce arose in the discussions. Pedro Gual, the Colombian plenipotentiary, presented to Anderson a project containing the unqualified most-favored-nation clause. Anderson amended this to include the conditional principle, and the article was accepted.[197] In the following year, Colombia concluded a treaty with Great Britain which provided that there should be no distinction between Colombian and British vessels when the latter carried British produce. The United States claimed, by virtue of its most-favored-nation treaty, the benefit of this stipulation, which was promptly granted by Colombia. By act of Congress of April 20, 1826, the reciprocal favor for Colombian vessels was provided.[198]

The second South American treaty was that with the Federation of the Center of America, concluded at Washington by Clay in December, 1825. This was the first treaty to contain the complete reciprocity rule, i.e., the provision for national treatment of vessels regardless of the origin of the cargoes.[199] Although the commerce of Central America was of no great value, the treaty became of considerable impor-

[196] Adams to Anderson, May 27, 1823, Manning, op. cit., I, 199-204; Clay to Poinsett, Sept. 24, 1825, ASP, FR, VI, 581; Protocol of Poinsett's conference with Mexican commissioners, Sept. 13, 1825, ibid., 583-585.
[197] Miller, Treaties, III, 163-194. For Anderson's account of the negotiation and the protocols of the conferences, see ASP, FR, V, 712-726.
[198] Adams to the House of Representatives, March 30, 1826, Richardson, II, 341-342; Statutes at Large of the U. S., IV, 154.
[199] Miller, Treaties, II, 209-238.

tance as a model for later treaties. Clay wrote of it in 1828 as follows:

It would leave each at perfect liberty, as each ought to be, to impose such duties as its wants or its policy might seem to require, whilst it would restrain either from laying upon the produce or manufactures of the other, higher duties than are exacted from other nations, on similar articles of their produce or manufacture. . . . According to its principle, whatever can be imported into or exported from the ports of one country in its own vessels, without any regard to the place of its origin, may, in like manner, and upon the same terms and conditions, be imported or exported in the vessels of the other country. This is the most perfect freedom of navigation. We can conceive of no privilege beyond it. All the shackles which the selfishness or contracted policy of nations had contrived, are broken and destroyed by this broad principle of universal liberality. The President is most anxious to see it adopted by all nations.[200]

Negotiations with Mexico encountered insuperable obstacles, although a considerable trade had developed between the two countries and needed treaty protection. Joel R. Poinsett, the United States minister at Mexico City, opened negotiations in 1825. He was provided with a copy of the Colombian treaty to use as a model. Clay, however, was not satisfied with that treaty's provision of most-favored-nation treatment for commerce. He wrote:

The rule of the most favored nation may not be, and scarcely ever is, equal in its operation between two contracting parties. It could only be equal if the measure of voluntary concession by each of them to the most favored third Power were precisely the same; but as that rarely happens, by referring the citizens of the two contracting Powers to such a rule, the fair competition between them, which ought always to be a primary object, is not secured, but, on the contrary, those who belong to the nation which has shown least liberality to other nations are enabled to engross almost the entire commerce and navigation carried on between the two contracting Powers.

Simple most-favored-nation arrangements were objectionable also because of the difficulty of determining in any given case whether a favor was granted gratuitously or for a concession.

[200] Clay to Tudor, March 28, 1828, *25th Congress, 1st Session, House Document 32*, 15.

For these reasons, Poinsett was ordered to use his best efforts to obtain a specific provision for national treatment of shipping in the direct trade, as in the British treaty of 1815.[201] The question of reciprocity in the indirect trade never entered into the discussions with Mexico. At the beginning of the negotiation, of course, the principle had not yet been adopted by the Department of State. No reason for its omission in later instructions has been found.

The Mexican plenipotentiaries immediately and firmly objected to the reciprocity provision, asserting that in the existing state of the Mexican marine the provision would benefit only the United States. Poinsett was obliged to accept most-favored-nation privileges.[202] Further, the United States minister had great difficulty in inducing the Mexican government to yield its intention to reserve the right to favor the trade of other Latin American states more than that of any other nation. Treaties containing the exception had been previously concluded with Colombia and Great Britain, though they remained unratified. Poinsett made the abandonment of the reservation a *sine qua non,* and his conduct was emphatically approved by Clay. Although the dispute caused the suspension of the conferences for a time, the Mexicans eventually yielded.[203]

A treaty was signed on July 10, 1826. However, neither government ratified it. The United States Senate objected to provisions discriminating against United States citizens of Spanish origin in Mexico, and regarding neutral rights. The Mexican government refused to accept the article providing for the rendition of fugitive slaves.[204] Conferences were re-

---

[201] Clay to Poinsett, March 25, 1825, *ASP, FR,* VI, 578-581.

[202] Protocol of 2nd, 6th and 7th conferences, Sept. 13, 1825, May 6, May 17, 1826, *ASP, FR,* VI, 583-585, 592-593; Poinsett to Alamán and Esteva, Sept. 18, 1825, *ibid.,* 585-586.

[203] Clay to Poinsett, Nov. 9, 1825, *ASP, FR,* VI, 582-583; Protocols of 2nd, 5th, 6th conferences, Sept. 13, Sept. 28, 1825, May 6, 1826, *ibid.,* 583-585, 588-589, 592-593; Poinsett to Rufus King, Oct. 10, 1825, Manning, *Diplomatic Correspondence,* III, 1634-1635; Manning, *Early Diplomatic Relations of the United States and Mexico,* 205-221.

[204] Manning, *Early Diplomatic Relations,* 224-231. The treaty is printed in *ASP, FR,* VI, 608-613.

newed in 1828, and a new treaty was drawn up and signed on February 14, 1828. At this time the Mexican government agreed to include an article providing for national treatment of shipping, but insisted on a separate article suspending the operation of the provision for ten years. This treaty was promptly ratified by the United States, but the Mexican Congress again refused to agree to the provision for the return of fugitive slaves, and to that for maintaining peace among the Indians along the international boundary.[205] American commerce, lacking treaty regulation, suffered severely as a result of unsettled conditions, arbitrary acts on the part of Mexican officials, and unstable government regulations.[206]

From the standpoint of existing and potential commerce with the United States, Brazil was the most important of the South American states. The establishment of treaty relations was especially desirable, too, because American trade was in a very unfavorable position. Pursuing the policy of the Anglo-Portuguese treaty of 1810, the Brazilian government admitted British and other European produce at an ad valorem duty of fifteen per cent, while the produce of the United States was taxed twenty-four per cent. Until 1828, however, protests against this legislation were unavailing.[207] Until that time, too, relations between the two countries were strained because of a dispute arising from American demands for indemnity for seizures of American vessels by the Emperor's squadrons blockading the Rio de la Plata during the war with the Argentine. These claims were settled in 1828, and William Tudor, the United States chargé, then proceeded to negotiate a commercial treaty. Clay instructed him to use the Central American treaty as a model, if Brazil's government

---

[205] Manning, *Early Diplomatic Relations*, 234-246; Poinsett to Clay, May 21, 1828, *25th Congress, 2nd session, House Doc.* 351, p. 210. For the treaty of 1828, see *ASP, FR*, VI, 952-957.

[206] Manning, *Early Diplomatic Relations*, ch. 8; Poinsett to Secretary of State of Mexico, Jan. 20, 1828, and to Clay, July 14, 1828, *25th Congress, 2nd session, House Doc.* 351, p. 219-222, 227.

[207] Clay to Condy Raguet, April 14, 1825, Manning, *Diplomatic Correspondence*, I, 238; Clay to Tudor, March 29, 1828, *25th Congress, 1st session, House Doc.* 32, 15.

would agree to its terms. Refering to the Brazilian tariff discriminations, Clay asserted that no equivalent could be granted for their elimination. "It has formed no part of our foreign policy," he wrote, "to subject this Government to any limitation as to the amount of duty which it may think proper to impose on foreign productions; and the President cannot authorize any deviation from our established policy in that respect. Foreign Powers have been content to treat with us upon the principle that their respective productions shall be received at the same rate of duty which is paid by the most favored nation, and what that should be has been left to the direction of Congress."[208] Only one difficulty arose in considering the commercial articles. The Brazilian plenipotentiaries insisted on reserving the right to favor trade with Portugal beyond that of other nations. Tudor offered strong opposition to the proposition, but finally, with Clay's authorization, acquiesced in its inclusion. At the time, as the envoy pointed out, there was no actual discrimination in favor of Portuguese produce or shipping. The treaty was concluded December 12, 1828.[209]

With the other South American republics, no negotiations of importance were undertaken. In the Argentine John M. Forbes, acting chargé, took occasion, in 1824, on the eve of the conclusion of the Argentine-British treaty, to warn the government that the United States would demand the same privileges conceded to other nations.[210] He was assured that no exclusive privileges would be granted, and was informed that the Buenos Aires government was prepared to conclude a treaty with the United States. Clay avoided a negotiation, however, saying that he wished to settle commercial affairs

[208] Clay to Tudor, March 31, 1828, *25th Congress, 1st session, House Doc. 32*, 18-19.

[209] Clay to Tudor, Oct. 23, 1827, March 29, 1828, March 31, 1828, *25 Congress, 1st session, House Doc. 32*, 7-12, 15-16, 18-19; Tudor to Clay, Aug. 5, Aug. 25, Sept. 30, Oct. 22, 1828, *ibid.*, 48, 55, 90-92, 105-106; Tudor to the Marquis of Aracaty, Aug. 9, Aug. 27, Sept. 15, 1828, *ibid.*, 65-70, 93-95, 98-101; L. F. Hill, *Diplomatic Relations of the U. S. and Brazil*, 70. For the treaty, see Miller, *Treaties*, III, 451-484.

[210] Forbes to García, Dec. 6, 1824, Manning, *Diplomatic Correspondence*, I, 642-643.

either by mutual legislation or by a negotiation at Washington. Forbes was very active in trying to secure a favorable reception in Argentine ports of American produce, particularly flour. He was successful in securing the repeal of a law excluding the latter article, but it was replaced with a prohibitive tariff. The Argentine-Brazilian war in the ensuing years delayed consideration of a commercial arrangement.[211] In Chile anarchical conditions interfered with commercial relations, and made negotiations inadvisable during the period. The principle restrictions which Heman Allen and Samuel Larned, the United States representatives, attempted to remove were high flour duties and a government tobacco monopoly.[212] In Peru, discrimination against cotton goods from the United States were removed in 1826 after strong remonstrances by the consul, William Tudor, but high duties remained a grievance.[213]

THE TARIFF IN FOREIGN RELATIONS

The rule established by Hamilton, that customs duties on merchandise must be the same for all foreign nations, was strictly adhered to as far as announced policy is concerned during the administrations of Monroe and Adams. In executive utterances and acts it was made clear that retaliative measures were directed against adverse shipping regulations and not against restrictions on the importation of American produce. It is quite obvious, however, that the refusal of the nations of Europe to receive freely American produce was a very powerful directive influence in the formation of the commercial foreign policies of the United States, especially tariff policy. The existing barriers to trade which aroused most resentment in the United States were those against agricultural produce, particularly wheat and flour. The cessation of

[211] Watt Stewart, "U. S.-Argentine Commercial Negotiations in 1825," *HAHR*, XIII (1933) 367-371.

[212] H. C. Evans, *Chile*, 30-34; Larned to Clay, Nov. 1, 1827, May 10, 1828, Manning, *Diplomatic Correspondence*, II, 1122-1123, 1128-1130.

[213] Tudor to Clay, June 12, 1825, Feb. 28, Nov. 21, 1826, Jan. 6, 1827, *24th Congress, 2nd session, House Doc. 167*, 67, 69-70, 114, 127-128; Tudor to J. M. de Pando, Nov. 2, 1826, Jan. 6, 1827, *ibid.*, 120-124, 141-142.

the war-time demand produced a very severe collapse of values of farm produce throughout the country. The price of flour at Baltimore, for example, declined between the years 1817 and 1821 from $11.43 to $5.28 per barrel.[214] This collapse was widely attributed to the European restrictive regulations—and particularly to the British corn laws. Congress was careful to give public recognition to this view. Twice during the period the State Department at the request of Congress made compilations of the commercial regulations of foreign governments, one purpose of which was to keep the grievance before the public.[215]

The protective tariff laws during this period were made possible by the votes of the farming states of Pennsylvania, Ohio, Indiana, Kentucky, and Missouri, where the argument was accepted that the surplus of farm produce could be absorbed only by the creation of a home market built up by the encouragement of domestic manufactures. In reporting to his government with regard to the tariff of 1824, Addington, the British minister, wrote:

I have only to add, that had no restrictions on the importation of foreign grain existed in Europe generally, and especially in Great Britain, I have little doubt that the Tariff would never have passed through either house of Congress, since the great agricultural states, and Pennsylvania especially, the main mover of the question, would have been indifferent if not opposed to its enactment.[216]

Officially, no complaint was ever made with regard to the British restrictions, and inequalities were seldom mentioned in the negotiations between the two countries.[217]

[214] *ASP, C&N*, II, 657.

[215] "Commercial Regulations of Foreign Countries," communicated to the Senate, Dec. 14, 1819, *ASP, C&N*, II, 199-384; *A Digest of the Commercial Regulations of the Different Foreign Nations* (Washington, 1824); Adams, *Memoirs*, V, 221-222.

[216] Addington to George Canning, May 30, 1824, PRO, FO, 5, vol. 185; see also *Annals*, XXXVI, 1924-1928, 1944-1946, XXXVIII, 243-247; Taussig, *Tariff History*, 63-64, 70-71, 74-75; Stanwood, *Tariff Controversies*, 143, 207-211, 213-216, 232, 239.

[217] The subject was discussed unofficially, of course. Rush reported from London in 1820: "In all circles where I mix, whether political or commercial, I do not cease to inculcate the truth, that our call for the products of the British

Several times during the period, representatives of the British government expressed dissatisfaction with the United States tariff. In the West India negotiation of 1824, in answer to the American complaint that United States shipping was at a disadvantage because of the limited list of articles admitted from the United States, the British negotiators asserted that "the rum and molasses of the British West Indies are, in point of fact, but barely admitted to the market of the United States."[218] In 1828, Lord Aberdeen jokingly complained to Barbour, the United States minister, that Great Britain had received very unkind treatment in the tariff of that year.[219] A more serious grievance was the discrimination between iron manufactured by rolling and that manufactured by hammering, which was incorporated in the tariff of 1816 and subsequent laws. Rolled iron was taxed $1.50 per hundred pounds and the hammered article only 45 cents. Since the British manufacturers had developed the rolling process, they felt that the discrimination was directed solely against them. Castlereagh was induced to instruct Bagot at Washington to protest against the discrimination as being in violation of the treaty of 1815, which stipulated that no higher duties should be levied on British goods than on the like articles of any other country.[220]

The Administration, without committing itself on the correctness of the British interpretation, was sympathetic, and apparently used its influence to secure equalization of the duties. A bill for the purpose was introduced in the session of 1816-1817 but was not acted upon. British protests continued to be made. In 1820, Henry Baldwin, chairman of the House committee on manufactures, prepared a letter for the British

workshops must become more and more abridged, if not from choice, from necessity, unless we are afforded the means of paying for them conveniently by a door being kept open to the easy and just reception in Britain of all the productions of our soil." Rush to Adams, March 16, 1820, Dispatches, Great Britain, XXIV.

[218] *ASP, FR,* V, 567.

[219] Barbour to Clay, Oct. 2, 1828, Dispatches, Great Britain, XXXVI.

[220] Castlereagh to Bagot, Sept. 6, 1816, PRO, FO, 5, vol. 113; Bagot to Monroe, Nov. 18, 1816, *ASP, FR,* IV, 159-160.

chargé, expressing the views of the committee on the subject. He defended the discrimination on the ground that the greater expenditure of labor and time in the hammering process and the better quality of the product was sufficient difference to justify separate rates of duty. The British Committee of the Privy Council for Trade then prepared a lengthy report describing the methods of manufacture and the qualities of the two products in an attempt to show that they were "like articles" within the meaning of the treaty. Stratford Canning made able use of this report in his correspondence with the Secretary of State.[221] In May 1822, Monroe recommended that Congress give the protest consideration, on the ground "that a liberal construction of those engagements [of the treaty of 1815] would be compatible with a conciliatory and a judicious policy."[222] Congress failed to see the subject in the same light as Monroe and Adams, however. The British protests reached a climax in 1824 with the threat of a similar discrimination against American cotton on the ground that the seeds were removed with a gin. At this time the House committee on commerce made an investigation of the subject and discovered that a considerable quantity of rolled iron was imported from Sweden and Russia. This disposed of the dispute, since the British government could no longer contend that British industry alone was being discriminated against.[223]

Of the commercial regulations of France, aside from the discriminations on shipping, those which constituted the greatest grievance in the United States were the discrimination against short staple cotton and the government monopoly of tobacco and strict limitation on the importation of American tobacco. Both these subjects were discussed in the negotiation preceding the treaty of 1822, but the United States was not

[221] G. C. Antrobus to Castlereagh, June 5, 1820, PRO, FO, 5, vol. 149; Castlereagh to Stratford Canning, Dec. 30, 1820, *op. cit.*, vol. 150, June 12, 1821, vol. 156; Stratford Canning to Adams, Nov. 26, 1821, March 5, 1822, Notes from British Leg., XII; Adams, *Memoirs*, V, 446.

[222] Monroe to House of Representatives, May 1, 1822, *ASP, FR*, IV, 869.

[223] George Canning to Addington, March 13, 1824, PRO, FO, 5, vol. 184; Adams, *Memoirs*, VI, 311, 333; Newton's report from the House committee on commerce, May 22, 1824, *ASP, FR*, V, 347-348.

prepared to offer sufficient compensation to secure alterations.[224] The French government complained of the American
methods of taxing wines, by which the wines of France were
taxed by specific duty amounting to a much larger percentage
of their value than the wines of other countries. In 1819, the
duties on the cheaper wines, which included most of the
French wines, were reduced to about half the former rate.[225]
The act was adopted partially in an effort to dispose the
French government to be more reasonable in its shipping
policy. Toward the end of the period, the French government again complained of the tariff on wines. It was asserted
that the treaty of 1822 had resulted so much to the advantage
of the navigation of the United States that additional compensation would have to be furnished to secure its continuance.
In 1828, another special wines act further reduced the rates
on French wines. The general tariff act of 1828 contained also
another concession requested by France: a higher rate of duty
on silks from the Orient than on those of Europe. In this case,
tariff concessions were made not in exchange for tariff concessions but for the continuation of favorable shipping regulations.[226]

[224] See above, p. 203.
[225] *Statutes at Large of the U. S.*, III, 310-314, 515.
[226] *Ibid.*, IV, 309; 270-275.

CONCLUSION

NATIONALISTS like John Quincy Adams[1] have contended that the commercial policy of the United States developed from motives of justice and considerations of fundamental truth. The view is hardly susceptible of historical analysis, but careful study leaves the impression that the government of the United States has been little less selfish in forwarding the interests of its nationals than that of any other country. Even though "reciprocity" promised the world cheaper transportation, it meant American supremacy in certain fields of foreign trade just as definitely as navigation laws meant Spanish or English monopoly. In the formulation of principles, eighteenth century political and economic thought was undoubtedly important. Benjamin Franklin, who exerted a marked influence on early commercial policy, was a thorough convert to Physiocratic doctrines, and some of his admirers have attributed to him a hand in the composition of the *magnum opus* of Adam Smith.[2] Thomas Jefferson, before the Revolution, saw in the British Acts of Trade and Navigation a usurping encroachment upon the "natural right" of the Americans to carry on a free trade with all parts of the world.[3] Reaction against the "oppressive" British trade regulations of the colonial period was probably of less influence than is often supposed. Recent students place little stress upon the injuriousness of the old colonial system in British America, and relegate the Acts of Trade and Navigation to a secondary position among the causes of the break with England. The merchants and other informed individuals were under no illusions

[1] See, for example, his letter to G. W. Campbell, June 28, 1818, *Writings*, VI, 367-368.

[2] Franklin, *Writings* (ed. Smyth), VII, 175-177; L. J. Carey, *Franklin's Economic Views*, 128-131, 139-166.

[3] Jefferson, "A Summary View" in *Writings* (ed. Ford), I, 421.

as to the advantages to commerce to be derived from a dissolution of the empire.[4]

The arguments of the free trade theorists were made to
serve one immensely important practical purpose at the beginning of the Revolution; that is, to meet the arguments of
the conservatives who pointed out the manifest commercial
advantages of the imperial connection. To the majority of
Americans, the propagandist's picture of a golden age of
commerce to follow the bursting of the restraining bonds of
the British laws was much more attractive. Jefferson's statement, to which reference was made above, was an early development of the theme, and, as the crisis developed through
1776, the argument was more frequently used by pamph-
leteers and writers for the newspapers.[5] From this sort of
propaganda arose the official viewpoint of the government
throughout the war period, which emphasized the expectation that free trade would open a great new era of commercial
development, and that Continental Europe stood to gain
much from the unshackling of American trade.

If the economists had not already developed the principles of economic liberalism, American statemen would have
been under the necessity of inventing them. There was no
practicable alternative policy for an independent America in
the eighteenth century. A weak, divided, poor country was in
no position to maintain a navy, to undertake the exploitation
of dependencies, or to engage in cutthroat trade rivalry. A
more reasonable supposition would be that an alliance with
France, providing for the exchange of exclusive commercial
privileges, might have been formed. It was determined, however, that the idea was "contrary to the very spirit of our
undertaking," and that America must be independent of the
whole world "as well in matters of government as in com-

[4] C. M. Andrews, *The Colonial Background of the American Revolution*,
122-129; A. M. Schlesinger, *The Colonial Merchants and the American Revolution*, 1-32, 91-93, 112-114.

[5] For extracts from pamphlets and editorials written in this tenor, see
Schlesinger, *Colonial Merchants*, 592-604. Paine's statement in *Common Sense*
is clear and emphatic. Thomas Paine, *Works* (ed. Van der Weyde), II, 125.

merce."[6] Diversity of economic interests and consequent class and sectional jealousies were among the strongest supports of liberalism. Planters became nervous at the prospect of their northern brethren acquiring a monopoly of the carriage of their staples. Spokesmen for the farmers regarded with self-righteous anger anything that could be construed as a tax upon agriculture for the benefit of mere trade.

The Revolution began with the nullification of the British trade and navigation laws, and the insurgents passed quickly to the stage of offering their commerce to other countries in exchange for aid against their enemy. The latter policy was pushed with unbounded enthusiasm. Nearly every government in Europe was importunately urged to accept a share in the putative wealth of American trade. This program bore little relation to reality, however, and the commercial phase was of very secondary significance in the dispositions leading to the final outcome of the war. The illusion of world-wide commerce was shattered on the establishment of peace. Great Britain relegated her former colonies to their rightful place among her maritime rivals. Other countries found little promise of profit in American trade, and retained their monopolies and restrictions. American state governments adopted counteracting regulations, and only clumsiness of the governmental machinery prevented Congress from adopting a thoroughgoing measure to establish reciprocity. Pretentious diplomatic efforts to limit the British monopoly of American commerce by establishing direct exchanges with the nations of the Continent were made. Although some success was attained in limiting monopoly and reducing duties in France, no practicable method of weaning American trade from the British market could be devised. The unsatisfactory status of foreign commerce during the Confederation Period contributed an immense incentive to the movement for the Constitution.

The formation of "a more perfect union" had the effect of inducing ministers to listen more graciously, perhaps, to

[6] See *ante*, p. 18, fn. 50.

American complaints, but European governments persisted in regulating their trade with a view solely to their own interests. Although Jefferson and Madison and their followers continued to work for a policy of bargaining with Continental Europe and for resistance to British monopoly, Washington's administration, under the leadership of Hamilton and with the support of the commercial interest, decided to give up the fight for reciprocity. Hostility toward British commerce would have endangered the neutrality of the United States, and impeded the settlement of other critical issues in the relations of the two countries. In the Jay Treaty the United States abandoned, in effect, the struggle for a share of the West India carrying trade, and yielded its power to increase the discrimination in favor of its own shipping and to purchase special concessions from other foreign governments.

The long period of the wars of the French Revolution and Napoleon changed considerably the point of emphasis in American commercial policy. The usual regulations which circumscribed American trade in time of peace, particularly in the colonies, were very generally removed. Each belligerent, however, made war on the supply trade of its enemies, even when carried on by neutrals. The protection of neutral rights rather than the securing of reciprocity was, therefore, the principal commercial objective of the United States. In the non-importation, embargo, and non-intercourse legislation, the federal government under Presidents Jefferson and Madison exercised to the fullest extent its power to regulate foreign trade, in an effort to force the warring powers, particularly Great Britain, to respect the right of the United States to trade with all belligerents.

In the new patriotic enthusiasm and national self-confidence which followed the successful outcome of the Second War with Great Britain, the United States adopted a policy of open warfare against the old colonial system and the remnants of mercantilism. Much of the hostility to European colonization in America expressed in the Monroe Doctrine had its origin, doubtless, in the government's long experience in fighting colonial commercial monopolies. During Monroe's and Adams' administrations, activities in aid of foreign commerce were limited almost entirely to the protection of merchant shipping. The growing manufacturing interest was able to convince a large proportion of the farmers that the further development of domestic manufactures through tariff protection was the proper means of counteracting European corn laws and other barriers to the disposal abroad of the agricultural surplus. Expansion of foreign markets was no longer an important part of American reciprocity policy, as it had been in Jefferson's time. The bitter wars of retaliation carried on against British restrictions in the West Indies and against the French discriminating duties constituted belated but effective execution of the frequent threats voiced by American spokesmen in the previous forty years. However, the country remained united behind the militant policy for only a short time, and the election of 1828 foreshadowed the decision to abandon commercial warfare.

BIBLIOGRAPHY

GUIDES AND OTHER BIBLIOGRAPHICAL AIDS

S AMUEL F. BEMIS' and Grace G. Griffin's comprehensive
Guide to the Diplomatic History of the United States
(Washington, 1935) is indispensable for the investigation of
any subject touching upon American foreign relations, broadly
interpreted. Although the writer's manuscript was complete
before the *Guide* was published, he profited from the com-
pilers' gracious permission to consult the work in manuscript
and galley proof. The bibliographical notes in a number of
publications hereafter listed, particularly monographs on
phases of foreign policy, have been helpful. The bibliographical appendix in E. R. Johnson and T. W. Van Metre, *History
of the Domestic and Foreign Commerce of the United States*
(2 vols., Washington, 1915) is of value. A very handy aid in
a specialized field is D. P. Myers, *Manual of Collections of
Treaties* (Cambridge, 1922). Miss Griffin's *Writings in
American History* (available through 1931) and *Social Science Abstracts* are necessary in surveying the literature upon
commercial policy. Adelaide R. Hasse, *Index to United States
Documents Relating to Foreign Affairs, 1828-1861* (3 vols.
Washington, 1914-1921) makes available an immense
amount of printed material, which would, without the *Index,*
be almost inaccessible because of its volume and haphazard
arrangement.

The series of guides to the materials for American history
in foreign archives prepared for the Carnegie Institution of
Washington are the initial aids to the use of the reproductions
of manuscripts from foreign archives in the Library of Congress. The guide to London archives by C. O. Paullin and
F. L. Paxson (Washington, 1914), M. D. Learned's guide to
German state archives (Washington, 1912), W. R. Shep-

herd's guide to Spanish archives (Washington, 1912), and R. R. Hill's *Descriptive Catalogue of Documents . . . in the "Papeles Procedentes de Cuba"* (Washington, 1916) have been most useful. Some aid in the use of French diplomatic materials is provided by *Inventaire sommaire des archives du Département des Affaires Etrangères* (6 vols. Paris, 1883-1920) and N. M. M. Surrey, *Calendar of Manuscripts in Paris Archives and Libraries Relating to the History of the Mississippi Valley to 1803* (2 vols. Washington, 1926-1928). The Library of Congress possesses a series of manuscript inventory lists of foreign archival materials of which photographic reproductions are on its shelves, in addition to an incomplete card catalogue of manuscripts. For manuscripts other than reproductions from foreign archives, the *Handbook of Manuscripts* (Washington, 1918) has been excellently supplemented by C. W. Garrison, *List of Manuscript Collections in the Library of Congress* (Washington, 1931). The calendars of the Jefferson, Madison, and Monroe papers, and the catalogue of the papers of the Continental Congress, published by the Bureau of Rolls and Library of the Department of State, are useful in examining those collections. The Van Tyne and Leland guide to the archives of Washington (2nd ed., Washington, 1907) is still very helpful in spite of its age.

MANUSCRIPT COLLECTIONS

United States Department of State, Washington, D.C.
> Instructions to Ministers
> Dispatches from Ministers
> Domestic Letters
> Notes to Foreign Legations
> Notes from Foreign Legations

Reproductions of Manuscripts in the Library of Congress
> Great Britain. Public Record Office, London.
>> Foreign Office, Series 4. Vol. II contains the papers relating to the commercial negotiations of 1782-1783. Vols. IV-XI contain the correspondence of Sir John Temple, Consul General; Phineas Bond, Consul for Pennsylvania and New York; George Miller, Consul at Charleston; John Hamilton, Consul

at Norfolk; and P. Allaire, a spy in the employ of Sir Arthur
Yonge. The years covered are 1783-1789.
Series 5. This series contains, chronologically arranged, the
dispatches of the British ministers to the United States to
their government, and the drafts of instructions from the For-
eign Office.
Colonial Office
Series 42. Vols. 68, 72, 73, 85 contain the correspondence of
George Beckwith.
Great Britain. The Shelburne Papers
Photo-copies of the originals now in the William L. Clements
Library, University of Michigan, Ann Arbor. Vols. 70, 72,
and 87 contain important documents on the peace negotia-
tions of 1782-1783.
France. Archives des Affaires Etrangères, Paris.
Correspondance Politique, Etats Unis. This series contains the
dispatches of the French ministers in the United States and
drafts of instructions issuing from the Ministry of Foreign
Affairs.
Mémoires et Documents, Etats Unis. Miscellaneous documents,
including lengthy memoranda on commercial relations between the United States and France by government officials
and others, memorials, and petitions.
Spain. Archivo General de Indias, Seville.
Papeles Procedentes de Cuba. These are the papers transferred
from the archives of Cuba. They contain the correspondence
of the first Spanish envoys to the United States, Juan de
Miralles and Francisco Rendón, and much material relating
to trade with Cuba and other Spanish colonies.
Spain. Archivo Histórico Nacional, Madrid.
Estado. This series contains the drafts of instructions to the
Spanish diplomatic representatives in the United States and
dispatches from them, *Consultas* of the *Consejo de Estado*, and
other materials relating to the diplomatic and commercial
relations of Spain and the United States.
Prussia. Preussisches Geheimes Staats-archiv, Berlin-Dahlem.
Königl. Geheimes Ministerial Archiv.
General Controlle. Tit. LVIII, No. 7. Acta betreffend den
Amerikanischen Handel und Krieg, 1776-1783. Vols. I and
II. Papers relating to Prussian-American relations during the
Revolution.
General Controlle. Repositur XI. 21a. Conv. 1. Amerika.

Verein. Staaten, 1778-1801. Papers relating to the negotiation of the treaty of 1785.

General Controlle. Repositur XI. 21a. Conv. 2. Amerika.
Verein. Staaten, 1795-1804. Papers relating to the treaty
of 1799.

Auswärtiges Amt. Abteilung II. Rep. 6. Handel. Nord-
Amerika. Vol. III contains the correspondence relating to the
treaty of 1828.

The Henry Adams Transcripts. Copies of documents in European
archives, made for Henry Adams, and now deposited in the
Manuscripts Division of the Library of Congress.

Miscellaneous

The Papers of the Continental Congress
The Thomas Jefferson Papers
The James Madison Papers
The James Monroe Papers

Letters of Members of the Continental Congress, Unpublished
material. These are the copies of letters of members of the Continental Congress in the possession of Dr. E. C. Burnett of the
Carnegie Institution of Washington, collected for the volumes
now being prepared for publication.

COLLECTIONS OF PUBLISHED DOCUMENTS

*State Papers: Government Publications, Treaties, Diplomatic Corre-
spondence, Legislative Journals and Debates, Statutes.*
United States

*American State Papers: Documents, Legislative and Executive, of
the Congress of the United States.* 38 vols. Washington, 1832-
1861.

Burnett, E. C., *Letters of Members of the Continental Congress.*
7 vols. to date. Washington, 1921-1934.

*Commercial Regulations of the Foreign Countries with Which the
United States Have Intercourse, Collected, Digested and Printed
under the Direction of the President of the United States, Con-
formably to a Resolution of the Senate of the Third of March,
1817.* Washington, 1819.

*Debates and Proceedings in the Congress of the United States . . .
from March 3, 1789 to May 27, 1824.* 42 vols. Washington,
1834-1856. Commonly known by the binder's title of *Annals
of Congress.*

*A Digest of the Commercial Regulations of the Different Foreign
Nations, with Which the United States have Intercourse, Pre-*

pared Comformably to a Resolution of the House of Representatives of the 21st of January, 1823. Washington, 1824.

A Digest of the Existing Commercial Regulations of Foreign Countries with Which the United States Have Intercourse, Prepared under the Direction of the Secretary of the Treasury, in Compliance with a Resolution of the House of Representatives of 3d March, 1831. 3 vols. Washington, 1833-36.

Diplomatic Correspondence of the United States . . . 1783-1789. 3 vols. Washington, 1837.

Documentary History of the Constitution of the United States. 5 vols. Washington, 1894-1905.

Farrand, Max, *Records of the Federal Convention of 1787.* 3 vols. New Haven, 1911.

Force, Peter, *American Archives.* 9 vols. Washington, 1837-1853.

Journal of the Executive Proceedings of the Senate of the United States of America from the Commencement of the First to the Termination of the Nineteenth Congress. 3 vols. Washington, 1828.

Journals of the American Congress from 1774-1788. 4 vols. Washington, 1823.

Journals of the Continental Congress, 1774-1789 (ed. W. C. Ford, G. Hunt, J. C. Fitzpatrick, R. R. Hill). 33 vols. to date. Washington, 1904-1936.

Journal of the House of Representatives of the United States. First to the Twentieth Congress. Washington, various dates.

Journal of the Senate of the United States. First to the Twentieth Congress. Washington, various dates.

Manning, William R., *Diplomatic Correspondence of the United States Concerning the Independence of the Latin American Nations.* 3 vols. New York, 1925.

Mayo, Robert, *A Synopsis of the Commercial and Revenue System of the United States, as Developed by Instructions and Decisions of the Treasury Department for the Administration of the Revenue Laws.* Washington, 1847. A compilation of summaries and quotations from the circulars issued by the Secretary and by the Comptroller of the Treasury.

Public Statutes at Large of the United States of America from the Organization of the Government in 1789 to March 3, 1845. 8 vols. Boston, 1845-1851.

Register of Debates in Congress . . . Dec. 6, 1824 to Oct. 16, 1837. 14 vols. Washington, 1825-1837.

Richardson, J. D., *Compilation of the Messages and Papers of the Presidents, 1789-1897.* 10 vols. Washington, 1896-1899.

Secret Journals of the Acts and Proceedings of Congress, from the First Meeting Thereof to the Dissolution of the Confederation. 4 vols. Boston, 1820-1821.

Miller, David Hunter, *Treaties and Other International Acts of the United States of America.* 4 vols. to date. Washington, 1931-1935. The definitive edition of United States Treaties, edited and annotated by the Historical Adviser, United States Department of State.

Wharton, Francis, *The Revolutionary Diplomatic Correspondence of the United States.* 6 vols. Washington, 1889.

Foreign Countries

Bond, Phineas, "Letters of Phineas Bond, British Consul at Philadelphia, to the Foreign Office of Great Britain, 1787-1789, 1790-1794," *AHA, AR,* 1896, II, 463-659; 1897, 454-568. Washington, 1897, 1898.

Bourne, H. E., "The Correspondence of the Comte de Moustier with Montmorin," *AHR,* VIII (1903), 709-733, IX (1903), 86-96.

British and Foreign State Papers. 125 vols. to date. London, 1832-1932.

"Correspondence of the Russian Ministers in Washington, 1818-1825," *AHR,* XVIII (1913), 309-345, 537-562.

Doniol, Henri, *Histoire de la participation de la France a l'établissement des Etats-Unis d'Amérique.* 5 vols. Paris, 1886-1892. Many state papers are printed *in toto,* and the text contains copious extracts from many others.

Frederick the Great, *Politische Correspondenz Friedrich's des Grossen* (ed. J. G. Droysen *et al.*). 43 vols. to date. Berlin and Leipsig, 1879-1935. The king touched upon the commercial aspects of the American war in numerous letters.

Great Britain, Board of Trade, "A Report of the Lords of the Committee of the Privy Council, Appointed for All Matters Relating to Trade and Foreign Plantations, on the Commerce and Navigation between His Majesty's Dominions and the Territories Belonging to the United States of America, 28th January, 1791." In *Collection of Interesting and Important Reports and Papers on the Navigation and Trade of Great Britain, Ireland and the British Colonies in the West Indies and America, Printed by Order of the Society of Ship Owners of Great Britain.* London, 1807.

d'Hauterive, Pierre Louis, Comte, and Ferdinand de Cussy, *Recueil des traités de commerce et de navigation de la France.* 10 vols., Paris, 1834-1844.

Hermelin, Samuel Gustav, *Berättelse om Nordamerikas Förenta Stater: Bref till Kanslipresidenten af Frh. S. G. Hermelin* (ed. C. E. B. Taube af Odenkat). Stockholm, 1894. Reports of the Swedish commercial investigator in the United States in 1784.

Houtte, Hubert Van, "American Commercial Conditions and Negotiations with Austria, 1783-1786," *AHR*, XVI (1911), 567-578. Contains several documents from Austrian archives concerning the proposal for a commercial treaty between Austria and the United States, 1785-1786.

Martens, Georg Friedrich von, *Recueil des traités d'alliance, de paix, de trêve . . . depuis 1761 jusqu'à présent.* Second edition. 8 vols., Göttingen, 1817-1835.

————, *Nouveau recueil de traités d'alliance, de paix, de trêve . . . depuis 1761 jusqu'à présent.* 16 vols. Göttingen, 1817-1824.

Napoleon I, *Correspondance de Napoléon Ier.* 32 vols. Paris, 1858-1869.

Schlitter, Hans, "Die Berichte des Ersten Agenten Oesterreichs in den Vereinigten Staaten" in *Fontes Rerum Austriacarum*, Abth. II, Bd. XLV. Vienna, 1891. Correspondence of the Baron de Beelen-Bertholff, Austrian commercial agent in the United States, 1784-1789.

Stevens, B. F., *Facsimiles of Manuscripts in European Archives Relating to America, 1773-1783.*

Turner, F. J., "English Policy Toward America, 1790-1796," *AHR*, VII (1902), 706-735, VIII (1902), 78-86. Documents from the British Public Record Office.

————, "Correspondence of the French Ministers to the United States, 1791-1797," *AHA, AR*, 1903, II. Washington, 1904.

Yela Utrilla, J. F., *España ante la independencia de los Estados Unidos.* 2 vols. Lérida, Spain, 1925. Volume II contains a valuable selection of documents from Spanish archives concerning Spain and the American Revolution.

Private and Miscellaneous Papers

Adams, John, *The Works of John Adams* (ed. C. F. Adams). 10 vols. Boston, 1850-1856.

Adams, John Quincy, *The Writings of John Quincy Adams* (ed. W. C. Ford). 7 vols. New York, 1913-1917.

Burnett, E. C., *Letters of Members of the Continental Congress.* 7 vols. to date. Washington, 1921-1934.

Cabot, George, *Life and Letters of George Cabot* (ed. H. C.

Lodge). 2d ed. Boston, 1878. Cabot was Senator from Massachusetts from 1791-1796. Because of his intimate knowledge of commerce, his opinion was often asked on policies to be pursued, particularly during the Federalist period.

Carey, Mathew, *The American Remembrancer.* 3 vols. Philadelphia, 1795-1796. Contemporary pamphlets, speeches, etc., relative to the Jay Treaty.

Deane, Silas, "Correspondence of Silas Deane, Delegate to the First and Second Congress at Philadelphia, 1774-1776" in Connecticut Historical Society, *Collections,* 1870, II, 129-368.

————, "The Deane Papers, 1774-1790" in New York Historical Society, *Collections,* 1868-1891. Vols. XIX-XXIII. New York, 1887-1890.

————, "The Deane Papers: Correspondence between Silas Deane, His Brothers and Their Business and Political Associates, 1771-1795" in Connecticut Historical Society, *Collections,* 1930. Vol. XXIII. Hartford, 1930.

Fitzmaurice, Edmond George Petty-Fitzmaurice, *Life of William, Earl of Shelburne, afterwards first Marquis of Lansdowne, with Extracts from His Papers and Correspondence.* Second edition. 2 vols. London, 1912.

Ford, Paul Leicester, *Essays on the Constitution of the United States, Published During Its Discussion by the People, 1787-1788.* Brooklyn, 1892.

————, *Pamphlets on the Constitution of the United States, Published During Its Discussion by the People, 1787-1788.* Brooklyn, 1888.

Franklin, Benjamin, *The Writings of Benjamin Franklin* (ed. A. H. Smyth). 10 vols. New York, 1905-1907.

Gallatin, Albert, *The Writings of Albert Gallatin* (ed. Henry Adams). 3 vols. Philadelphia, 1879.

Hamilton, Alexander, *Industrial and Commercial Correspondence of Alexander Hamilton Anticipating His Report on Manufactures* (ed. A. H. Cole). Chicago, 1928.

————, *The Works of Alexander Hamilton* (ed. H. C. Lodge). 12 vols. New York and London, 1904.

Higginson, Stephen, "Letters of Stephen Higginson, 1783-1804," *AHA, AR,* 1896, I, 704-841. Washington, 1897. A wealthy Boston merchant, Higginson was member of Congress from Massachusetts in 1783. His letters contain much information on commerce and commercial policy.

Huskisson, William, *The Speeches of William Huskisson.* 3 vols. London, 1831.

Jay, John, *Correspondence and Public Papers of John Jay* (ed. H. P. Johnston). 4 vols. New York, 1890-1893.

Jefferson, Thomas, *The Writings of Thomas Jefferson* (ed. P. L. Ford). 10 vols. New York and London, 1892-1899.

————, *The Writings of Thomas Jefferson* (Memorial ed., A. A. Lipscomb, editor-in-chief). 20 vols. Washington, 1903-1904.

King, Rufus, *The Life and Correspondence of Rufus King* (ed. Charles R. King). 6 vols. New York, 1894-1900.

Maclay, William, *The Journal of William Maclay: United States Senator from Pennsylvania, 1789-1791.* New York, 1927.

Madison, James, *The Writings of James Madison* (ed. Gaillard Hunt). 9 vols. New York, 1900-1910.

Marraro, Howard R., ·"Philip Mazzei, Virginia's Agent in Europe, the Story of his Mission as Related in his Own Dispatches and Other Documents." *Bulletin of the N.Y. Pub. Lib.*, XXVIII, 155-175, 247-274, 447-474, 541-562. Mazzei was sent to Tuscany during the Revolution by the State of Virginia for the purpose of securing a loan.

Monroe, James, *The Writings of James Monroe* (ed. S. M. Hamilton). 7 vols. New York, 1898-1903.

Paine, Thomas, *The Life and Works of Thomas Paine* (ed. W. M. Van der Weyde). 10 vols. New Rochelle, N.Y., 1925.

Plumer, William, *William Plumer's Memorandum of Proceedings in the United States Senate, 1803-1807* (ed. E. S. Brown). New York, 1923.

Rush, Richard, *Narrative of a Residence at the Court of London.* London, 1833. Second edition. Discursive memoirs of the first fifteen months of his seven-year term (1817-1825) as United States minister to Great Britain, including brief notes of the negotiations in which he participated.

"Warren-Adams Letters, Being Chiefly a Correspondence among John Adams, Samuel Adams, and James Warren, 1743-1814," Mass. Hist. Soc., *Collections*, vols. 72-73. Boston, 1917-1925.

Washington, George, *The Writings of George Washington* (ed. W. C. Ford). 14 vols. N.Y. and London, 1892.

MONOGRAPHS AND SPECIAL STUDIES

[Adams, John Quincy], "The British Colonial and Navigation System," *American Quarterly Review*, II (1827) 267-306. A review of British and American commercial policies and regulations from 1783-1825, directed to the defense of Adams' policy against British and American critics.

Andrews, Charles M., *The Colonial Background of the American Revolution*. Revised edition. New Haven, 1931. A brilliant interpretation of colonial history and the Revolution in terms of the imperial relationship.

Baasch, Ernst, "Beiträge zur Geschichte der Handelsbeziehungen zwischen Hamburg und Amerika" in *Hamburgische Festschrift zur Erinnerung an die Entdeckung Amerikas*, I, No. 3, 91-256. Surveys the commerce of Hamburg with the Western Hemisphere during the 18th and 19th centuries. The author makes excellent use of Hamburg, Bremen, Lubeck, Breslau and Netherlands archives.

Bates, William W., *American Navigation*. Boston, 1902. An historical account which relies upon Congressional debates and selected published documents. Opposes policy of reciprocity as injurious to American navigation.

Baxter, James P., 3rd, "Our First National Shipping Policy" in *United States Naval Institute Proceedings*, XLVI (August, 1920) 1251-1264. A study, based upon secondary materials, which concludes that the growth of American shipping in the early 1790's was due to discriminating duties.

Beard, Charles A., *An Economic Interpretation of the Constitution of the United States*. New York, 1913.

Bell, Herbert C., "The West India Trade before the American Revolution," *AHR*, XXII (Jan., 1917), 272-287. A model study, from British and American sources, of the mechanism of the trade: kinds of vessels, routes, methods of sale, remittance and insurance.

————, "British Commercial Policy in the West Indies, 1783-1793," *EHR*, XXXI (July, 1916), 429-441. A careful review of the development of British policy preceding the act (28 Geo. III, c. 6) permanently regulating the trade between the United States and British dominions.

Bemis, Samuel Flagg, *The American Secretaries of State and Their Diplomacy*. 10 vols. New York, 1927-1929. The most detailed complete survey of American foreign relations yet published, but the biographical essays vary greatly in merit.

————, *The Diplomacy of the American Revolution*, New York, 1935. A compact, readable, thorough account, making use of the more important European and American archival sources.

————, *Jay's Treaty*. New York, 1923. Adequate treatment is given to the commercial aspect of Anglo-American relations in the critical early period of the national government.

————, *The Pinckney Treaty*. Baltimore, 1926. Commerce in the early relations between Spain and the United States is treated in Chapters II to V.

————, "Relations between the Vermont Separatists and Great Britain, 1789-1791," *AHR*, XXI (1916), 547-560. Account of efforts of the Allen brothers to bring Vermont under the protection of Great Britain in order to provide a trade outlet via Lake Champlain and the St. Lawrence.

Benns, F. Lee, *The American Struggle for the British West India Carrying Trade, 1815-1830*. Bloomington, Ind., 1923. The standard treatise on the subject, founded on a wide investigation of published documents and newspapers. Critical of American policy as conducted by John Quincy Adams.

Benson, Adolph B., *Sweden and the American Revolution*. New Haven, 1926. Swedish archives are listed in the bibliography, but the short account of commercial relations in chapter III is based on printed materials, largely American.

Bond, Beverley W., *The Monroe Mission to France, 1794-1796*. Baltimore, 1907. The author concludes, from a study of State Department MSS and the Monroe Papers, that both Monroe and the Administration were to blame for the unfortunate outcome of Monroe's mission.

Brown, David Walter, *The Commercial Power of Congress Considered in the Light of Its Origin*. New York, 1910.

Brown, George W., "The St. Lawrence in the Boundary Settlement of 1783," *Canadian Historical Review*, IX (1929), 223-238. Holds that the American commissioners refrained from demanding the navigation of the St. Lawrence in order to avoid discouraging, by seeking a competing trade route, the British policy of making liberal territorial concessions in the hope of retaining commercial domination of the West.

————, "The St. Lawrence Waterway as a Factor in International Trade and Politics, 1783-1854" in University of Chicago, *Abstracts of Theses, Humanistic Series*, VIII. Chicago, 1927.

Burnett, E. C., "London Merchants on American Trade, 1783," *AHR*, XVIII (July, 1913), 769-780. A reprint of a report by a committee of London Merchants, preceded by a detailed account of Pitt's bill for regulating trade with the United States.

————, "Note on American Negotiations for Commercial Treaties, 1776-1786," *AHR*, XVI (April, 1911), 579-587. A brief record, derived almost entirely from the Journals of Congress and the published American diplomatic correspondence.

Carey, Lewis J., *Franklin's Economic Views*. New York, 1928.

Carlson, K. E., *Relations of the United States with Sweden*. Allentown, Pa., 1921. A carelessly prepared account, through 1827, which makes some use of State Department MSS, and published Swedish materials.

Chandler, Charles Lyon, *Inter-American Acquaintances*. Sewanee, Tenn., 1915. A series of discursive essays by a veteran American diplomat, which contain some significant facts about early trade and diplomatic relations between the United States and Latin American countries.

Clark, George L., *Silas Deane, A Connecticut Leader in the American Revolution*. New York, 1913.

Clauder, Anna Cornelia, *American Commerce as Affected by the Wars of the French Revolution and Napoleon, 1793-1812*. Philadelphia, 1932. An account derived from merchants' letters, court decisions, state papers, customs records, and newspapers.

Coe, Samuel Gwynn, *The Mission of William Carmichael to Spain*. Baltimore, 1928. Carmichael, chargé d'affaires in Spain from 1782 to 1795, was entrusted with only routine matters in the relations of the two countries.

Conrotte, Manuel, *Intervención de España en la independencia de los Estados Unidos*. Madrid, 1920. A brief survey of Spanish policy toward the United States through 1795, with an appendix containing selected documents from Spanish archives.

Corwin, Edward S., *French Policy and the American Alliance of 1778*. Princeton, 1916. A scholarly and lucidly written interpretation, for which the author has drawn liberally from Doniol.

Coxe, Tench, *An Enquiry into the Principles on Which a Commercial System for the United States of America Should be Founded*. Philadelphia, 1787. A pamphlet published on the eve of the meeting of the Constitutional Convention, and possibly of influence in the deliberations of that body.

Crandall, S. B., *Treaties, Their Making and Enforcement*. New York, 1904.

Cresson, W. P., "Francis Dana: An Early Envoy of Trade" in *New England Quarterly*, III (1930), 717-735. Account of Dana's mission to Russia during the Revolution. Sympathetic toward Dana.

Crittenden, Charles Christopher, *The Commerce of North Carolina, 1763-1789*. New Haven, 1936. An account, supported by thorough and wide research, of the details and trends of internal and external trade, excellently presented.

Dangerfield, Royden J., *In Defense of the Senate: a Study in*

Treaty Making. Norman, Okla., 1933. Largely a statistical analysis of Senate procedure in dealing with treaties, with interesting charts and tables, showing tendencies, 1778-1928.

Doniol, Henri, *Histoire de la participation de la France à l'établissement des Etats-Unis d'Amérique.* 5 vols. Paris, 1886-1892.

Edler, Friedrich, *The Dutch Republic and the American Revolution.* Baltimore, 1911. Emphasizes diplomacy and neglects commerce. Uses Sparks, Bancroft, and Stevens transcripts from Dutch and other foreign archives.

Evans, Henry Clay, *Chile and Its Relations with the United States.* Durham, N.C., 1927. A brief, well-written summary from independence through the World War.

Farrand, Max, "The Commercial Privileges of the Treaty of 1803," *AHR,* VII (April, 1902) 494-499. Discusses the commercial articles from the constitutional point of view.

Fogdall, Soren J. M. P., "Danish-American Diplomacy, 1776-1920," *University of Iowa Studies,* VIII, No. 2. Iowa City, 1922. Gives a brief narrative of the negotiations of 1777-1783 and 1825-1826, for which some use was made of Danish archives, but not of those of the United States Department of State.

Garlick, Richard Cecil, Jr., *Philip Mazzei, Friend of Jefferson: His Life and Letters.* Baltimore, 1933.

Giesecke, Albert A., *American Commercial Legislation before 1789.* Philadelphia, 1910. Concentrates on colonial and state legislation, without extensive use of collateral material.

Gottschalk, L. R., "Lafayette as Commercial Expert," *AHR,* XXXVI (1931), 561-570. Facts regarding two memoranda prepared by Lafayette on American trade, and the text of one of them.

Graham, G. S., *British Policy and Canada, 1774-1791; A Study of 18th Century Trade Policy.* London, 1930. An important study, showing relationship of Canada to British commercial policy toward the United States.

Guttridge, George Herbert, *David Hartley, M. P., an Advocate of Conciliation, 1774-1783.* Berkeley, 1926. Makes use of the Hartley MSS.

Hayden, Ralston, *The Senate and Treaties, 1789-1817: the Development of the Treaty-making Functions of the United States Senate During Their Formative Period.* New York, 1920.

Haworth, P. L., "Frederick the Great and the American Revolution," *AHR,* IX (1904), 460-478. An examination of Prussian policy, resulting in the conclusion that Frederick felt no sympathy for the American cause.

Hill, Lawrence F., *Diplomatic Relations between the United States and Brazil*. Durham, N.C., 1932. Treats the period from 1808 to recent times, with only very slight attention to commercial relations. Based largely on State Department MSS.

Hildt, J. C., *Early Relations of the United States and Russia*. Baltimore, 1906. Covers period from 1776 to 1824, with some slight attention to commercial relations.

Hoekstra, Peter, *Thirty-seven Years of Holland-American Relations, 1803-1840*. Grand Rapids, 1917. An excellent study making adequate use of both Dutch and American sources.

Holroyd, John Baker, Lord Sheffield, *Observations on the Commerce of the American States with Europe and the West Indies*. London, 1783.

Holt, W. Stull, *Treaties Defeated by the Senate: a Study of the Struggle between President and Senate over the Conduct of Foreign Relations*. Baltimore, 1933. Gives proper emphasis to partisan politics among the motives in Senate action on treaties.

Hornbeck, Stanley Kuhl, *The Most-Favored-Nation Clause in Commercial Treaties: Its Function in Theory and in Practice and Its Relation to Tariff Policies*. Madison, 1910. Contains a lengthy, though not thorough, historical introduction.

Hoskins, Halford L., "Hispanic American Policy of Henry Clay, 1816-1828," *HAHR*, VII (1927) 460-478. Shows that after becoming Secretary of State, Clay was somewhat disillusioned as to the meaning of the Spanish American Revolution.

Hovde, Brynjolf J., *Diplomatic Relations of the United States with Sweden and Norway, 1814-1905*. Iowa City, Iowa, 1920. A brief, lucid summary from American published sources.

Hunt, Gaillard, *The Department of State of the United States: Its History and Functions*. New Haven, 1914.

Hunter, William Columbus, *The Commercial Policy of New Jersey under the Confederation, 1783-1789*. Princeton, 1922. A study of this type for every state is needed.

Jameson, J. F., "St. Eustatius in the American Revolution," *AHR*, VIII (1903), 683-708. The story of the Dutch West India island which became the depot supplying the United States with war materials.

Johnson, E. R., Van Metre, T. W., Huebner, G. G., and Hanchett, D. S., *History of the Domestic and Foreign Commerce of the United States*. 2 vols. Washington, 1915.

Kapp, Friedrich, *Friedrich der Grosse und die Vereinigten Staaten von Amerika*. Leipsig, 1871. Uses documents in Prussian archives to show, among other things, that Frederick was greatly interested in American markets for Prussian produce.

Koulischer, Joseph, "Les traités de commerce et la clause de la nation la plus favorisée du XVIe au XVIIIe siècle" in *Revue d'histoire moderne,* VI (1931), 3-29. This and the following article constitute the best available history of the development of the most-favored-nation formula.

————, "Die Meistbegünstigung in den Handelsverträgen im Wandel der Zeiten," *Zeitschrift für die gesamte Staatswissenschaft,* Vol. 89 (1930), 540-572.

Levasseur, E., *Histoire du commerce de la France.* 2 vols. Paris, 1911-1912. Succinct account of commerce and commercial policy.

Lindeman, Moritz, "Zur Geschichte der alteren Handelsbeziehungen Bremens mit den Vereinigten Staaten von Nord Amerika" in *Bremisches Jahrbuch,* X (1878), 124-146. A thorough study derived from materials in the archives of Bremen and Prussia.

Lingelbach, W. E., "England and Neutral Trade," *Military Historian and Economist,* II (1917), 153-178. A scholarly review of the development of British policy toward neutrals from Elizabethan times to the World War, with emphasis on the *Essex* decision of 1805.

————, "Saxon-American Relations, 1778-1828," *AHR,* XVII (1912), 517-539. Relates the efforts of the Saxon government to establish commercial relations with the United States, as shown by Saxon and American documents.

Luthin, Reinhard H., "St. Bartholomew; Sweden's Colonial and Diplomatic Adventure in the Caribbean," *HAHR,* XIV (1934), 307-324. Treats briefly of the trade between the United States and St. Bartholomew, and the negotiations resulting in the treaties of 1816 and 1827.

McClendon, R. E., "Origin of the Two-thirds Rule in Senate Action upon Treaties," *AHR,* XXXVI (1931), 768-772. Emphasizes the importance of the effect of the Jay-Gardoqui agreement regarding the Mississippi.

Manning, William R., *Early Diplomatic Relations between the United States and Mexico.* Baltimore, 1916. Complete and authoritative, with a detailed record of early commercial relations and negotiations.

Maxwell, Lloyd W., *Discriminating Duties and the American Merchant Marine.* New York, 1926. Written from published documents, to prove that the United States has never resorted to discriminating duties except in self-defense, and that discrimination is a bad merchant shipping policy.

Melvin, Frank E., *Napoleon's Navigation System.* New York,

1919. Gives considerable attention to the influence of the United States and its commerce in the development and decline of the Continental System.

Monaghan, Frank, *John Jay*. New York, 1935. Probably the definitive biography of Jay.

Moore, David R., *Canada and the United States, 1815-1830*. Chicago, 1910. Contains a short chapter on commercial relations.

Nevins, Allan, *The American States During and After the Revolution, 1775-1789*. New York, 1924. Summary treatment of state commercial policies.

Nichols, R. F., "Trade Relations and the Establishment of the United States Consulates in Spanish America, 1779-1809," *HAHR*, XIII (1933), 289-313. An account of the conditions and volume of the commerce between the United States and the Spanish colonies, especially Cuba, during the war-time relaxations of the Spanish exclusive system, with particular attention to the careers of the American commercial agents in the colonies.

Nussbaum, F. L., "American Tobacco and French Politics, 1783-1789" in *Political Science Quarterly*, XL (1925), 497-516. An aspect of the struggle to encourage Franco-American commerce by liberalizing the French commercial system.

————, *Commercial Policy in the French Revolution: a Study of the Career of G. J. A. Ducher*. Washington, 1923. Traces the predominant influence of Ducher in the development in the French navigation system and customs administration during the Revolution.

————, "The French Colonial Arrêt of 1784" in *South Atlantic Quarterly*, XXVII (1928), 62-78. The attempt of the French monarchy to readjust its colonial system to the new situation created by an independent America—an attempt which the author aptly shows to have been satisfactory to neither the Americans nor the French commercial interests.

————, "The Revolutionary Vergennes and Lafayette versus the Farmers General" in *Journal of Modern History*, III (1931), 592-604. Another chapter of the story of the French government's efforts to turn the American alliance to the advantage of French commerce.

Page, Thomas Walker, "The Earlier Commercial Policy of the United States," *Jour. of Political Economy*, X (1902), 161-192. Treats the period from the Revolution to about 1830 in a very general way.

Parks, E. Taylor, *Colombia and the United States, 1764-1934*.

Durham, N.C., 1935. Gives very little attention to commercial relations in the early period.

Perkins, Dexter, *The Monroe Doctrine, 1823-1826*. Cambridge, 1927. This author recognizes the important influence of commerce in the formulation of the non-colonization principle, but not in the policy of forbidding European intervention in Spanish America.

Pitkin, Timothy, *Statistical View of the Commerce of the United States*. Revised edition. New Haven, 1835. Narrative account with statistical tables from official sources for period from 1783 to 1835.

Pratt, E. J., "Anglo-American Commercial and Political Rivalry on the Plata, 1820-1830," *HAHR*, XI (1931), 302-335. An excellent account of American and British trade with the Argentine, and the rivalry of merchants and diplomatic agents in forwarding the interests of their respective countries.

Ragatz, L. J., *The Fall of the Planter Class in the British Caribbean, 1763-1783*. New York, 1928. A brilliant and authoritative contribution to economic and social history.

Renaut, Francis P., *La politique de propagande des américains durant la guerre d'indépendance, 1776-1783*. Paris, 1922-1925. 2 vols. Suggestive essays on the mission of Dana at St. Petersburg and of C. W. F. Dumas in the Netherlands, based principally on Wharton, with some use of French, English, and Dutch archives.

————, *Les Provinces Unies et la guerre d'Amérique*. 3 vols. Paris, 1924-1932.

Rippy, James F., *Rivalry of the United States and Great Britain over Latin America, 1808-1830*. Baltimore, 1929. This work contains much information on commercial diplomacy not available elsewhere in print.

————, *Latin America in World Politics*. Revised edition, New York, 1931.

Robertson, William Spence, *Hispanic American Relations with the United States*. Washington, 1923. A comprehensive and scholarly survey from the beginning of the independence movement to recent times. A revised edition to include the work of recent students is needed.

Schlesinger, A. M., *The Colonial Merchants and the American Revolution, 1763-1776*. New York, 1918. Indispensable for the commercial aspects of the American Revolution.

Schlitter, Hans, *Die Beziehungen Oesterreichs zu den Vereinigten Staaten von Amerika*. Innsbruck, 1885. Treats the attempt of Austria and Russia to mediate between Great Britain and the

Bourbon kingdoms, and the commercial negotiation with the Jefferson Commission. The appendix contains many documents.

Sears, Louis Martin, *Jefferson and the Embargo*. Durham, N.C., 1927. Shows that the Embargo was the natural outgrowth of Jefferson's pacifism, and examines the effect of enforcement at home and abroad. Derived from a thorough study of the Jefferson Papers and contemporary newspapers.

Sée, Henri, "Commerce between France and the United States, 1783-1784," *AHR*, XXXI (1926), 732-752. Utilizes papers from French national and provincial archives, some of which are printed in full.

Setser, V. G., "Did Americans Originate the Conditional Most-Favored-Nation Clause?" in *Journal of Modern History*, V (Sept., 1933), 319-323. Presents evidence that the so-called "American" form of the most-favored-nation clause, first appearing in the Franco-American treaty of 1778, was of French origin.

Seybert, Adam, *Statistical Annals of the United States of America, 1789-1818*. Philadelphia, 1818. A systematic summary of American official statistics to 1818, compiled by a Pennsylvania congressman for the use of the national legislature.

Sherman, William R., *Diplomatic and Commercial Relations of the United States and Chile, 1820-1914*. Boston, 1926. Good material from the United States State Department amateurishly presented.

Stanwood, Edward, *American Tariff Controversies in the Nineteenth Century*. 2 vols. Boston and New York, 1903. Convenient summaries of Congressional debates, with some pamphlet, newspaper, and other material. Little attention is paid to the tariff in foreign relations.

Stephenson, O. W., "The Supply of Gunpowder in 1776," *AHR*, XXX (1925), 271-281. A significant article, which demonstrates the necessity which the patriots were under to carry on sufficient foreign trade to provide a supply of munitions of war.

Stewart, Watt, "The Diplomatic Services of John M. Forbes," *AHR*, XIV (1934), 202-218.

————, "United States-Argentine Commercial Negotiations of 1825," *HAHR*, XIII (1933), 367-371.

Taussig, F. W., *The Tariff History of the United States*. New York and London, 1931. 8th edition. A series of brilliant essays, evaluating each of the tariff acts from 1789-1931. The period from 1789 to 1824 is treated only sketchily.

Tazewell, Littleton W., *A Review of the Negotiations between the United States of America and Great Britain Respecting the Commerce of the Two Countries, and More Especially Concerning the Trade of the Former with the West Indies.* London, 1829. A series of letters by the Virginia Senator originally published anonymously in the Norfolk (Va.) *Herald,* and reprinted in England as an endorsement of British West India policy. A superficial, partisan indictment of John Quincy Adams. Reviews subject from the colonial period to 1827.

Temperley, Harold, "The Later American Policy of George Canning," *AHR,* XII (1906), 779-797. Traces Canning's efforts to "defeat certain claims and pretensions of the Monroe Doctrine."

Thomas, Benjamin Platt, *Russo-American Relations, 1815-1867.* Baltimore, 1930. Gives only passing notice to commerce.

Tucker, Henry St. George, *Limitations on the Treaty-making Power under the Constitution of the United States.* Boston, 1915.

Urtasún, Valentín, *Historia diplomática de América.* Pamplona, Spain, 1920. A spiritedly written account of the diplomacy of the American Revolution by an Argentine scholar, based upon wide study of published materials and some use of French archives.

Updyke, Frank A., *The Diplomacy of the War of 1812.* Baltimore, 1915. Full treatment from British and American printed materials and manuscripts.

Van Tyne, Claude H., *The Causes of the War of Independence.* Boston and New York, 1922. A highly authoritative account of the "growth of the spirit of independence which made Americans discontented with their subordinate position in the Empire."

————, "French Aid before the Alliance of 1778," *AHR,* XXI (1925), 20-40.

————, "The Influences Which Determined the French Government to Make the Treaty with America, 1778," *AHR,* XXI (April, 1916), 528-541. The author concludes that Vergennes abandoned the policy of secret aid in favor of military participation because he was convinced it was necessary to forestall an alliance of the United States and Great Britain against France.

————, *The War of Independence.* Boston and New York, 1929. The narrative ends, unfortunately, with the conclusion of the alliance with France.

Walker, W. H., *Franco-American Commercial Relations, 1820-*

1850. Hays, Kansas, 1931. A very useful monograph, with much statistical material, dealing with the large subject of French commercial relations with the entire Western Hemisphere.

Warren, Charles, *The Making of the Constitution.* Boston, 1928. A weighty counterbalance to Beard's *Economic Interpretation of the Constitution.*

Weeden, W. B., *Economic and Social History of New England.* 2 vols. Boston, 1890. Volume II contains suggestive accounts of commerce during the Revolutionary and Confederation Periods.

Westermann, J. C., *The Netherlands and the United States, Their Relations in the Beginning of the Nineteenth Century.* The Hague, 1935. An extraordinarily thorough and comprehensive work which emphasizes the period from 1813 to 1820.

Whitaker, Arthur Preston, *The Mississippi Question, 1795-1803.* New York, 1934.

————, *The Spanish-American Frontier, 1783-1795: the Westward Movement and the Spanish Retreat in the Mississippi Valley.* Boston and New York, 1927. This and the preceding book contain a brilliant and thorough account of Spanish Louisiana in American diplomacy and the westward movement, with occasional informative references to commerce.

Wood, George C. *Congressional Control of Foreign Relations During the American Revolution, 1774-1789.* Allentown, Pa., 1919.

Woolery, W. K., *The Relation of Thomas Jefferson to American Foreign Policy, 1783-1793.* Baltimore, 1927. Considerable attention is given to Jefferson's work for commercial reciprocity.

Yela Utrilla, J. F., *España ante la independencia de los Estados Unidos.* 2 vols. Lérida, Spain, 1925. Vol. I contains a useful narrative of Spain's part in the diplomacy of the American Revolution.

Zimmerman, James Fulton, *Impressment of American Seamen.* New York, 1925. The standard history of the practice of impressment as applied to United States citizens and its influence on Anglo-American relations.

Zook, George F., "Proposals for New Commercial Treaty between France and the United States, 1778-1793," *South Atlantic Quarterly,* VIII (1909), 267-283. A brief, factual account derived from printed sources, principally American.

INDEX

Aberdeen, Lord: on the West India trade, 238; on the U. S. tariff, 253.

Adams, John: on non-intercourse, 9; on trade and the friendship of foreign nations, 11; on debates in the Continental Congress, 11 and *n*; on a treaty with France, 12; and the treaty plan of 1776, 15-16; on relations with France, 17-18; as envoy to the Netherlands, 32; as plenipotentiary for a treaty with Great Britain, 35-37; and the peace negotiation of 1782, 40-41; in the British negotiation of 1783, 45; recommends a navigation act, 55; on the Swedish treaty of 1783, 56*n*; and report on trade, 59; on the French treaty of 1778, 74*n*; English mission of, 81, 97-98; urges retaliation, 98; and relations with France, 1797-1800, 138-139.

Adams, John Quincy: as minister to the Netherlands, 135, 148; as minister to Prussia, 145; and the treaty with Prussia, 1799, 146; fails to renew the Swedish treaty of 1783, 146; as minister to Russia, 181; and commercial policy after 1815, 183; and the British commercial treaty of 1815, 186, 187; and the Netherlands arrangement of 1818, 191, 193; fights for the reciprocity plan, 200-201; on French demands in Louisiana, 201, 202; and the Neuville negotiation, 1821-1822, 203-205; and the French treaty of 1822, 205-207; and relations with Portugal-Brazil, 209, 210; and relations with Spain, 212, 213; and reciprocity with Sweden and Norway, 215; recommends complete reciprocity to Congress, 216; and relations with Denmark, 217; on relations with Russia, 220-221; West India policy of, 223-225; and Castlereagh's West India proposals, 225-226; defends U. S. retaliatory laws, 232; and the West India trade in the campaign of 1828, 239; and retaliation in the plaster of Paris trade, 241; Latin American policy of, 243-244; and the tariff on rolled iron, 254.

Adams, William, 186.

Addington, Henry Unwin, on U. S. tariff policy, 252.

Adet, P. A., and a proposed treaty with France, 126, 138.

Africa, Northern, U. S. dealings with, 2.

African slave trade, and the West India trade, 53.

Alberg, Duke d', and the Barlow negotiation, 179.

Alexander, W., plan of, for marketing French manufactures in the U. S., 84.

Allaire, P., British secret agent in N.Y., 111*n*.

Allen, Heman, U. S. minister to Chile, 251.

Alliance: European, opposed in the U. S., 12, 13, 15-16; commerce and the Franco-American, 14-15; not envisaged in the treaty plan of 1776, 17; opposed by Hamilton, 102; against the British navigation laws proposed, 113, 134; U. S. tariff and tonnage laws and the French, 119-120; as the price of Spanish trade concessions, 133.

American System, 172, 183.

Ames, Fisher, on Madison's program of retaliation, 118.

Anderson, Richard C., and the Colombian treaty of 1824, 246.

Apollon case, 204, 206.

Appleton, J. J., and the Swedish treaty of 1827, 216-217.

Argentine: war of, with Brazil, 249; U. S. relations with, 250-251.

Armstrong, John, and the French treaty proposal, 1805, 174.

Articles of Confederation: New Jersey